THE COMMUNITY BUDGET FOR AN ECONOMIC AND MONETARY UNION

Also by Paul Bernd Spahn

CHANCEN UND RISIKEN DES FINANZPLATZES FRANKFURT
IM GEMEINSAMEN MARKT-ENTWICKLUNGSAUSSICHTEN
DES FINANZSEKTORS IN HESSEN (*with Gerhard Bauer*)

DIE BESTEUERUNG DER PERSÖNLICHEN EINKOMMEN IN DER
BUNDESREPUBLIK DEUTSCHLAND

DIE DUALISTISCHE WIRTSCHAFTSSTRUKTUR DER ENTWICK-
LUNGSLÄNDER UND DIE INFLATION

DIE VEREINIGTEN STAATEN VON AMERIKA (*with Willi Adams, Ernst-
Otto Czempiel, Berndt Ostendorf, Kurt L. Shell, Michael Zöller, eds*)

SOCIALVERTRAG UND SICHERUNG – ZUR ÖKONOMISCHEN
THEORIE STAATLICHER VERSICHERUNGS- UND UMVERTEILUNGS-
SYSTEME (*with Gabriele Rolf and Gert Wagner, eds*)

STEUERREFORM ALS GESELLSCHAFTSPOLITISCHE AUFGABE DER
NEUNZIGER JAHRE (*with dieter Döring, eds*)

"L'EUROPE SANS RIVAGES" 40 ANS APRES (*with Raymond Barre,
Gilbert Blardone, Gérard Destanne de Bernis, Rénato di Ruzza, Daniel
Dufourt, Marie-Christine Leroy, Maurice Pangaud, René Sandretto*)

LITTAUER MODEL FOR GERMANY, AN ECONOMETRIC
SIMULATION MODEL FOR ALTERNATIVE FISCAL POLICIES

MIKROSIMULATION IN DER STEUERPOLITIK (*with Heinz-Peter Galler,
Helmut Kaiser, Thomas Kassella and Joachim Merz*)

THE FUTURE OF COMMUNITY FINANCE (*with Luigi Spaventa,
L. Koopmans, Pierre Salmon and Stephen Smith*)

PRINCIPLES OF FEDERAL POLICY CO-ORDINATION IN THE
FEDERAL REPUBLIC OF GERMANY: BASIC ISSUES AND
ANNOTATED LEGISLATION

PUBLIC EXPENDITURE TRENDS (*with Michael Keating and Jean-Pierre
Poullier*)

The Community Budget for an Economic and Monetary Union

Paul Bernd Spahn
Professor of Public Finance
University of Frankfurt/Main

First published 1993 by
THE MACMILLAN PRESS LTD
Houndmills, Basingstoke, Hampshire RG21 2XS
and London
Companies and representatives
throughout the world

ISBN 0-333-58646-8 hardcover

A catalogue record for this book is available
from the British Library.

Copy-edited and typeset by Grahame & Grahame Editorial, Brighton

Printed in Great Britain by
Ipswich Book Company Ltd
Ipswich, Suffolk

To Sigrid, Béla, and Maria

Contents

List of Tables

List of Abbreviations

CAP	Common Agricultural Policy
COMECON	Council for Mutual Economic Assistance
EC	European Community
ECSC	European Coal and Steel Community
ECU	European Currency Unit
EEC	European Economic Community
EFTA	European Free Trade Association
EFTS	European Federal Transfer Scheme
EGGFA	European Guidance and Guarantee Fund for Agriculture
EIB	European Investment Bank
EMS	European Monetary System
EMU	Economic and Monetary Union
EPS	EC Pension Scheme
ERDF	European Regional Development Fund
ESCB	European System of Central Banks
ESF	European Social Fund
Euratom	European Atomic Energy Community
GATT	General Agreement on Tariffs and Trade
GDP	Gross Domestic Product
GNP	Gross National Product
LDC	Less Developed Country
M3	Money Demand (including cash, demand and time deposits, and savings)
NATO	North Atlantic Treaty Organisation
NCI	New Community Instrument
PAYE	Pay As You Earn
R&D	Research and Development
UK	United Kingdom
US	United States
VAT	Value-Added Tax
WEU	Western European Union

Preface

Community public finance and European integration are intrinsically linked for both economic and political reasons. In the aftermath of the Maastricht summit the intended deepening of economic integration calls for major changes in the EC budget the various dimensions of which are explored in the present volume.

Based on a review of basic recommendations derived from the theory of fiscal federalism, important aspects of multilayer government finance and of intergovernmental relations are discussed drawing on the experience of existing federations – Australia, Germany, Switzerland and the United States. It is obvious that an Economic and Monetary Union (EMU) will have repercussions on the Community budget, which will have to ascertain new functions stemming from the centralisation of government responsibilities while observing the 'subsidiarity principle'.

Basic questions raised in this book relate to the future financing of the Community budget under EMU. A systematic analysis of revenue instruments for asserting the functioning of the Community budget is provided. Traditional taxes are analysed as to their possible contributions to financing the EC budget. Also new revenue instruments are discussed, for instance an EC surcharge on national energy taxes, an EC ecotax on carbon emissions, and an EC corporate cash flow tax which exhibits interesting effects both as to allocative aspects of capital formation and growth in the Community and as a contribution to a positive regional policy fostering the development of poorer regions; it thus supports the objective of achieving 'cohesion' in the Community quasi-automatically.

Furthermore, in so far as the impact of EMU on central banking policies is discussed to the extent that it affects seigniorage, a revenue source for national government budgets so far. Seigniorage of a future European System of Central Banks is likely to become an interesting own revenue source for the EC. The book concludes with a number of recommendations regarding the reform of Community institutions.

The book has immensely benefited from discussions of a study group on the future of Community finance under EMU that has met in Brussels several times during 1990 through 1992. I wish to thank all members of that group – inside and outside the Commission – for their stimulating thoughts.

It is obvious, however, that this book does not commit any one of them nor any institution, and that the author bears full personal responsibility for the ideas expressed in this volume.

PAUL BERND SPAHN
Frankfurt

Introduction

1 Introduction

It is simply a matter of time before the European Economic and Monetary Union (EMU) will be realised – notwithstanding a great number of pending political and economic obstacles to the forming of such a union and of uncertainties regarding the historical process itself – even after the Maastricht accord. EMU – the creation of a monetary zone with one single currency in Europe – will have a pervasive impact on many facets of political and economic decision-making within the Community, many of which have been studied by the Commission in its 'One market, one money' report (Commission of the European Communities 1990). A single European currency will almost instantaneously rival the US dollar as the predominant international means of exchange. It will alter world financial flows, improve efficiency conditions at both the national and international level, and it is likely to stabilise price levels for most of the countries adhering to EMU.

EMU has, also, implications for public finances of individual member countries and for fiscal federal relations within the EC. Some of these problems have been discussed in the Commission's report (Commission of the European Communities 1990, ch. 5, pp. 100–35). In particular the Commission has looked into the impact of EMU

- on new demands for fiscal policy at the national level (given the loss of autonomy in monetary and exchange-rate policies);
- on the long-term consistency of common monetary policy and fiscal policies of member countries (in particular with regard to unsustainable budgetary positions of some member states);
- on fiscal discipline and on the necessity to coordinate fiscal policies among member governments;
- on the implications of converging inflation rates for the revenue structure of member states' budgets (in particular through the loss of revenue from seigniorage);
- on the cost of public borrowing – notably during transition to price convergence (given that present interest rates carry inflation expectations); and finally
- on questions relating to efficient taxation and the provision of public goods, on spillover effects in the cross-frontier incidence of taxing and spending, as well as on tax competition and tax harmonisation.

1

This book tries to shed some light on some of the consequences of EMU for the distribution of functions and the sharing of public revenues between central (Community) and regional (member states') budgets within the EC. Starting from theoretical considerations regarding the principles for assigning taxes to and designing grant systems for multilevel government, different federal financial constitutions inside and outside Europe are briefly examined in order to draw from their experience for the further development of federal financial relations within the EC. Finally, scenarios are developed that it is hoped will contribute to the further advancement of existing arrangements relating to the sharing of public revenues within the Community for the conditions prevailing under EMU – taking some limiting basic political choices into account.

2 Multilevel Government Finance

2.1 FISCAL FEDERALISM AND THE 'LAYER-CAKE' VIEW

2.1.1 The Philosophy of Federalism

'Federalism' has become a fashionable term, not only in Europe but in many parts of the world. Yet eager politicians and the media quickly fraught the word with compassions, anxieties, and prejudice. Nowadays the term 'federalism' is even – for some – a shorthand for centre government dominance and a threat to national and regional sovereignty. Such misconceptions are especially popular in the Anglo-Saxon world – possibly with regard to the US federal government having continually extended its grip on American states. Yet, recently, suspicion against centre dominance has become more widespread as Eastern European states have reacted against centralist rule, and Western Europeans have started to discuss the implications of the Maastricht accord.

Despite the obvious corruption of the term, it will be used in this book in its original sense: federalism – from Latin: *foedus* meaning treaty – will, then, denote various forms of voluntary agreements among governments that, typically, respect mutual state sovereignty, even where new supraregional governments are formed. This traditional interpretation of the term is – by its nature – the opposite of central government dominance and hostile to the erosion of subcentral sovereignties. It emphasises the role of decentralised decision-making, it respects different cultural and individual traditions, and it lauds regional diversity. In its vertical dimension, federalism is the institutional equivalent to the 'subsidiarity principle'. As to horizontal intergovernmental relations federalism reflects the regional dimension of democracy. The opposite to federalism – the legitimacy of which is always based on freely negotiated treaties – would be coercive government – sometimes of course appearing in 'federal' disguise. Such degenerated forms of 'coercive federalism' do exist, yet they do not warrant any discussion here.

Treaties are hence the essence of any federal structure. They are necessary for a federation but not sufficient. Treaties could of course function entirely at horizontal levels, reflecting economic and political bargaining among states. Even where multilateral, such horizontal agreements need not necessarily be 'federal'; NATO or GATT are appropriate examples. Although such treaties may restrict national policies they usually maintain national sovereignty through opting-out clauses, veto-power, or the unanimity rule.

A federal treaty has more of a constitutional nature: by integrating their economies and by coordinating their policies *all* participating nations will reach a higher degree of freedom as they improve conditions for social and economic development – conjointly as well as for each individual state. Although the initial treaty requires freedom of choice, unanimity among signatories and a broad consensus among citizens of the respective jurisdictions, the treaty – once adopted – will imply stronger commitments for member states. A federation is not simply a 'club' to be joined or quitted. Integration through federation is more binding than membership. This is because secession would imply heavy costs for *all* partners that have been investing in a common cause, hence it must be associated with high penalties for seceding members – excluding the cost of war of course.

Typically, federal constitutions do not address the issue of secession. Despite the long-term nature of the engagement a right of secession *in principle* should, however, be constituent to the notion of federalism. Without it, the welfare-improving character of the treaty for *all* members could not be tested. Where the possibility of a negotiable secession with compensation payments for sunk costs of the federation applies, however, no member can be forced to accept negative net benefits resulting from the treaty in the longer run. This in itself would induce the federation and its members to act conformingly and to share the fiscal surplus resulting from federation equitably so as to avoid secession. Concepts of federalism are thus prone to establishing regional fairness and to securing economic and social cohesion to the benefit of all jurisdictions.

Most federations that have evolved organically have indeed never had to face this ultimate test of their political stability. This may serve as an indication that federations have realised regional fairness as well as economic and social cohesion to a large extent. The realisation of these objectives is less obvious for unitary states; and regional interests have certainly been disregarded in formerly socialist countries where coercive federal structures were superimposed in order to disguise central dominance.

It is largely the experience of Eastern European disintegration and of some – albeit limited – regional conflicts in unitary states of the Western world that have spurred the interest in devolution and the decentralisation of powers. It is widely acknowledged today that the emphasis on administrative clarity and cost effectiveness through centralising the government sector will entail costs in terms of economic inefficiencies and inequities that tend to undermine the very nature of the social contract and create political instability. Greater economic and political integration must thus be assessed in view of the cost-benefit trade-off associated with the design of federal institutions.

2.1.2 The 'Layer-Cake' View of Federalism

The theoretical literature on fiscal federalism is heavily influenced by the 'layer-cake' idea.[1] According to this view, consumption of government services can be defined over – ideally distinct – geographical areas forming separable layers of constituencies for each public good. Larger constituencies supersede smaller regions, forming higher layers of government responsibility whenever this is warranted by a larger geographical distribution of public goods. Efficiency considerations then require regional governments to decide on Pareto-efficient levels of public services for their respective jurisdictions rather than to provide these services at uniform levels of output across all regions.[2] Public constituencies would thus, ideally, be formed and delineated in accordance with the local distribution of 'internal' benefits derived from government activities, and the efficient outcome would reflect both specific preferences as well as the ability to pay of taxpayers within each region. As a consequence there would be no conflict between governments at the vertical level – neither for the provision of public goods nor for its financing (which would obey the principle of benefit-taxation).[3]

In the real world, regions cannot be delineated neatly according to that view – even abstracting from given political boundaries – and this mainly for two reasons.

- *For each regional public good* there may be spillovers by which neighbouring regions are affected through public activities in other regions. This calls for cooperation among the respective governments and/or financial compensation for regional benefit spillovers – giving rise to a system of horizontal grants or transfer payments. It does not require interventions by the centre government.
- Governments usually provide *a full set of public goods* for their constituencies – not separable, specific regional goods. It is, then, most unlikely that taxpayers' preferences are sufficiently homogeneous *for all public goods* to be consumed within any one region.

Correspondence between the taxpayers' willingness to pay and the provision of each public good cannot be achieved under these circumstances.

However, if individual preferences of taxpayers do not conform with the local supply of government services, people are free to move into other constituencies in order to enhance personal (and social) welfare, according to the Tiebout (1956) view.[4] Again no central policy intervention is needed to maximise social welfare, except for 'framework legislation' creating and guaranteeing the conditions for mobility of goods and services as well as of factors of production – and hence for greater efficiency – within the whole federation.[5] This does not necessarily call for a widening of central responsibilities at the level of policy implementation.[6]

The 'layer-cake' model stresses the vertical division of independent government functions. The larger the geographical distribution of benefits derived from a public good, the higher will be the level of government providing that good. Higher levels are encouraged to act only to the extent that lower levels of government cannot provide services efficiently (*subsidiarity principle*). The central government's responsibilities are thus rather limited.[7]

On the other hand, the vertical separation of government functions leaves ample room for independent policies at each level of responsibility, emphasising cooperation among governments at the horizontal level. The model has no scope for equalisation payments or intergovernmental grants – except for those warranted by horizontal regional benefit spillovers. Moreover, all government services can be attributed to regional governments, and these are free to design their respective tax systems independently – and in accordance with benefit-pricing rules.

2.1.3   Normative Aspects of Federalism

The model sketched is the economist's *only positive* contribution to the theory of fiscal federalism. It is wholly based on efficiency considerations, disregarding distributive aspects entirely. Its conclusions are strong but very restricted in scope, because they disregard a number of important aspects restricting federal financial relations in practice. It should be noted, however, that any deviation from this model will necessarily imply *normative* (or value) judgements which are dictated by historical, political, psychological and social traditions and processes.

Normative judgements are, however, crucial for the design of federal financial relations to the extent that they reflect *consensus views* within the polity. There are essentially two types of processes leading to political consensus among regional authorities: those based on *mutual benefits*, and those based on *nuisance potentials* or concepts of *fairness*.[8]

Mutual benefits – As an example of the first type of consensus, the case of extreme economic discrepancies among regions leading to large interjurisdictional migration may be considered. For the economist migration is a (value-neutral) precondition for enhancing efficiency. From a political aspect, however, large flows of migrants may not be acceptable. Migration can cause enormous social problems resulting from mounting political tensions in labour-receiving regions, and social and economic disruptions in labour-losing areas. Even under economic considerations migration may entail social costs due to agglomeration effects on one hand, and to the emergence of non-viable regional economies on the other. It could lead to regional inequalities as to the provision of public goods and to imbalances between (infrastructure) capital and labour – given that land, fixed capital and other (cultural) inputs to regional production and social life are essentially immobile.

Thus there is a common interest of both labour-attractive and unattractive regions to restrict labour mobility in order to avoid the costs of too rapid transformations of local economies and an unacceptable corruption of regional cultural heritage. If these costs are thought to outweigh the efficiency gains from migration there is a strong case for a consensus on monitoring and discouraging migration through opposite economic incentives or even institutional barriers.

This consensus is wholly based on perceived *mutual benefits* to the regions concerned. If a wider concept of Pareto-optimality is adopted these political ingredients of intergovernmental arrangements can be incorporated into the traditional benefit-pricing model. Restricting mobility generates 'political stability', and, if this is considered to be a 'good' for citizens in all regions concerned, conforming political action can be regarded as forming an input to a generalised social production function, correcting for regional externalities and hence increasing general welfare.

Yet this type of government intervention may be effected entirely at the horizontal level – through bilateral or multilateral treaties among states. The case for central government intervention is relatively weak here – unless the costs of producing stability would be lowered by a central provision of the service.

Nuisance potential and fairness – As to the other type of consensus-forming process one should consider that the bargaining strength of regions within a federation may vary considerably. There are many avenues toward correcting distortions in bargaining power through the forming of regional coalitions and log-rolling. But if regional interests are too specific, and log-rolling potentials are low, there is always the threat of regional interests being ignored. If bargaining processes among regions are considered to be 'unfair', however, minority regions may have recourse to nuisance strategies or retaliation by which they can impose heavy costs on other regions without being able to pursue their interests directly;[9] they start exploiting their 'nuisance potentials'.[10] It then becomes the interest of the dominant regions to accept certain demands made by weaker states in order to avoid those potential costs and to preserve political stability. In this case, central government intervention may be warranted because there is the need for an impartial arbiter in the bargaining game (participating states themselves being always interested parties).[11] It is obvious, though, that the central government's role as an impartial arbiter must be accepted by minority regional governments. Since we are in the realm of normative judgements, this may not necessarily be the case.[12]

Again, fairness – as a normative ingredient – is usually *not* incorporated in the concept of Pareto-efficiency; yet, as before, it could be interpreted as forming an input into a more general social production function, creating gains from political stability. Redistribution of resources among regional governments then becomes a factor of production.

It is in this sense that the central government may have to intervene in order to increase general welfare and to avoid the threat of social unrest, losses in economic potential, political instability or even secession within a federation.[13] This redistributive goal has been accepted by the EC. It was officially adopted through the Single European Act (article 130), where 'cohesion' is seen to form a guiding principle for Community policies.

2.1.4   Centralisation vs Decentralisation

Multilevel finance, together with the subsidiarity principle, tends to limit the scope for centralising government functions. Centralisation is warranted only if specific government services can be supplied more efficiently at the centre level. The case for centralising functions is usually difficult to make. Theoretically, the layer-cake model would support centralisation only for three reasons:

- homogeneous preferences of voters/consumers for public services across regions;
- wider public-goods characteristics of a government service;[14] and
- lower transaction costs through economies of scale in the provision of public goods.

Homogeneous preferences are a necessary but not sufficient argument for centralising government activities in order to enhance efficiency. Even though preferences may be homogeneous throughout Europe it may still be efficient to provide public services at the lower tiers of government if this is more cost-effective or if preferences are more clearly identified at the regional level. Moreover, the argument is weak for the EC, given that preferences for public goods still appear to be very heterogeneous at present, and that maintaining diversity within Europe is widely accepted as a policy objective – leading to a better quality of life for citizens within the whole federation.

By far the most important argument rests on public goods. If the Community is to extend its responsibilities for the provision of supranational government services – for example, defence – this will strongly reinforce centripetal forces in Europe. But centralising functions by political decisions based on a broad consensus among national governments has to be thoroughly distinguished from the alleged automatic attractiveness of the central budget that is sometimes emphasised in the literature.[15]

While it is obvious that a conscientious decision to centralise functions must entail a strengthening of the central government's own resources – corresponding to reduced needs for resources at subcentral levels – the alleged automatism leading to a 'concentration process' for public resources remains to be validated empirically (Pryor 1968, pp. 70–9; Oates 1972, p. 210; Pommerehne 1977, p. 306; Nutter 1978, p. 90–4; Oates 1991).

For the following analysis we do not pay attention to occasional political rhetoric that aims at painting the EC Commission a voracious Leviathan *per se*, eager to get hold of public resources of nation states. This view may reveal itself to be entirely based on 'gut feelings', not on objective evidence. Yet it seems to be clear that the Community will evolve by increasingly shifting responsibilities onto the central government, and, where deliberate decisions of this kind are being taken, the consequences for financing such services have to be considered as well. As to multilevel government finance much depends therefore on the scenario for the distribution of functions within a future European Community.

Despite the importance of public goods and their role for a possible concentration process, the argument is not sufficient for centralising the supply of public goods on efficiency grounds. There may be simultaneous countervailing forces favouring decentralised government services – for example, a lesser degree of administrative effectiveness of the central government, or diseconomies of scale in the central provision of these goods. The residual economic argument for centralising power within a federation rests largely on transaction costs. If central decision-making is shown to reduce coordination costs the role of a central government is strengthened.[16] Yet, essentially, this argument is more in favour of centralised coordination; it does not necessarily support an increase in the central government's outlays or expenditure functions. The centre's role could be restricted to coordination; and services would continue to be supplied by national governments. This model has been shown to work successfully even in the realm of defence (NATO). It is also typical of the horizontal approach to federalism adopted in the Federal Republic of Germany and, to some extent, in Switzerland (see chs 3.2 and 3.3 below).

In addition to the economic costs of decentralised coordination there may exist 'political transaction costs'. It has been argued that smaller government units are more likely to respond to the demands of special-interest groups and to political pressure, which may entail inefficiencies and slower economic growth. Mancur Olson went as far as to stipulate that 'the efficiency of an economy may be increased either by making narrow special-interest groups weaker or by making the government stronger in relation to them' (Olson 1983b, p. 23; see also Olson 1983a, ch. 6). This argument points toward greater centralisation of responsibilities, not necessarily, again, toward the central provision of public services. It seems to be rather convincing though.[17]

It should be noted, however, that most arguments for centralising government functions are related to the expenditure side; they rarely stem from taxation. There is little support for a centralisation of government functions based on pure revenue aspects. Taxes seem to follow expenditures under the benefit-pricing rule implicitly – which is thought to be the key to economic efficiency in the public sector. The main rationale for centralised tax collection is again based on higher transaction costs or the political costs of decentralised tax collection. Yet although there may be economies of scale in central tax collection it is often overlooked that this may warrant central tax administration, not the assignment of the proceeds from taxation to the central government. The choice between own taxes, shared taxes and grants in multilevel federal finance is examined more thoroughly in ch. 2.2.

2.1.5   Some First Conclusions

As far as the vertical distribution – and notably the centralisation – of functions in a federal polity is concerned, economic theory offers little guidance. The thrust of the arguments is on efficiency with regard to the provision of public goods, and on transaction costs. Considering efficiency aspects as well as normative political considerations, the division of functions between the centre and the states' governments is seen to be determined as follows.

- There is a strong case for centralising the provision of generalised public goods the benefits of which can be attributed to the whole federation. Historically, a shared consensus on forming a regional defence pact has usually been at the cradle of existing federations – with the notable exception of the EC. Apart from defence and foreign policy the case for generalised public goods is difficult to make, which explains the reduced size of the EC budget measured as a percentage of Community GDP. As to the future development of the EC budget much depends on the political will to concentrate and to join efforts in defence and foreign policy in Europe.

- Based on mutual gains from internalising regional spillovers there is a case for coordination and cooperation among regions. The central government can play an active role by supporting these processes through information and standardisation policies as well as through providing a legal and political framework for coordination. As can be seen from the German model of federalism – to be discussed later in more detail – a horizontal division of functions may result by which the central government provides support through framework legislation and the states retain the power to implement these policies according to their preferences and within the general restrictions set by the centre. Central government activities do not require much budgetary means under such institutional arrangements.[18]

- Political costs may emerge through regional competition for factors of production causing social disruptions and political unrest through large-scale migration, for instance. This may jeopardise 'cohesion' within the EC. Again, emerging problems may be settled by the regions concerned;[19] yet there is a case for the central government helping to smooth adjustment processes – for instance by the setting of minimum standards for public services in order to contain interjurisdictional migration. Coordinative functions of that type do not require large increases in budgetary means however.

- There is a different type of social cost based on the power of any one region to impose costs on the federation through political frictions and retaliation if federal arrangements are thought to be unfair. It is in the interest of the Community to avoid such costs and to establish equality of opportunities by setting minimum standards for the provision of public goods. Where these cannot be met through own financial resources there is a case for the central government engaging in redistributive activities through asymmetrical vertical-equalisation grants and/or asymmetrical financial contributions from regions to the financing of central government activities. Activities of this type may lead to an expansion of the EC budget in the future.

- Similarly, in a Community evolving at multiple speeds, the more dynamic member states may have to 'bribe' the smaller ones to join the bandwagon of common policies within the EC. This approach may help to reduce political frictions and hence costs to the Community. In order to render these policies feasible it may be necessary to channel funds through the EC budget in order to 'blur' direct compensation payments. Furthermore, asymmetries in the distribution of means may be objected to on political grounds, or central funds may have to be rendered accessible to *all* regions for legal and constitutional reasons. This must lead to a 'churning' of resources through the central budget, which is a dreadful thought to the economist eager to dispel fiscal illusion rather than fostering it through such devices. It should be noted, however, that political acceptance and stability *is* a public good, and that fiscal illusion created through 'churning' may be the price to be paid for achieving it.

- Finally, the central government may play an active role in protecting national governments against special-interest groups and lobbying within their respective jurisdictions. This may, again, warrant greater responsibilities on the part of the Commission in the setting of a framework for national legislation; it does not necessarily entail a greater EC budget though.

There may be a further case for central government intervention that is not usually addressed in the traditional model of fiscal federalism. Regional economic and political integration – especially under EMU – may require the centralisation of payment or funding functions in Europe, respectively a clearing system to be exerted by the Commission. For instance, existing proposals for a coordinated system of value-added taxation in Europe require the creation of a regional clearing mechanism. A possible future pension fund for European workers and employees may also become reasonable under EMU. A number of such funds could be directly related to EMU. Also, there may be the need for a central unemployment insurance fund in order to mitigate regional unemployment caused by asymmetrical shocks. Furthermore, it may well be that parts of existing national public debts *vis-à-vis* national Central Banks will not be transferred onto the con-solidated balance sheet of the European System of Central Banks (ESCB).

Excessive parts of the national debt of any one member country may then be shifted onto 'wind-up funds' that will be used to reschedule and redeem existing debt under national governments' responsibilities without affecting coordinated monetary policies. These 'wind-up funds' are likely to remain under national responsibility; they may require EC intervention in the form of financial contributions to the redemption of the debt however.

Such funds or clearing functions may be regarded as being 'off budget' (as they are, indeed, in many countries, for instance pension funds or public health insurance funds), and they should be governed by a strict *quid pro quo* principle or other 'rules of the game' as in the case of pure clearing funds. It should be noted in passing that the agricultural guarantee fund – which evokes strong regional *'juste-retour'* thinking – would also qualify to be treated in this fashion: by being put 'off' the EC budget to be run separately under its own specific 'rules of the game' (Spaventa/Koopmans/Salmon/Smith/Spahn 1986).

2.2 OWN TAXES, SHARED TAXES AND GRANTS

2.2.1 Tax Assignment

Any federation has to deal with the vertical as well as the horizontal assignment of financial resources to its different governments.

2.2.1.1 Assigning taxes vertically
The vertical distribution of funds[20] usually follows the distribution of functions among different layers of government: the smaller the competence of the centre, the more reduced will be the scope for defining its own resources. The vertical distribution of funds thus reflects – to some extent – the degree of centralisation within a federal state.[21]

Yet apart from the question of the vertical structure of expenditures there is the issue of the vertical assignment of tax instruments. The question is, here, whether certain taxes are better suited to be assigned to the central government than others (or to regional governments, and *vice versa*), or whether tax assignment is simply a matter of convenience.

A useful starting point to discuss this issue is found in Musgrave's systematic treatment of the question (Musgrave 1983, Oates 1991). He would assign the following taxes to the central budget:

- Taxes with highly progressive rates – Such taxes are expected to entail perverse incentives for migration between regions if levied at

the regional level. This is consistent with Musgrave's contention that the distribution function should be exerted by central governments.
- Taxes on highly mobile tax bases (like portfolio capital) – Such taxes are expected to distort locational patterns of economic activity if levied at the regional level.
- Taxes on tax bases that are distributed across jurisdictions in a highly unequal fashion (like natural resources) – Such taxes are expected to lead to geographical inequities and to entail allocative distortions if levied at the regional level.

On the other hand, subcentral authorities should exploit the following revenue sources.

- Taxes on regionally immobile tax bases – Such taxes do not exhibit 'excess burdens' – they are hence neutral as to regional locational decisions.
- Taxes relating to specific regional benefits – Such taxes (like user taxes and fees) create, again, little incentive for moving across jurisdictions.

Musgrave's criteria – although very useful – seem to be heavily influenced by the assignment of taxes in the United States. They may not be sufficient for discussing the assignment of taxes within the Community. It is debatable, for instance, whether progressive subnational taxation does in fact lead to perverse migration effects. Tiebout migration seems to be exaggerated by economists – given that individuals may incur high mobility costs and are usually more or less firmly tied to their regional cultural heritage.[22] And in more extreme versions of the 'public choice' perspective of federalism it is suggested that only regions should levy income taxes – because the extent of the redistribution that can be achieved is constrained by factor mobility and regional competition (Brennan/Buchanan 1983). Moreover there is at least one important counter-example to the United States, a federation with regional income taxation: Switzerland. Why should another not be formed by the EC?

Furthermore, Musgrave's criteria seem to imply inconsistencies. For instance the contention that natural resources should be taxed by the centre seems to collide with the rule that regional governments should tax regionally immobile tax bases. This is explained by Musgrave's mixing efficiency and distribution arguments, and by a potential conflict between these goals. It is not at all clear whether regional taxation of natural resources does in fact lead to inequities or allocative distortions. If a residence-oriented income tax dominates in a federation, regions rich in natural resources may find themselves deprived of any substantial revenue source unless allowed to tax their resources.[23] Furthermore, exploiting natural resources often entails 'excess profits' that can be taxed without leading to allocative distortions. And finally, regional immobility of tax bases alone is not sufficient to warrant regional taxation. Often the tax base is malleable ('putty-clay' model of investment), and even where it stays 'put', regional taxation may cause severe economic damage to the region: the closure of plants or – in the case of natural resources – ruinous competition with other regions disposing of similar resources. The necessary condition for efficient origin-based regional taxation is the existence of excess profits – not regional immobility.

If value-laden distributional effects of the Musgravian criteria are put aside, the essence of the allocative argument seems to lie, again, in benefit-pricing. We shall elaborate on this, adding some specific elements that may be inherent in Musgrave's concept: the instrumental use of taxes, as well as the tax-competition and the regional-arbitrariness arguments.

The benefit-pricing argument. As mentioned before, the layer-cake view would attribute own taxes to each level of government according to the regional distribution of benefits derived from public services provided by each layer of government. Each level would be free to chose its own tax base, and there would be no competition at the vertical level. There could even be concurrent taxation by different layers of government – which is in fact the case for the income tax in the United States, in Canada and in Switzerland.

Theoretically one would want to distinguish two aspects of taxation: (i) revenue effects and (ii) instrumental aspects.

Public revenue raising should ideally be neutral in that it distorts neither economic decisions (*efficiency neutrality*) nor the distribution of incomes (*distributive neutrality*).[24] It then has a pure income effect. Although full neutrality is never achieved, the emphasis is on revenue generation to finance public services, not on allocative, distributive or other policies through the use of tax instruments.

However, if revenue raising is the sole objective of taxation at the centre level, a similar result could also be achieved through unconditional bloc grants to be handed to the centre by the states. This is essentially the solution adopted for the German *Reich* at its inception;[25] it is equally the solution found for the EC at present (since the sharing of VAT and the 'fourth' and 'fifth' levies could all be interpreted as general revenue grants). The question is, therefore, whether direct access to regional tax bases has advantages over unconditional revenue grants to be accorded to the central government.

On pure revenue considerations the advantages of direct taxation powers by the centre *vis-à-vis* unconditional bloc grants may be twofold: (i) the greater degree of political independence of the centre; and (ii) a visible link between the provision of public goods provided by the centre and the corresponding financial burden imposed on taxpayers.

- Greater political independence involves, again, value judgements. A strong central government may be desirable for some; it may be vehemently rejected by others. Given the reluctance of regional governments to forego sovereignty – as expressed in the subsidiarity principle – and even a renaissance of regional politics – notably in Eastern Europe – it is questionable whether central taxation can be based on such an argument. To the extent that financial stability is needed to ascertain a smooth functioning of the central government's functions this could equally be achieved through firm financial commitments by regional authorities to supply funding, commitments that could even take the form of 'constitutional' guarantees. Under pure revenue aspects a centralisation of taxation powers does not seem to be necessary.
- The link between the taxpayers' bills and the provision of public goods is the economists main avenue towards establishing efficiency and at the same time containing the size of the public sector (Brennan/Buchanan 1977, 1980). Fiscal sovereignty at each layer of government is expected to dispel fiscal illusion, which is thought to mobilise taxpayers' resistance against undesired high levels of government expenditure.

Such conclusions are drawn from an analogy to the paradigm for the efficient supply of private goods under market conditions. Samuelson (1954, 1955) has established rules for the Pareto-optimal supply of public goods; he has also brought to the fore that these requirements are difficult to meet in practice, however.

Pareto-efficiency for public goods requires the planner to be informed on individual preferences, and to set (Lindahl-) tax-prices according to individual marginal benefits; the sum of these taxes should equate marginal costs. Tax-prices usually vary among taxpayers according to their willingness to pay.[26] Furthermore, the model is based on the assumption of a first-best economy (in particular there are no distortions inherent in the tax system), governments provide only one public good (or there are homogeneous regional preferences as to a given bundle of public goods), and a collective welfare function prevails allowing interpersonal comparisons of individual utility.

These conditions are impossible to meet in practice. And even if they were met: the link between the taxpayers' bills and the provision of public goods would not be sufficient for centralising taxing powers. This link could be rendered visible at the level of regional taxation, for example through a regional piggy-back tax (or surcharge) for the central government's budget.

As regards revenue raising in the pure sense, the economist's points for central taxation seem to be rather weak indeed.

The instrumental-approach argument. Where the instrumental approach to taxation dominates, the emphasis is on the economic effects of taxation – not on revenue raising. For instance, if taxes are used for stabilisation purposes, tax proceeds of a boom period may have to be immobilised in order to be spent during a recession.[27] Redistributive taxation may collect resources from one group of taxpayers for the support of other groups. Taxation may also be targeted to allocative objectives – creating, for instance, incentives to reduce pollution from certain economic activities. If the latter goal is achieved through tax instruments, the conflict with the fiscal objectives of taxation is most obvious: the revenue-raising effect of an efficient pollution tax is ideally zero.

It is interesting to note that, originally, the emphasis of the EC budget was mainly on revenue raising. The proof for this is the bloc-grants means of financing large shares of the budget. The very fact that the EC budget is not allowed to run deficits prevents the Commission from engaging in stabilisation policies. The EC has little power to 'legislate' on taxes and it only has restricted access to own tax bases. Neither regionally redistributive taxation nor taxation aiming at allocative objectives is thus feasible.

Yet more recent developments have introduced and strengthened the instrumental approach to taxation at the Community level. To the extent that central expenditure functions – notably those related to price guarantees within the realm of Common Agricultural Policy (CAP) – were seen to distort supply reactions of European farmers, corrective actions were taken through the use of agricultural levies. There is thus a strong precedent for using taxation as an instrument for Community allocation policies.

Contrary to the pure revenue-raising aspect, the case for central taxes based on the instrumental approach is rather strong. The question, therefore, is which central policies will become more important in the future and to what extent will it be necessary to hand over conforming tax instruments to the Community level, enabling it to perform its functions effectively.

This question will have to be discussed more specifically in the last chapter of this book.

The tax-competition argument. There is a further dimension to the problem of assigning taxes vertically that has become more and more important in recent years: the increasing regional mobility of tax bases. Notably, the difficulty of imposing capital income from portfolio investments acts as a constraint to effective taxation at the regional level – because taxpayers can avoid taxation by moving the tax base from high-tax to low-tax jurisdictions. These reactions are tied to the so-called 'tax-competition' phenomenon. Under these circumstances regional governments are inclined to compete for mobile tax bases by mutually reducing tax rates. The result is a beggar-thy-neighbour policy, a Nash-game, the equilibrium outcome of which is the undertaxation of capital. This would then entail a suboptimal provision of public goods within all regions (Giovannini 1989).

The argument is often stressed in view of tax harmonisation within the EC under EMU, where exchange rates cease to compensate for differences in tax rates. It could also be interpreted as a centripetal force working in favour of centralised tax collection.

The problems of tax competition and tax harmonisation cannot be dealt with here in full.[28] They are especially complex with regard to taxing the proceeds from production – labour and capital income. With relatively immobile factors of production in the early days of the Community this problem did not seem to be urgent. Where mobility was important, governments were quick to react by installing controls – if they were not already existing, as in the case of capital income. But with capital and labour markets becoming more and more integrated, and exchange-rate risks disappearing under EMU, tax avoidance may in fact become a serious problem within the Community.

One way out of the dilemma could be uniform taxation within the federation – which is the model adopted in Germany for instance. Uniformity of tax rates would avoid regional 'tax arbitrage' and hence discourage tax-avoidance strategies and the unproductive derouting of capital flows for purely institutional reasons. While the necessity of uniform taxation within a federation has been proved to be wrong as long as price elasticities are below infinity,[29] the argument strongly holds for the harmonisation of tax bases rather than rates (Sinn 1990), and it is most powerful as regards the flows of portfolio investment in globalised capital markets where price elasticities do in fact approach infinity. But even if the uniformity approach were accepted – as in Germany – this does not necessarily imply centralising the proceeds from taxation. All it requires is central tax legislation or some form of tax coordination.

Tax coordination is, indeed, the soft approach to avoiding tax competition within a federation while retaining decentralised tax legislation. The smaller the discrepancy between effective regional tax rates the lower the incentive to move tax bases across regions. The Community has embarked on that avenue by proposing bands of tax rates for certain excise taxes and for VAT or rate floors.

Tax coordination may be an intermediate step towards achieving full tax harmonisation in the long run. As markets develop, tax competition may reappear with falling transaction costs. Only where convergence of tax rules is complete will all forms of tax competition within the Community vanish. Full tax harmonisation may in the longer run be the future of VAT – which is increasingly being considered as a revenue-raising instrument *par excellence*. A unitary income tax is, however, likely to be politically unacceptable for a long time.

Income taxation is very heterogeneous; it is heavily intertwined with national social policy; it is subject to large differences in collective value judgements – especially on redistribution; and it is often a symbol of national sovereignty. Nevertheless, pressure for harmonising the taxation of capital income will mount as competition for international resources increases. In particular, governments may eventually accept a unitary corporation tax affecting excess profits or rents within the Community. This point will have to be developed more fully below. Again this does not necessarily imply central tax legislation or central tax collection.[30]

The regional-arbitrariness argument. Tax competition within a federation also relates to a discussion on which taxes should be centralised and which taxes should remain at the state (and local) level for technical reasons.[31] Obviously the more difficult it is to define a tax base at the regional level the more appropriate this base becomes for central taxation. In particular, if the regional distribution of tax bases is arbitrary it becomes questionable to apportion the proceeds from taxes to regional governments.

At the Community level this can best be demonstrated for customs duties. Customs duties are levied on international transactions at uniform rates throughout the Community. From a fiscal point of view it is rather arbitrary whether a foreign supplier goes through country x or y when accessing the European market. Regional apportionment of tax proceeds would reflect this regional arbitrariness: it would favour regions that specialised in foreign trade, and it would disfavour all other regions irrespective of the final use of the imported goods. It is for these reasons that the proceeds from these taxes have been handed over to the Commission even though tax collection remains at the state level.

A similar reasoning applies to agricultural levies used for CAP. Import levies and export subsidies are instrumental to protecting the agricultural sector *in toto*. Again it is rather arbitrary in which region they are applied. Consequently the proceeds from those levies – as well as related expenditures – have been transferred to the Commission under these auspices.[32]

Similar problems may emerge for value-added taxation. If a destination-type VAT with a tax credit is used in a federation where no interior fiscal frontiers exist, a regional apportionment of taxes is questionable on the basis of the proceeds from these taxes. Again there may be regions specialising in the production of exportable goods, whereas others thrive on import-refining industries. Governments of the former regions would receive comparably little revenue from VAT (or even experience negative incomes if they have to credit taxes paid to other governments in the federation that are higher than own tax collection); governments of the latter regions would collect taxes on imported goods even though final consumption was mainly outside the region.

It may be for these and similar reasons that VAT is usually a tax collected by the central government or – as in the case of Germany – jointly by federal and state governments, and that apportionment of taxes to regional governments is independent from regional tax proceeds – for instance those based on a per capita formula.[33] It may also explain why a share of VAT has been transferred to the EC budget. VAT is therefore another strong candidate for coordinated or even centralised taxation. However, the argument is not sufficient for handing over VAT entirely to the central government. As is seen from both German and EC examples, VAT can also become a shared tax between centre and regional governments.

A similar reasoning could apply to business income taxes (of a residence type) for multinational companies – since the attribution of taxable income to different plants is absolutely arbitrary.[34] The argument is less stringent for business income taxes of an origin type. It is true that the location of firms and their network of regional plants within the federation should not be dictated by tax considerations; and there are also strategies for moving the taxable base from one region to another. Yet the harmonisation of business taxes of an origin type is mainly based on the tax-competition argument, and hence the case for centralising these taxes is rather weak.

More recently a case has been made for centralised pollution taxes in as much as the effects of pollution cannot be confined to regions, and discrepancies in regional environmental charges may entail ruinous tax competition among states failing to achieve environmental efficiency. This argument is in fact related to a number of arguments for centralising or coordinating tax collection: the regional-arbitrariness, the tax-competition, the instrumental, and the benefit-pricing approaches alike. We shall pursue this idea in the last main chapter of this book.

The economies-of-scale-in-collecting-taxes argument. As has been noted in ch. 2.1.4, there may be economies of scale in collecting and administering taxes at the centre level. The main rationale for this was based on the higher transaction costs or political costs of decentralised tax collection. It was argued earlier that the dimensions of the tax-assignment problem are more important with regard to the rights to legislate and to levy taxes, and that tax administration seems to be subsidiary in nature. Therefore the argument seems to be less relevant here. Moreover it is questionable whether it is convincing in the context of Community finance, where tax administration is likely to remaine at the level of Nation states – at least for the foreseeable future.

The case for economies of scale in central tax collection, regarding its possible impact on a future EC budget under EMU, is not discussed here at length. Nevertheless a few remarks seem to be in order since they may have a bearing on related issues discussed later in this book.

- Central tax administration for reasons of economies of scale should not be confounded with central tax administration under the instrumental approach. It may well be true that tax legislation and tax administration can become heavily intertwined – because of enforcement problems, for instance. Yet in this case the dominant argument for centralising taxation powers still rests on *tax legislation* not on its administrative side aspects.

- Central tax administration does not necessarily imply the assignment of the proceeds from taxation to the central government. The EC could eventually collect and administer taxes on behalf of member states – as the latter may act on behalf of the EC. Assigning the proceeds from taxes can in fact fully be separated from tax administration.

- If central tax administration and collection is chosen for any reason, be it economies of scale or legislative reasons (instrumental purposes), this may be compensated for by the system of multilayer finance to be adopted within the federation. In principle, any system of tax collection may be acceptable to member states – since the right to administer taxes and the right to absorb the proceeds from taxation are fully separable. However, it may entail additional provisions in the form of vertical clearing mechanisms that reorient cashflows to the revenue structures adopted.

Vertical cashflows resulting from the divergence between the right to collect taxes and the right to retain tax yields should be distinguished from vertical tax adjustment warranted for other reasons – for instance a discrepancy between tax proceeds and expenditure needs. The latter will be addressed more fully in the next chapter.

2.2.1.2   The case for tax sharing

Within the layer-cake model any necessary vertical adjustments of tax proceeds can always be effected through a change in tax rates and/or tax bases at any one level of government. Tax proceeds ideally follow the expansion of government functions – the benefit-pricing or correspondence approach remaining the general guiding principles. It was emphasised, however, that these principles are far from being operational for an effective Pareto-efficient allocation of public goods. In addition the vertical distribution of funds is often blurred by contradictory value judgements. For instance, some authors expect a more centralised government to lead to larger public sectors; others express the opposite view. For some, centralised taxation is an evil; others view it more positively. The lack of consensus on the vertical distribution of funds may entail vertical tax competition or an over-exploitation of tax bases. It is, then, in the interest of all governments to avoid such a situation by imposing constitutional constraints on taxation at the vertical level.

The constitutional separation of taxation powers found in most Western federations largely corresponds to the layer-cake idea. Yet even though an initial assignment of taxes through the constitution may be in line with the division of outlay functions among tiers of government, the distribution of public revenues may have to be continuously readjusted in order to cope with the following dynamic problems.

- The assignment of taxes may not correspond to the central government's obligations in the area of demand management.
- Taxes may react differently to the swings in the business cycle and to growth, and hence the development of public funds may jeopardise a steady, continuous, needs-oriented expansion of government services.
- The vertical distribution of tax yields may not follow the development in the vertical distribution of functions among the tiers of government.
- There may be political changes in the distribution of functions that fail to be reflected in the distribution of financial means among the tiers of government, requiring some governments to react to the change.

Problems related to compensatory finance in a federal setting are not dealt with here.[35] As far as the correspondence between outlays and revenues is concerned there is a multitude of reasons why it may be undermined in the longer run: for instance, easier access to debt finance may relax the budget constraint for one level of government compared with others; this may lead to an asymmetrical expansion of government outlays through government debt (the case of the US federal government). More generally speaking: softer budget constraints usually render governments more vulnerable to the demands of specific-interest groups, with an asymmetrical expansion of functions among the tiers of government. Low revenue elasticities for taxes assigned to one tier of government may combine with highly elastic outlays either as a function of a higher proportion of services (health, education) or as a result of a widening of functions through alien legislative interference (the case of German municipalities with regard to *Sozialhilfe*).[36]

It is for these (and other) reasons that Germany, for instance, has moved away from assigning taxes to independent levels of government, increasingly using shared or joint taxes. Taxes can, in principle, be assigned jointly to all levels of government. Tax yields can then be distributed vertically using any formula imaginable. There may also result desired (and undesired) implicit horizontal equalisation effects – by the very nature of the formula adopted – if the distribution of funds works asymmetrically among regions. Joint taxes or revenue sharing are therefore flexible as to both vertical readjustments and a regional redistribution of means.

Tax sharing needs a strong political consensus among all governments concerned; and it requires an institutional setting for revising distribution formulae in view of changing demands. These institutions must also effectively protect regional minority interests from the outset, and they must guarantee a fair dealing for the settling of conflicts and disputes among parties concerned.

Tax sharing is the horror of the 'layer-cake' economist because it destroys the link between taxation and the provision of public goods. Scepticism as to the viability of benefit-taxation in general has already been expressed above (see ch. 2.1.4). Furthermore, the economist's argument is questionable to the extent that a neat vertical division of functions remains a theoretical construct. And the vertical distribution of functions often reflects value-laden political decisions – not simply efficiency considerations. But, even based on pure theoretical grounds, concern over destroying this link is unfounded to the extent that the emphasis is on revenue raising, that is, on the income effect of taxation. In this case tax sharing among governments – notwithstanding non-neutral effects of taxation – may become a public zero-sum-game – with no further incentive effects on the economy.[37]

The fear that tax sharing may nourish a 'Leviathan' central government is also unfounded. On the contrary: an institutional tax-sharing formula may avoid over-exploitation of tax bases more effectively than any alleged constraining power of the revenue-expenditure link exerted by the median voter.

If taxes are to be used as policy instruments, however, a clear-cut and visible pattern of tax incidence *is* desirable and any sharing formula blurring these effects must become counterproductive. It is therefore important, again, to underline instrumental aspects of taxation when defining the scope for further revenue sources to be handed over to the Commission.

2.2.1.3   Regional inequities and perequation

The other problem to be solved in a federation regards the horizontal distribution of taxes. Again, the theory of fiscal federalism tends to favour independent tax policies within different regions. States may be free to define different tax bases, they may fix different rates and accord different tax concessions to their citizens. Taxes are seen as 'prices' for government services, and, again, independent benefit-pricing rules are seen to foster efficiency within the public sector.

From the political aspect taxes can be targeted toward specific national policy goals. They are used for income redistribution, for family and employment policies, and so on. Administratively, they become intertwined with social security arrangements; they are combined with other taxes to a varying degree (corporation taxes, payroll taxes); and they are operating within different institutional and political settings. Regional taxation is thus essential for preserving existing patterns of social traditions and cultural heritage.

Yet, from a horizontal aspect, the assignment of taxes to regions may cause undesired economic effects: different levels of taxable capacity may entail different individual tax burdens for a given level of public services (or imply different levels of services for a similar tax burden). Moreover, the taxable capacity of poorer regions is restricted. This must lead to a lower provision of public goods (human and fixed-capital infrastructure); and this, again, tends to preserve existing regional discrepancies in economic potential. This consequence may be experienced as unfair by poorer regions, rendering social and political cohesion more difficult. It therefore, jeopardises regionally balanced growth in the federation. The problem may be accentuated by tax-competition phenomena, and there are likely to occur further inequities within the federation where interregional tax loopholes exist.

If political stability or fairness are seen to be factors of production these phenomena justify corrective actions through the redistribution of funds. For the EC the basis for implementing such policies is embedded in article 130 of the Single European Act, where the aim of 'cohesion' is emphasised; Germany goes even a step further stressing – in its Constitution – the 'uniformity of living conditions' for the federation.

Redistributive policies are, again, normative to a large extent. Furthermore, they tend to destroy desired links between taxes and expenditures. As has been more fully discussed above, 'cohesion' – even as a vague concept – can lead to horizontal equalisation grants – as in the German case – or to asymmetrical vertical grants and to regional tax concessions. The design of intergovernmental grants will be discussed in the next chapter.

2.2.2   Grants and Equalisation

2.2.2.1   *The nature of grants*
Federal fiscal relations are typically characterised by the existence of intergovernmental grants – the transfer of resources among governments within a federal polity.[38]

A thorough distinction should be made between intergovernmental grants and intergovernmental financial flows. Grants always imply a transfer of real resources from the granting to the grantee government. Whether grants take the form of financial compensation or other forms of assistance (for example unpaid services) is unimportant. On the other hand, there may be intergovernmental financial flows that are different from grants. These may originate, for instance, from one government collecting taxes on behalf of another (discrepancy between *Ertragshoheit* and *Durchführungshoheit*), which entails the need for financial clearing. Or financial flows may result from payments for services received according to a strict *quid pro quo* principle.[39]

Grants may be either for general purposes – that is, they are available for spending at the discretion of the recipient government – or for specific purposes – available only for spending on particular programmes designated by the granting government. Furthermore, grants can be conditional or unconditional.[40] Grants are therefore classified as in the table overleaf.[41]

S-grants are usually given for allocative reasons when the level of the provision for specific services to be supplied by the grantee government is low and the granting government wants to raise it. If grants are unconditional, their effects on the aided function are uncertain, since these grants usually release own funds of the receiving government which would have been spent on the aided programme anyway. To the extent that S-grants free resources for other uses as the granting government thinks fit, their effects are indistinguishable from general purpose grants.

	Unconditional	*Conditional*
General Purpose Grants	G-grants	G*-grants
Specific Purpose Grants	S-grants	S*-grants

S*-grants tend to affect the function of recipient governments to a much larger degree, because national priorities can be more clearly defined as conditions for the aid.[42] Furthermore, this type of grant may mobilise additional funds for the aided programme, for instance through matching requirements. Open-ended matching grants are often seen to follow the standard prescription for Pigovian subsidies, where the matching term indicates the benefits to residents of other jurisdictions. The grant therefore, serves to internalise these benefits into regional decision-making (Break 1967).

G-grants are usually given for equalisation purposes or as a substitute for own revenue collection by regional governments (as in Australia). G*-grants are also often used for allocative purposes when the income elasticity of demand for public services is high at the state level. Conditions attached are rather weak in these cases, for example they may be required to be spent on fixed-capital formation only.

Grants may take the form of horizontal or of vertical transfers of means. Horizontal grants are used to shift resources among regional governments at a given level. Vertical grants involve different levels of government, and they may be downward as well as upward oriented.

2.2.2.2   Horizontal grants

The case for horizontal grants between governments is often made on the basis of regional spillovers. These grants may operate on a voluntary basis among states without an intervening third party. They thrive on the mutual benefits to be realised through such a scheme. In the case of horizontal grants that compensate for public services provided by neighbouring regional governments a market-like *quid pro quo* principle may be applied, which is the economist's delight. It is expected to enhance efficiency. In fact there are many examples of horizontal cooperation of this type – even among EC member states – yet the case is more complex than it appears at first sight.

- Horizontal cooperation based on mutual benefits among states only functions for the provision of goods – whether rival in consumption or not – to which the exclusion principle can be applied. Exclusion may, however, be politically unacceptable – for instance, university education only for members of the region; or technically unfeasible – which is generally the case for regional public goods. Under these circumstances there may be a free-rider incentive for regional governments, leading to a break-down of cooperation and to a failure to achieve Pareto-efficient outcomes. This may require central government intervention.
- Furthermore, taxable capacities of some regions may be too low, preventing them from cooperating effectively in horizontal joint public ventures. Again, corrective measures are needed at the horizontal level.
- And finally, there is the case of regional inequities leading to political instability, which may warrant intervention on the grounds of regional fairness or social and economic 'cohesion'.

The first two issues cannot be resolved through horizontal grants. They necessitate central government intervention. If a free-rider strategy is adopted at the regional level horizontal grants are inappropriate to internalise benefits from spillovers. The same is true if cooperation is hindered by an effective budget constraint on a regional government benefiting from spillovers: horizontal grants given to ease this constraint may then be considered equivalent to conceding regional spillovers directly and without compensation. If there is a deadlock on an infrastructural project caused by the inability to pay of a regional constituency benefiting from spillovers this can only be resolved through vertical grants.[43]

The third issue, regional perequation of diverging taxable capacities, may equally be achieved through vertical grants. This will be addressed in the next chapter. Yet correcting regional imbalances can equally be effected among regional governments themselves – through horizontal grants. Such grants require coordinative action; yet they do not necessarily imply central government involvement.[44] An institutional example of horizontal perequation can be found in Germany's *Finanzausgleich*.[45]

Perequation does not compensate for regional spillovers: it is a purely redistributive device implying political or value judgements. As has been argued earlier, equalising measures can also be subsumed under the

Pareto-concept – to the extent that such devices act as a safeguard for political stability within the federation. It is obvious that a strong consensus on more general benefits to be reaped from equalising public revenue is needed among participating states for such a scheme to become operational. Yet horizontal grants may also be based on nuisance potentials of any one region if the federation has an interest in preserving stability and in avoiding possible disruptions. In this sense the concessions of the EC accorded to the United Kingdom and Germany in the Fontainebleau agreement may also be understood as implicit horizontal grants – especially since the reduction in the British contribution is made up by all member states, except Germany, in accordance with their respective percentage share of VAT payments.[46]

Horizontal grants may take different institutional forms: they may be arranged bilaterally or multilaterally; they may be negotiable or based on firm constitutional rules; they may be once-and-for-all payments or be granted on a regular basis; the amount may be determined *ad hoc* or calculated using complex distribution formulae; there may be full annual clearing of grants or a revolving fund to be managed in accordance with specific needs (for instance a public investment fund).

More important than the institutional peculiarities of the arrangements are the criteria guiding horizontal equalisation. Basically two approaches may be distinguished: one attempts to equate taxable capacities; the other stresses equal opportunities on the basis of specific needs for public services. The German *Finanzausgleich* in its present form emphasises taxable capacity as a yardstick for equalisation. Consequently horizontal grants are pure G-grants with no strings attached to the receiving government. This may make sense as long as the costs of providing public services are comparable across regions, and as long as the basket of public goods supplied is fairly homogeneous – which was true for West Germany before 1990.

If the aim is equal opportunities and the costs of providing specific public services differ significantly among regions, horizontal grants must be corrected on the basis of cost indices (for example wages) for a given basket of goods. Balancing fiscal capacities without taking these differentials into account would result in over-compensation.[47] If ever the EC should adopt horizontal grants she is likely to opt for corrective cost elements in the distribution formula, given the fact that there are large discrepancies in the cost of providing services in different regions of the EC. This is true despite the fact that EMU will eventually lead to more homogeneous cost levels within Europe.[48]

If the aim is equal opportunities and the baskets of goods supplied by regional governments differ widely there is a further problem involving nearly insurmountable interpersonal and interregional comparisons of value judgements. The problem is then to define the content of 'equal opportunities' in terms of a specific basket of public services to be supplied under different geographical, climatic, cultural, ethnic, religious, economic, social and other circumstances. Problems of this kind are familiar to politicians in Australia, Canada and the United States, where large regional discrepancies exist. Whereas the US makes no attempt to perequate regional differences of this type, Australia regularly reviews these discrepancies through a specific independent body, the Commonwealth Grants Commission. This Commission monitors the provision of public goods in each state, recommending financial assistance for specific purposes on the basis of perceived regional needs. It is obvious that these judgements are heavily influenced by 'merit-good' considerations (in the Musgravian sense), which are unlikely to be resolved through horizontal cooperation. They usually rest on the notion of a benevolent patriarch or dictator – which is a way of circumscribing central government intervention.

For the Community – even with converging unit costs under EMU – horizontal equalising grants are unlikely to become acceptable given the variety of cultures and the specific needs of different regions. Equalisation is more likely to become the realm of central government intervention, taking the form of asymmetrical vertical-grants-in-aid programmes and, possibly, of tax sharing – with corresponding implicit redistribution formulae (like the tax sharing of VAT in Germany). This must have a bearing to the central government's budget. Moreover, different options for vertical grants will have to be studied in order to identify which type may be most appropriate for achieving common policy goals, notably the fostering of regional development projects and a more balanced economic expansion of the EC as a whole.

2.2.2.3 *Vertical grants*

Federal fiscal relations are typically characterised by vertical flows of funds which are usually more important than horizontal grants. The distinction between specific purpose and general revenue grants also applies to this type of grant, as does the distinction between conditional and unconditional assistance.

To the extent that unconditional vertical grants are a substitute for own revenues at any one level of government, they can be used as a corrective for imbalances in the vertical assignment of taxes among levels of government. As has been argued above, pure revenue redistribution within the government sector may become a public zero-sum-game which – given certain premises – may have no incentive effects on the economy. Vertical G-grants may thus become an essential ingredient in the fiscal federal machinery, correcting for imbalances between expenditure functions and assigned revenues.

In principle two extreme philosophies could be adopted for vertical G-grants: a central tax collection with downward-oriented G-grants (which is essentially the Australian model); and a decentralised tax collection with upward-oriented G-grants (which was the model of the German *Reich* of 1871, and is at present the approach to financing the EC budget). There may be variants to this that allow some discretion for rate policies at the receiving end. Instead of downward G-grants the states may be allowed to impose surcharges on central taxes (basically the Canadian model); or conversely the centre may be allowed to levy piggy-back taxes on top of state taxes.[49]

Revenue sharing (as in the German model) may be seen as a special form of G-grant arrangement.[50] The distinction of shared taxes from own resources is warranted on the grounds that their apportionment onto participating governments usually does not reflect local taxable capacity.[51] This then implies regional perequation effects.

The pure vertical redistribution of public resources correcting for imbalances in the assignment of taxes can in fact be implicitly combined with equalisation – both for revenue sharing and vertical grants. Tax sharing formulae, as well as the rules governing the distribution of vertical grants, can be designed in such a way that taxable capacity below average leads to a relatively higher apportionment of funds correcting existing inequities. The per capita distribution of VAT among the German states implies such an equalising effect. It may be reinforced by asymmetrical vertical G-grants at the discretion of the federal government.

Again there is no place to discuss the multitude of vertical grant schemes which implicitly embody equalisation effects. These may entail pure revenue effects as they may – through matching requirements – alter relative prices with the objective of correcting for existing disincentives (or of creating additional incentives). There may be strings attached to the grants, which may be binding or 'soft' (freeing resources that would have been spent anyway).

The advantages of such vertical grant schemes (as of tax sharing) are sometimes seen to be of a conflict-resolving nature. True, they tend to blur the economist's favourite revenue-benefit link, yet this may be accompanied by the disguising of social conflicts within a federation, thus enhancing political stability and preserving the framework conditions for stable economic growth. The economic profession may be divided on the issue of fiscal illusion in the context of federal finance. Clear-cut fiscal sovereignties with a transparent division of functions among government may be praised for enhancing process efficiency; they may however jeopardise the social contract on which the operating economy is based. Casual empiricism indicates that politicians have chosen to sacrifice the narrower concepts of process efficiency by creating an arsenal of instruments geared toward achieving political stability – of which fiscal illusion is just one tool.

2.2.3 Political Aspects of Tax Assignment

It is important to note that any one of the models discussed in this chapter does in fact convey symbolic messages that must be in accordance with traditions and existing consensus views if political frictions in the federation should be avoided. This is why history has generated such widely differing institutional arrangements for existing federations that cannot be transplanted from one cultural setting to another.

For instance, both the Australian and the Canadian models of federalism may be interpreted as the states being at the mercy of the central government.[52] This may be heavily resented by member states – as can be seen from the Canadian case. Corrective measures may then have to be taken in order to satisfy regional demands (for example through specific purpose grants based on needs criteria, as in the Australian case). It is obvious that neither the Australian nor the Canadian model of federalism is suitable for guiding fiscal federal reforms in Eastern Europe – the former Soviet Union, Czechoslovakia or Yugoslavia. It conveys too much central political power, a message that is not acceptable to Eastern European states at present.

On the other hand, the German tax-sharing model conveys the message of homogeneity and cooperation among the different layers of government. Again, this symbol may be rejected by Eastern European federations in transition. It may also be resisted as a guiding principle for reforming the EC budget.

Finally there are established federal constituencies that emphasise regional diversity by jealously defending the states' sovereignty against the mounting power of central governments. Some of them have been successful in their endeavour (Switzerland), whereas others have been less fortunate (the United States). With regard to the financing of public budgets in more decentralised federations, the question arises whether revenue collection can be effectively coordinated under such conditions or whether this might not lead to a costly 'tax jungle' – which is the administrator's nightmare (and the economist's delight?).

The EC is still relatively young, and is a federation *in statu nascendi*. Although important basic decisions have already been made, it is still unclear which direction the EC may follow after the achievement of EMU. The following chapter tries to evaluate some of the experiences found in Western federations that may be useful for the revamping of EC federal financial arrangements and the financing of the Community budget under EMU.

Obviously there is a short and a longer-term perspective. The recent renaissance of regional political and cultural identities in both Eastern and Western Europe is likely to restrict the political choice to models of decentralised tax collection for the immediate future. More centralised models may come; but the time is certainly still 'not ripe'.

3 Federal Financial Constitutions Compared

The following chapter tries to evaluate some experiences from existing federations that may be useful for the discussion of the EC budget under EMU. An arc is drawn between two extreme models: one that puts regional constituencies at the mercy of the centre; and another that leaves the centre depending on the mercy of states. These two models are discussed in relation to the Australian and the EC experiences – although it is clear that history never obeys the *Ideal typus* of any model. The exercise demonstrates – among other things – that the notion 'at the mercy' is applicable neither to Australian nor to European federalism.

Two intermittent models are also briefly looked at: one that emphasises both central and regional governments' independence as well as regional diversity; another that stresses the notion of federal-state cooperation as well as unity and uniformity. These are the cases of Switzerland (and to a certain extent the United States) and Germany. Switzerland and Germany are not only models of federalism that may influence developments in Europe more strongly than the American and Australian experiences; they also bear directly on the key question to be resolved in any constitution of a future European federation under EMU: how unity can be achieved without sacrificing regional diversity and state sovereignty. The exercise demonstrates – *inter alia* – that the EC federal machinery has already absorbed a number of elements taken from these two federations, notably from Germany (for example the subsidiarity principle, the role of the Council, revenue sharing). A number of issues remain to be resolved, however, where benefits can be reaped from looking more closely into these two European federations.

3.1 AUSTRALIA: THE STATES AT THE MERCY OF THE CENTRAL GOVERNMENT?[1]

3.1.1 General Characteristics of the Australian Federation

Australia[2] was formed as a federation at the beginning of this century. The aim of the states in joining their efforts politically was twofold:

defence, and a more intensive economic cooperation and trade on the Australian continent.[3] The latter argument bears resemblance to the motive for creating the EC in the second half of this century.

Among the six major federal countries in the Western world, Australia is by far the most centralised with regard to revenue sources. The Commonwealth accounts for approximately four-fifths of national tax revenue for most years since the Second World War. Approximately three-fourths of the remaining taxes accrue to the states directly; the local government sector's share in taxation (and responsibilities) is extremely small compared to other federations – and even compared to unitary states.

The vertical imbalance between tax assignment and expenditure functions is very acute in Australia. The Commonwealth's own revenues greatly exceed its outlay responsibilities. On the other hand, the states – retaining control over almost all major government functions (except defence, foreign affairs, interstate matters and social service benefits) – are denied access to the two major sources of revenue in Australia: income taxation and sales taxes on goods.[4] Australian states thus largely depend on revenue transferred to them by the Commonwealth. This is effected predominantly through general revenue sharing – unconditional bloc grants – and specific purpose payments – categorical grants. In 1987–8 the states relied for half of their revenue needs on Commonwealth grants (Groenewegen 1991). This has led some authors to speak of the states as depending 'on federal largesse' (Bird 1986, p. 125) or of the Commonwealth's 'financial domination over the states' (Mathews/Jay 1972, p. 291). This interpretation needs further elaboration.

3.1.2   Vertical Tax Assignment and 'tax reimbursement' grants

Tax assignment in Australia – as in Switzerland – may be seen as strictly following the layer-cake approach, each level of government being reserved its own tax base. But it also demonstrates vividly what may result from such a prescription: a severe lack of vertical fiscal balance. Contrary to Switzerland, the Australian federal government controls virtually all lucrative taxes.

A number of historical events have led to the central government continually eroding state competences in taxation. These are the main steps in this process.

• At its inception, in 1901, the federation transferred exclusive powers on customs and excise revenues to the Commonwealth as constitutional rights. Starting in 1908,[5] the High Court has consistently interpreted these powers more and more generously in favour of the central government. Sales taxes (a major state tax in the United States) would be considered unconstitutional at the state level in Australia.

- In compensation for the loss of customs duties and excise taxes the states were originally given three-quarters of collected revenue – which was relatively more important then than today (*section 87 of the Constitution*). Yet, on the expiry of the clause, the central government did not continue this form of tax sharing. It accorded per capita financial assistance instead (1911–27), a grant that was rapidly eroded in real terms by inflation.[6]

- An offer was made in the early 20s by the Bruce-Page government to vacate the area of personal income taxation – leaving it exclusively to the states. This failed on the rejection of New South Wales (all other states had accepted). A similar move to hand over smaller taxes and to reduce income taxation was equally discarded at a Premiers' Conference in 1926. The states then had no desire to administer unpopular taxes.

- A change in the provision of financial assistance, through the *Financial Agreement* of 1927, led to the Commonwealth intruding on state sovereignty: the (unconditional) per capita grants were transformed into annual contributions towards interest charges on the public debt of states. The Agreement also introduced greater Commonwealth control of state borrowing through the establishment of a Loan Council.

- A system of fiscal equalisation for the financially weaker states, involving special grants from the Commonwealth, was introduced in 1933.

- The most important development during World War II was the taking over, in 1942, of all income tax by the Commonwealth as a wartime emergency measure. The federal government, 'having tasted the delights of full control of this great revenue machine, wanted to retain that control' (Bird 1986, p. 110) – and was successful in doing so.[7]

- Financial compensation for the loss of the income tax was given through 'tax reimbursement grants', which became – with amendments – the cornerstone of intergovernmental fiscal arrangements in Australia. This issue will be addressed in more detail in chapter 3.1.3.

- The only (minor) reversal of this centripetal trend came in 1971 with the handing over of payroll taxation to the states.[8]

- Since World War II there has been a massive increase in specific purpose payments to the states in the main functional fields for which they have constitutional responsibility, such as education and health.[9]

The Commonwealth government now collects all major taxes in Australia: taxes on income, profits and capital gains (70 per cent of all taxes collected in 1988),[10] sales taxes (16 per cent), and customs duties (5 per cent). The states and municipalities collect payroll taxes, stamp duties, motor vehicle taxes, gambling taxes, franchise taxes, land taxes and property taxes (municipal rates) that contribute relatively little to total tax revenue.

Irrespective of these historical facts the distribution of revenue sources in Australia is found to be more or less consistent with Musgrave's criteria for vertical tax assignment in a federation. There is a strict separation of taxable sources, avoiding tax competition among governments. Moreover, since the Australian tax system relies heavily on (progressive) income tax, it is obvious that the main revenue source should be centralised on the grounds of fiscal stability and regional equity.[11] As a matter of fact, the discussions centring around the introduction of uniform income-tax legislation in 1942–3 owed a good deal to the very uneven tax incidence of state income taxes. It was also tainted with arguments in favour of Keynesian demand management and central control of the economy, and of general welfare (Mathews/Jay 1972, pp. 180–83). More recently, in 1990, a Premiers' Conference essentially reconfirmed this assignment of taxes on similar grounds,[12] but the position is now being reviewed as part of a general process of reforming intergovernmental relations.

As to the contribution of taxes and grants to total revenue at each level of government, Table 3.1 may be indicative (for 1987–8).[13] It shows the heavy dependence of states (and to a lesser extent of local governments) on vertical grants: nearly 50 per cent of state revenues are supplied by the Commonwealth, and 20 per cent of municipal income.

3.1.3   Financial Assistance and Revenue Sharing

By far the most important single revenue source of subcentral governments in Australia is grant money. These grants are paid in the form of general purpose financial assistance, which is explained by their historic roots as 'income tax reimbursements' following the implementation of uniform income taxation in 1942. The *Tax Reimbursement Act* provided the legal basis for grants to any state which abstained from levying income tax.[14] In addition, half of Commonwealth assistance is in the form of tied grants (for health, education, roads and public housing).

Table 3.1   Sources of revenue for each level of government in Australia (in per cent)

Revenue source	Commonwealth	State	Local
Own tax revenue	89	32	56
Net operating surplus	4	11	7
Other	7	8	12
Total own source revenue	100	51	75
Payments from			
Commonwealth	–	49	19
States	–	–	7
Total revenue	100	100	100

Totals may not add up correctly due to rounding.

The more recent history of general revenue assistance to the Australian states falls into three phases:

- from 1959 to 1976, when general revenue funds were given to the states under the label of 'financial assistance grants';
- from 1976 to 1985, when such revenue was transferred to the states through revenue sharing; and
- from 1986 onward (when financial assistance grants were reintroduced).

Financial assistance grants were increased annually (from 1959 to 1976) by a formula stressing – for each state – three factors: (i) population changes, (ii) average wage increases, and (iii) a so-called 'betterment factor',[15] designed to allow the states to expand their relative level of services. On their reintroduction, these grants have been determined 'by fiscal equalisation factors based on revenue/expenditure disabilities for different states while the size of the pool is determined by a percentage growth rate set to reflect specified real (inflation-adjusted) changes in assistance which can be negative when fiscal restraint is called for' (Groenewegen 1991). From 1990 onward the Commonwealth has agreed to maintain the real value of such grants in order to provide greater certainty in the funding of state budgets.

The revenue-sharing interlude had been initiated by Fraser's 'New Federalism' policies. Sharing was first adopted for the income tax alone. The pool was formed applying first a fixed, later an increasing proportion of the tax proceeds collected in the states. This led to the states' revenues being determined by factors similar to those used for financial assistance grants before. Later, revenue sharing was extended to federal tax receipts as a whole, which somewhat lowered the rate of growth of the states' revenue pool (since revenue elasticities of other Commonwealth taxes are typically lower than those for income tax).[16]

As noted before, the revenue-sharing experiment was abandoned largely because of uncertainties over the Commonwealth's planned tax policies and for political reasons – since the states had found themselves to be 'more vulnerable to unilateral federal decisions on tax policy' (Bird 1986, p. 116).

It should be mentioned that, in addition to general revenue funds, the Commonwealth supplies financial assistance in the form of specific purpose grants. These are given for social services (health, education), social security and welfare, economic services (roads, transport, industry assistance, water resources) and other services (like housing and urban renewal, regional development, disaster relief and debt charges). As has been argued in chapter 2.2.2, it is questionable whether the budgetary effect of specific purpose grants is different from that of general purpose grants – a pure revenue effect – to the extent that they may free tied resources for general purposes at the state level. Some specific purpose grants in Australia are provided with matching requirements however. My own studies found that these grants are associated with substantially increased state-local taxation.[17] This indicates conforming additional increases in state-local expenditure (or saving) through expenditure requirements and relative-price effects. In any case the specific nature of the grants has an impact on the horizontal regional distribution of these resources, subject however to the Grants Commission taking grant differentials for most of the recurrent specific purpose grants into account when assessing general revenue grant relativities.

3.1.4   Equalisation and the Commonwealth Grants Commission

The horizontal distribution of government resources among the Australian states depends on a number of factors.

- On the distribution of *general revenue grants* (respectively tax-sharing funds). Since the distribution formula chosen for allocating these funds leads to varying weights being attached to different states, a gradual change in the relative provision of state revenue may result. The distribution of Commonwealth grants – both general revenue and specific purpose – depends almost wholly on the Grants

Commission's assessment of states' relative taxable capacity and their relative expenditure needs (see below).

- On the distribution of *specific purpose grants*. This hinges on several factors, including the historical distribution which was often arbitrary or reflected state expenditure policies and the Commonwealth's policy priorities (for example road construction, university education). Specific purpose payments are not always granted on the basis of relative economic advantage or needs.
- On the distribution of the *states' own tax bases*.
- On the distribution of the *states' loan moneys* (which are centrally controlled in Australia; see chapter 3.1.5 below).

This intergovernmental redistribution of funds may be put under the heading 'asymmetrical vertical grants' – except for states' own revenue. Yet – similarly to Germany – the Australian system also comprises a specific equalisation scheme that is designed to mitigate large regional inequities. But the equalisation process is carried much further in Australia where relative costs of providing standard services and relative specific purpose grant differentials are taken into account as well as relative revenue-raising capacities. These relativities are assessed by the Commonwealth Grants Commission following detailed submissions from and exhaustive discussions with the states and the Commonwealth Treasury.

The Commission was set up in 1933 and charged with the task 'of enquiring into and reporting on applications by the states for financial assistance under Section 96 of the Constitution' (Mathews/Jay 1972, p. 154). The Commission defines its own role as ' . . . an independent, impartial and authoritative arbiter in relation to distributional aspects of fiscal federalism' in Australia (Commonwealth Grants Commission 1983, p. 160).

Over the years, the Commission developed and refined criteria for horizontal fiscal equalisation. The guiding principle for supplying special grants was initially that of regional 'financial needs'. The formulae adopted cannot be discussed here in full, yet a few points are worth mentioning.

- For many years, the system was restricted to 'claimant' states the needs of which were compared to the two 'standard' states (New South Wales and Victoria). The horizontal review was hence only partial. With some states ceasing to claim special grants the scope for equalisation through the Grants Commission was further reduced. The special grants recommended by the Commission – whose recommendations were always accepted by the Commonwealth – were relatively small because they reflected the distribution of the financial assistance grants and because the financially weaker states were also the states with the smallest populations. The special grants were financed from the Commonwealth budget and did not affect the total amount of the financial assistance grants.

- Both 'revenue needs' and 'expenditure needs' were assessed comprehensively for all recurrent revenue/expenditure categories. This was different from the formula governing German *Finanzausgleich* for instance, which essentially emphasises aggregate fiscal capacity, leaving expenditure functions aside.[18]

However, the needs criteria developed by the Commission had (and have) some more general bearing on the philosophy governing horizontal equalisation in Australia – even for general financial assistance. This point was ostensibly made clear when the Commission was asked to review the initial allocation of tax-sharing funds introduced in 1976 through the New Federalism Policy. The Grants Commission's detailed reports on tax sharing led to a great deal of controversy in Australia, and the initial reactions were described 'as cold, if not actively hostile' (Bird 1986, p. 138). This was mainly for two reasons: (i) a full review of state relativities was to define losers and winners of the proposed redistribution exercise – which always meets political resistance; (ii) the report was so specific in many ways – for instance addressing outlays on shark and crocodile protection (Commonwealth Grants Commission 1985, Vol. II, p. 66) – that people started to wonder what this might have to do with the transfer of general revenue to states – although it has to be acknowledged that a systematic assessment had to include *all* state revenues and expenditures.

The Commission may in fact have overstressed its mandate in this exercise. Some authors considered this work to have weakened the status of the Grants Commission. Yet it should not be forgotten that, undoubtedly, the Commission has been 'the cynosure of federal finance specialists throughout the world' for over fifty years (Bird 1986, p. 142). What may have been overlooked over its achievements was the fact that the recommendations were initially bearing only on a small proportion of redistributive means – special grants – and that these grants were far from being comprehensive equalisation payments, either quantitatively or as to their coverage of regions. When the recommendations started addressing a broader range of issues, the obvious came to the fore: that horizontal equalisation is essentially a political process. This process may follow the advice of 'independent experts' – but only as long as it suits existing political interests.

Another lesson to be learned from the Grants Commission's tax-sharing exercise is that too specific horizontal redistribution formulae for substantive amounts of general revenue to be distributed are likely to meet political resistance. *Qui nimium probat nihil probat*. It is more likely to jeopardise any move aiming at establishing a greater degree of cohesion.[19]

Nevertheless the basic methodology developed by the Commission with the assistance of the states and the Commonwealth Treasury – the equalisation model for assessing general revenue grant relativities – has been accepted by all parties, the main issues between them being the extent to which the equalisation process should be carried out – a political question – and the details of revenue and expenditure assessments – involving technical and data considerations. While the political question – the extent of equalisation – needs to be determined by governments, it is generally accepted in Australia that an independent body is more likely to achieve an equitable distribution of grants than a process of political bargaining by governments of different political complexions and different fiscal strengths. The present system developed in Australia because of the perceived unfairness of the previous arrangements.

The distribution model which has been used in Australia since 1981, replacing the special grants arrangements, thus embraces all states and territories and determines the distribution of the total amount of Commonwealth general revenue grants. It involves the calculation of grant relativities by reference to the relative per capita revenue-raising capacities of all recurrent own-source revenues, the relative per capita expenditure needs (costs of providing standard services) of all recurrent expenditures and the differential per capita amounts of most recurrent specific purpose grants (those for the expenditures which have been equalised). In effect each state's or territory's share of the total Commonwealth general revenue grant depends on its standardised deficit, which is the product of its population and its per capita grant relativity. The latter is assessed as its per capita standardised expenditure minus its per capita standardised own-source revenues, plus (or minus) its differential per capita specific purpose grants.

Separate assessments are made for some 30 revenue categories, more than 60 expenditure categories and more than 20 grant categories. The grant relativities are assessed following a major review every five years. Methodological issues are also reviewed between the major inquiries.

An advisory body similar to the Commonwealth Grants Commission could also be considered as an element within the EC budgetary process. Such an institution could be extremely useful in developing recommendations to politicians on more informed regional and programme-related 'needs criteria'. Policy guidelines could be set to constrain such recommendations in advance, and parliament could even introduce firm budgetary limitations by putting a ceiling on regional and structural funds to be allocated. A paper prepared for the McDougall Committee (Mathews 1977) suggested action along these lines and developed a partial equalisation model similar in structure to the Australian distribution model.

3.1.5   Constraints on Deficit Financing

A full discussion of revenue instruments would have to include loan moneys to be raised at vertical levels of government as well. Loan money – if not controlled – may contribute to the softening of budget constraints at all levels of government; loan control is thus most delicate for multilayer government finance. Moreover, government borrowing is intertwined with monetary policy and macroeconomic demand management (through its impact on capital markets). Effective control on public sector borrowing is hence a major concern for all federations – notably for EC monetary policy under EMU.

Although the thrust of this study is not on public sector borrowing under EMU, a few remarks on the situation in Australia seem to be in order.

State borrowing (general government as well as state business enterprises) is determined by the Loan Council – not only the total amount but also the allocation among Australian states. This Council was set up through the *Financial Agreement* of 1927. It provides essentially what may be called a 'joint-decision-making' machinery, yet the Loan Council's decisions have predominantly reflected Commonwealth interests throughout its history.[20] Again the impression of the Australian states being at the mercy of the Commonwealth is restated.

The 1980s have brought about an increase in 'off-programme' borrowing activities at all levels of government. In the early 1980s it appeared that the Australian Loan Council was relaxing control. Furthermore, the states had increasingly developed devices to circumvent Loan Council control. State budget constraints had thus been softened quite considerably. And the constraints on regional loan financing appeared to be softer than it seemed at first sight. Nevertheless the Commonwealth retains control over the total borrowing programme, and – more recently – has introduced a new global-limits formula which has been used restrictively.[21] At present, consideration is given to allowing 'corporatised' government business enterprises to be freed from Loan Council borrowing limits.

3.1.6 The States at the Mercy of the Commonwealth? An Attempted Answer

The lack of flexible tax resources under state control is often cited as constituting a severe problem for multilevel government finance in Australia. Yet it is questionable whether the states have really been 'at the mercy' of the Commonwealth in this respect. A number of factors point toward the states having been able to preserve – and even extend – their responsibilities.

- General revenue grants based on quasi-constitutional rules and institutional inertia ('no one should lose a benefit once received') provide a secure revenue source covering half of state resources on average. This is prone to foster a stable environment for state policy decisions and for long-term planning of public sector developments. In recent years, however, general revenue grants have been cut substantially in real terms.

- If the states had continued to impose their own income taxes they would probably have received less revenue than they obtained through general revenue assistance. This was certainly true for the post-war period until the mid-sixties (Mathews/Jay 1972, p. 317); it was most likely to be true for the initial tax-sharing phase in the 1970s. The fact that the Commonwealth was able to reverse these trends on several occasions is not an argument for centre dominance; it is, rather, an indication that intergovernmental financial control may work even without the often cited tax/outlay link (see below).

- Specific purpose payments have almost certainly released states' own funds, in certain policy areas, that could be used for general purposes. This is true in spite of matching requirements in some instances. Matching requirements may, however, sometimes have introduced biases in the structure of state government outlays – creating, for instance, an incentive to increase expenditure on university education relative to primary and secondary schooling. Deploring this type of inefficiency is justified; yet it calls for a revision of the set of matching requirements associated with specific purpose grants – not for a revision of the whole system of federal finance, and this has generally been accepted in Australia. Recently the major growth in tied grants has been in areas where the states' own expenditures are limited and so free up very little state money. And matching requirements have come to play an insignificant role nowadays.

- Special grants and, later, the general revenue equalisation arrangements have helped to ease the budgetary constraints of the poorer states.
- The states have recently started to exploit more heavily some of their own resources – notably user charges, resource taxation and business franchise tax revenue.
- The consistent reduction in the Loan Council's role in controlling state borrowing has further contributed to easing budget constraints at state levels.

There is no doubt that the states do play an important role in Australia, and are *resilient* – not only because such a role is firmly established in the Constitution. The Commonwealth cannot ignore them and cannot keep cutting back grants to them. It is forced to reach broad agreements with the states (Fletcher/Walsh 1991) in order to preserve political stability. An outside observer of Australian federalism may well come to the conclusion that ' . . . overall, the pattern of Australian fiscal federalism seems to be fairly stable' (United States Advisory Commission 1981, p. 78).

Despite this positive interpretation of the effects of multilevel finance on state sovereignty in Australia, a number of writers continue to underline the inefficiency of these provisions – notably by stressing the missing tax/expenditure link or accountability supposed to enhance fiscal responsibilities at each level. On the grounds of the analysis given in chapter 2 of this book, the importance of this link may be debatable – in particular for smaller vertical fiscal imbalances. The question is whether the vertical imbalance in Australia is severe enough to warrant such concern.

It should not be overlooked, for that matter, that the political process regarding the vertical distribution of funds under revenue sharing or general purpose assistance may also generate a corrective response – that may be different from the traditional median-voter model, leading however to similar results. The Commonwealth government may thus come under direct pressure from its own electorate to constrain the overall level of taxation; and it may thus be encouraged to pass this pressure on to states by demanding a revision of the revenue-sharing formula. Not only can it be shown that such revisions have been taking place in Australia; the mechanism may in fact be fully appropriate for a polity in which 'neither the Senate nor the Cabinet provides adequate regional representation at the national level, because they are primarily dominated by party rather than by regional considerations' (Bird 1986, p. 130, referring to Mathews 1978 and Solomon 1982).

The analysis shows that federal financial arrangements in Australia have been preserving and securing state independence and that the lower tier of government is far from being at the mercy of the Commonwealth.

3.2 SWITZERLAND (AND THE US): EFFECTIVE TAX COORDINATION OR 'TAX JUNGLE'?[22]

3.2.1 General Characteristics of the Swiss Confederation

Of all the federations in the world Switzerland has by far the oldest tradition. The spirit of state independence dates back to the famous 'Everlasting Alliance' between the three founding states in 1291, yet this freedom was *de jure* granted only in 1648. In 1815 the Congress of Vienna confirmed this independent political status, and the Swiss Confederation – which had grown through associating (and conquering) a number of further regions (cantons) – was then established in its present boundaries. In 1848 a federal Constitution was adopted for Switzerland, which until then had consisted of a loose confederacy of regions.[23] The present Confederation and its philosophy date back to this first Constitution – although it has been amended several times since, notably through the important overhaul of 1874 that was strongly influenced by the United States' model of federalism.

The basic ingredients of the Swiss Confederation are the following.

- The cantons[24] represent a variety of ethnic, cultural, linguistic and religious groups within a small territory reflecting wide geographic and economic disparities. The situation resembles very much the EC *en miniature* – rendering Switzerland an extremely useful study case for possible future Community developments.
- The cantons are legally sovereign states unless this sovereignty is explicitly limited by the Constitution.
- The vertical distribution of functions largely reflects the layer-cake approach – at least intentionally. The Constitution does not only assign responsibilities (or expenditure functions) to each level of government; it also attempts to restrict these functions by assigning specific revenue sources as well. The economist's favourite tax/expenditure link is hence firmly entrenched in the Swiss Constitution. In particular, central government is prevented from levying any tax unless it is written into the Constitution.
- The tax/expenditure link is strengthened further by the political system of 'direct democracy'. Voters are not only asked to elect

representatives; they are frequently called to the polls to decide on all proposed constitutional changes and on specific pieces of legislation[25] (including projects to amend federal tax financing). Federal referenda must be approved not only by a majority of voters, but also by a majority of the cantons.

- Regional diversity in combination with cantonal sovereignty and direct democracy have led not only to different levels in the provision of regional public goods but also to a variety of regional tax laws. For the income tax, for instance, where sovereignty is shared by the Confederation and the cantons, there are 26 + 1 different tax codes with varying definitions for tax bases, for exemptions and deductible items, and for tax rates. In addition, the communes – which have no tax sovereignty – may tax by piggy-backing on cantonal taxes with varying annual coefficients.

A few first remarks – correcting some prejudices likely to exist with regard to the Swiss Confederation – may be in order:

- Neither direct democracy nor tax competition have led to the public sector being more 'limited' in Switzerland than in other Western nations. In 1988, total public expenditures (including social security) were 34 per cent of GNP (Dafflon 1991). The Swiss government may thus be somewhat smaller than the average for federal countries; however, it is not significantly less important than in other federations.
- A large proportion of cantonal public expenditures is fixed by federal law. In this case regional governments act as agencies of the centre – according to the German model of horizontal federalism.
- Direct democracy – the results of which often run across party lines – is felt as a constraint at the level of public decision-making, requiring compromise and virtual consensus among all parties. At the political level the sharing of power is institutionalised through a proportional representation of parties (*Proporz*), 'whereby a balancing of interests has become the dominating principle' (Bieri 1979, p. 14). The direct link between government and administration on one hand, and those affected by legislation, is subtly arranged through consultation procedures. These specific forms of cooperative federalism are further supported by the fact that every matter requires the consent of both Houses of parliament, the National Council (House of Representatives) and the Council of States (Senate). All these arrangements may run counter to the idea of a clear-cut separation of responsibilities.
- Furthermore also the tax/outlay link is blurred by many provisions in

the Swiss federal machinery, notably by revenue sharing and specific purpose grants with equalisation provisions.[26]

The Swiss model of federalism, with its competing taxation powers at the two levels of government and its diversity in federal fiscal arrangements, creates enormous problems of tax coordination, tax competition and harmonisation (Dafflon 1986). The variety and complexity of subnational tax systems is only rivalled by that of the United States, where tax competition as well as vertical and horizontal tax coordination has been a major concern for years (Bird 1986, pp. 173–7). This has induced some authors to speak of a 'tax jungle', stressing the administrative costs that are associated with such a system. Their quest is for harmonisation and uniform (standardised) tax rules. Yet the model has also thrilled those economists who praise the particular features of Helvetian federalism as fostering small government and exhibiting large efficiency gains in the economy. This group of addicts is well prepared to bear higher administrative costs in the interests of greater diversity and efficiency.

This ongoing controversy among proponents of uniformity and proponents of diversity is very familiar to observers of EC federalism. This may warrant a bit more elaboration on the specifics of Swiss federalism.[27]

3.2.3 Vertical Tax Assignment, Federal and State Taxation

As mentioned before, the Swiss Constitution makes a serious attempt to separate taxation powers vertically. According to the fathers of the Swiss Constitution the central government was to collect all indirect taxes; cantonal and municipal governments were attributed all direct taxes. The idea that the central government should collect customs duties, excises and general consumption taxes seems to be firmly entrenched in the minds of constitutional lawyers – proven by developments in Australia, in Germany, and, *in nuce*, in the EC – although there are also exceptions, notably the United States.[28] However, it sometimes runs counter to economic arguments, notably to Musgrave's criterion emphasising the assignment of progressive taxes to the central government, in view of their importance for stabilisation purposes.

Over the years the Confederation has acquired powers in the realm of income taxation however – similarly to developments in West Germany. As in Germany, this was mainly dictated by revenue needs, not by fiscal management. In the Swiss case the federal income tax was introduced during World War I – in the disguise of a 'defence tax'. World War II has seen the introduction of another important federal tax: the wholesale

Table 3.2   Sources of revenue for each level of government in Switzerland (in per cent)

Revenue source	Confederation	Cantons	Communes
Taxes on income and wealth	41	50	50
Taxes on consumption and expenditures	52	3	
Monopolies, licences, revenue from property	4	5	6
Total own source revenue	97	59	57
Grants-in-aid and reimbursements	–	21	15
Revenue sharing	–	6	2
Indemnities and sales	3	14	26
Total revenue	100	100	100

Totals may not add up correctly due to rounding.

sales tax. Both 'emergency taxes' stayed on – as is usually the case – and they were later sanctioned by a constitutional amendment. However, the Constitution fixes maximum rates for these federal taxes, and 'sunset' dates are established for their expiring.

Today the following vertical assignment of taxes is found in Switzerland.

- Indirect taxation on expenditures, excises and customs duties are exclusively federal.
- Tax bases of direct taxes on personal income and wealth, and on business income and wealth, are exploited concurrently by all levels of government, the Confederation, the cantons and municipalities – with priority given to the cantons.
- As a matter of principle '(e)ach tier of government is endowed with a full or partial tax authority for a number of taxes and not only one. Cantons and communes have also the right to levy user charges and fees for thoses services where this is appropriate' (Dafflon 1991).
- The cantons have an exclusive right to tax motor vehicles.

As to the contribution of taxes and grants to total revenue at each level of government, Table 3.2 may be indicative (for 1988).[29]

The bestowal of independent taxation powers to each layer of responsibility enables the federal as well as regional governments to discharge their respective functions effectively without being dependent on each other. Unlike Australia, cantonal dependence on grants is low in Switzerland: it amounts to an average of 21 per cent of their budgets. If revenue sharing is included it is 27 per cent. It should be noted, however, that the figure for grants comprises 7 ½ per cent of municipal contributions to cantonal services – hence upward-oriented vertical grants. If these grants are deducted, the total dependence of cantons on the Confederation is below 20 per cent of their budget receipts.

3.2.4   Equalisation, Revenue Sharing, and Specific Grants-in-Aid

As in Australia, there is a strong tendency incorporated in the Swiss federal machinery to equalise differences in taxable capacity through asymmetrical vertical grants provided by the central government. The objective is 'to enable the cantons to provide similar levels of services without need for a too heavier tax burden in some cantons than in others' (Dafflon 1991). This principle is firmly established in the federal law on equalisation of 1959. The principle of 'uniformity of living conditions' – the cornerstone of German equalisation arrangements – is not adhered to in Switzerland (Bieri 1979, p. 12).

The redistributive aims are mainly achieved through three types of vertical financial adjustments:

- federal tax reimbursements;
- tax sharing; and
- specific purpose grants (usually conditional grants-in-aid).

Similar to Australia at the inception of the federation, the Swiss Confederation reimburses part of the revenues collected from customs duties (yet only on fuel and petrol). This reflects the fact that the Confederation has delegated certain responsibilities to the cantons (especially road building), to be administered by them on behalf of the central government. The horizontal incidence of these payments is very complex since they are mainly related to cantonal expenditures on road construction and improvement. Although financial assistance is calculated in accordance with these functions (and on a fiscal-capacity yardstick to be discussed below)[30] these transfers are essentially unconditional – exhibiting a mere income effect.

Tax-sharing means – that have become more important recently under pressure from cantonal governments – can also be interpreted to form unconditional general revenue grants. They are basically distributed in accordance with regional revenue collection, population, and with the canton's relative fiscal 'needs' – measured in terms of a statistical yardstick. Tax-sharing revenue thus forms part of an asymmetrical vertical perequation scheme which is closed-ended. The scheme could be imagined as working in two stages: (i) the federal contribution may be thought of as entering a 'closed pool'; (ii) horizontal perequation is then achieved through rules similar to those of the German *Finanzausgleich*.[31]

Tax sharing in Switzerland comprises three revenue sources. In 1992 the cantons will receive (i) 30 per cent of the federal direct tax on income and profits; (ii) 10 per cent of the withholding tax; and (iii) 20 per cent of a tax on exemption from military service.[32] The latter tax share is distributed horizontally on a tax origin base without equalisation provisions. The direct tax share is allocated partly on a tax-origin base, partly according to the fiscal-capacity yardstick to be discussed below. Revenue sharing from the withholding tax is allocated to the cantons according to population for one half, according to fiscal capacity for the other.

Traditionally, vertical intergovernmental transfers in Switzerland have been dominated by conditional grants-in-aid to be applied in accordance with the policy priorities of the donor government. Conditional grants given to cantons by the Confederation are usually closed-ended, with strings attached in the form of matching requirements. Some grants are provided with 'pass-through' attachments, that is they have to be handed down to municipalities – sometimes with mandatory additional funding from the canton. In addition to providing funds for specific state functions according to national priorities, federal conditional grants are also intended to have some equalising effect. As for tax reimbursement grants and for tax sharing, their horizontal allocation is thus partly based on a cantonal fiscal capacity measure.

Measurement of the cantons' fiscal capacity has been modified several times. The actual formula comprises four ingredients (Dafflon 1991).

- *The canton's (adjusted) fiscal revenue per capita* – This includes cantonal and local tax revenue from all sources (adjusted for differences in tax effort in order to obtain comparable figures).
- *The canton's GDP per capita* – Not only cantonal fiscal resources are stressed in the formula, but also private income (which seems to be a natural indicator of fiscal capacity); this is different from Germany and Australia, where only public revenue is considered in the formulae governing horizontal perequation.
- *Regional (cantonal and local) tax effort* – In a federation which

accords a large degree of tax discretion to regional governments, no canton can be allowed to benefit from higher grants by reducing its own fiscal effort below an acceptable level. Otherwise this would be an incentive to exploit other regions through the lowering of tax rates. A similar correction for horizontal perequation is made through special grants in Australia; in Germany – with its uniformity in taxation – such a criterion is not applied (and would not make much sense).

• *The canton's specific expenditure requirements* – These enter the formula in a rather inambitious way – similar to expenditure needs in the German *Finanzausgleich*. Differences in the costs of providing services in mountainous regions are expressed by an indicator measuring the relative importance of agricultural areas below 800 metres; another proxy for differences in costs is relative population density. These indicators may appear to be extremely crude in comparison with the criteria for assessing relative expenditure needs as developed by the Commonwealth Grants Commission in Australia.

Despite these provisions for horizontal perequation through asymmetrical vertical revenue sharing and grants, equalisation is generally less important in Switzerland than in other Western federations – except the United States. The main outcome seems to have been to increase the amount of subsidies given to poorer cantons, a virtually self-perpetuating category (Frey 1977, pp. 98–100). As one prominent writer on Swiss federalism has concluded ' . . . equalization in grant programs is of subsidiary interest only' in Switzerland (Dafflon 1989, p. 213).

3.2.5 Constraints on Deficit Financing

In principle, each public constituency in Switzerland is autonomous and independent in its budgetary procedures. Yet this does not mean that there is no effective budget constraint leading to irresponsible deficit spending. The idea of 'sound financing' of public budgets is firmly entrenched in people's minds, determining the consensus view that governs fiscal federal arrangements in general. It excludes soft financing through money creation legally. Moreover, obligatory finance referenda, or the threat of calling to the polls in the case of facultative referenda, acts as an effective constraint on loan financing – as it does on taxation. The dominant rule on borrowing allows loan finance only for investment purposes on a pay-as-you-use basis – as in Germany. At the local level, borrowing is limited by law in most cantons, associated with investment financing, and restricted to balancing capital budgets (including interest payments and amortisation of the debt).

According to the Constitution, cantonal laws or municipal decrees, the following can be subject to referenda: 'engagement credits or project appropriations, the estimates (of the budget) as a whole, individual payment credits or annual appropriations, or loans' (Bieri 1979, p. 70). Despite the fact that the importance of finance referenda has declined, the eventuality of such referenda and a broad consensus on the issue seems to work as an effective constraint on public deficit financing. Furthermore, 'efforts are now . . . being made to expand the people's rights, either through well-balanced regulations or changes in the Constitution' (Bieri 1979, p. 70).

The Swiss attitude toward soft financing is thus in sharp contrast to the US model, where no constitutional limits to government debt exist. As long as there was a fiscal-conservative consensus on the 'sound financing' of the US budget this did not pose major problems. Yet this consensus was sacrificed to the benefit of other conservative values – increased military spending and lower tax rates – during the 1980s, with devastating effects on the size of the federal budget deficit. Attempts made by Congress to constrain the deficit, in 1986 (*Gramm-Rudman Act*) and at a summit in October 1990, do not seem to have been effective so far.[33]

3.2.6   Effective Tax Coordination or 'Tax Jungle'? An Attempted Answer

It is not astonishing that the model of Swiss federalism has intrigued so many economists. On a small scale, 'unity in diversity' can be studied for a very heterogeneous society. And the model studied resembles the economist's layer-cake ideal in many respects – going even beyond the federal arrangements of the other 'model federal country', the United States, in some dimensions, direct democracy for instance.

The Swiss pattern of federalism comes in fact closest to the United States model: the vertical separation of taxation powers; vertical competition in exploiting certain tax bases (like income); regionally different tax rules (notably of income taxes); a large number of conditional grant programmes with implicit – yet far from systematic – and limited equalisation effects; restricted scope for revenue sharing; and the absence of a comprehensive attempt at horizontal perequation: all bear resemblance to the US federal machinery. At the institutional level, the legislative process of the Confederation requiring the consent of both Houses of parliament – with the haggling over matters that go back and forth until a compromise is reached – is very familiar to politicians in the United States.

There are, of course, also significant differences between the two federations – apart from size. The main difference between Switzerland and the United States regarding financial arrangements is in tax assignment: the thrust of income taxation is at the federal level in the US, whereas it is at the subcentral level in Switzerland. Yet, notwithstanding such differences regarding the emphasis laid on income taxation at various levels, the Swiss Confederation has problems very similar to those of the United States in dealing with regional disparity, with vertical (and horizontal) tax competition and with fiscal harmonisation. Even some of the constitutional provisions trying to cope with intercantonal double taxation or prohibiting special taxation of industries (Articles 46.2 and 31 of the Swiss Constitution) evoke conforming instruments embodied in the United States' federal arrangements (like the *immunity doctrine* or the *due process of law clause* of the *Fifth Amendment*).

The fact that indirect taxation is central and that direct (in particular personal and corporate income) taxes are levied at the cantonal level – with formidable administrative and compliance complexities due to differences in the definition and measurement of the tax base, of taxable objects and subjects, and of taxing procedures – renders the Helvetian model also of particular interest to the student of EC federalism.

It is interesting to note that the Swiss federation has not chosen the EC approach for VAT and excise taxation defining floors for tax rates within the federation in order to contain effective tax competition. It did not have to – because indirect taxation is uniform, and is assigned to the centre. For the income tax this approach is neither applied in Switzerland nor is it proposed by the EC; it may also be inappropriate for this tax in general – which is progressive and exhibits large variations in the definition of tax bases because of different philosophies on the notion of comprehensive income and on distributive objectives.

Attempts made in Switzerland in the mid-seventies to introduce a uniform federal income tax with cantonal participation, or to impose uniform cantonal direct taxes throughout the country, were both defeated. Following a constitutional amendment in 1977, the *Confoederatio* seems to have chosen the avenue of some formal harmonisation of income taxes though. But – despite several attempts – it has not been successful in pursuing this goal effectively and consequently income tax harmonisation is still on the political agenda in Switzerland.[34] Formal harmonisation of direct cantonal and communal taxation can be expected to be enforced in the near future – following recent legislation[35] – as from 1 January 1993.

If one lesson can be learned from the Swiss experience it is that 'systems based on a strong reliance on cantonal sovereignty *can* work, even though it will likely result in wildly different – though widely accepted – personal (and other) tax systems' (Bird 1986, p. 67). The picture of a 'tax jungle' is thus inappropriate. It may have been created by centralist interest groups to evoke resentments against a decentralised public decision-making process; yet it fails the test of an objective investigation into the workings of such a diversified tax system.

One feature of Helvetian federalism has very much supported this financial structure and its underlying decision-making process, however, a feature that may still be absent from the EC platform: an inherent tendency toward consensus and compromise, and a strong commitment to the securing of minority interests.

Political decisions are seldom reached without prior consensus among all parties in Switzerland, and it would not be acceptable to decide on policy issues that are likely to meet resistance from substantial minority groups. Helvetian cooperative federalism means effective coordination at the horizontal level (through ministerial conferences, for instance), and vertical consulting procedures among political parties, economic and social groups and the tiers of government, through institutionalised procedures (*Vernehmlassungsverfahren*). In spite of this, established coordinative bodies (as in the German collective decision-making machinery, where party politics also plays a greater role) are missing in the Swiss model. The Helvetian brand of 'cooperative' federalism is closer to Japanese consensus-forming procedures and collective choice according to the first principle of the 19th century Japanese Constitution: '*Harmony stands above all*'. This principle has brought about effective policy coordination in a highly diversified policy structure, as it has fostered political stability, economic growth and general welfare.

3.3   GERMANY: UNITARY FEDERAL DOMINANCE OR COOPERATIVE FEDERALISM?

3.3.1   General Characteristics of the German Federation

Contrary to the Australian and Swiss histories, German federalism is rather young. In its present form it dates back to the period after World War II only. Its initial shape was strongly influenced by the Allies, notably by the American model of federalism, yet it also includes typical German elements that pre-date Nazi centralism. Furthermore, developments in Germany have consistently moved away from the original federal machinery established after the war.

A superficial glance at the German arrangements may detect many features of a unitary state.[36] There is a strong central government with an extensive area of influence. There is uniformity in legislation on almost all important issues. There is a uniform tax system. Based on collective welfare arguments or equity the Germans strive for a uniformity of living conditions in the whole nation, notably for national average standards in the provision of public goods (rather than for minimum standards).[37] Another characteristic is the strong coordination of policies among the different layers of government, which was equally guided by the uniformity-of-living-conditions principle. This principle will thus have to be kept in mind when discussing present federal arrangements in Germany.

Of course there are elements that vindicate the official title of the federation: the existence of intermediate levels of government, sixteen *Länder* or states (after unification), and a local government sector the importance of which cannot be over-emphasised;[38] yet the impression of a 'unitary federation' remains strong.

The present Constitution of Germany makes little attempt to divide government functions among the tiers vertically. At the central level emphasis is laid on legislative functions, the allocation of financial resources and the formulation of policy guidelines. The states and local governments are generally in charge of implementing and administering these policies. Lower levels of government often 'execute' policies on behalf of higher levels, and financing is sometimes tied to the function executed, leading to corresponding grants (or better: cost restitution). However, it may also have to be provided by the lower tiers themselves without any contribution from the top.[39] Central administration is thus relatively underdeveloped (except for specific functions like defence, foreign affairs etc.), and the states bear the brunt of administrative costs (including tax administration), which tend to grow comparably faster, since such services are relatively labour-intensive.

On the other hand, municipalities have to spend a large share of capital expenditure in such fields as communal services (sewerage etc.), health, sports and recreation, schools, housing and road construction. This particular division of functions – central decision-making with decentralised execution – has been labelled the 'horizontal' approach to federalism – in contrast to the 'vertical' model of the Anglo-Saxon world (Spahn 1978).

Despite the fact that the original constitutional power is with the states,[40] the lower tier of government has experienced a continuous erosion of its original competences, to the benefit of the central government. The few remaining policy areas where state governments are autonomous in the sense of a clear vertical division of functions are culture, education, law and order, parts of environmental and health policies as well as regional economic policy, but even in these areas state competence has been eroded as a result of larger responsibility sharing and 'joint-decision' mechanisms introduced into the Constitution in 1969. This has recently led to initiatives aimed at recouping some of the lost ground – also as a response to stronger centripetal forces through Western European integration.[41]

At the level of financial arrangements the horizontal distribution of functions is matched by the prevalence of revenue sharing. All major taxes (income, corporate income, value-added taxes) are joint taxes, that is, they accrue jointly to the federal and state governments. Legislation on taxes is uniform and centralised. State parliaments have essentially no power to legislate on taxes any more (Stern 1980, pp. 1118ff), despite the fact that some smaller taxes continue to be assigned to state or local governments. All taxes are assessed according to the same national tax code – in particular as regards the tax base.[42] Recent attempts to differentiate between the income tax rates in the Western and Eastern parts of Germany have met severe criticism, and the proposals were successfully resisted.[43]

Uniform taxation is typical for the German federal machinery. In economic terms uniform taxation may in fact be desirable from both distributive and allocative aspects. Uniformity of tax rules stresses the argument of regional fairness or equity; it also simplifies tax coordination from administrative points of view. More importantly, it avoids tax competition among regions, which would lead to distorting effects on the flow of capital, on migration and on cross-border shopping. This again fosters social cohesion and it tends to equate taxable capacity as long as the regional flows of resources resulting from market-oriented arbitrage remain unimpeded. Allocative aspects furnish strong arguments in favour of uniformity in national tax legislation. They are, however, not sufficient to explain the assignment of taxes to different layers of government or tax sharing in particular.

In political terms uniform taxation may be debatable, since it seems to restrict state sovereignty. As regards Germany it may seem astonishing that a federal organisation has in fact produced a political consensus leading to uniformity of tax rules and even to the sharing of joint taxes on the basis of standardised criteria for the apportionment of revenues. This can only be understood when looking at the specific rules governing the process of federal legislation and the means by which the states inject their voice into this process (Spahn 1977b).

3.3.2 The Role of the State House (*Bundesrat*)

Virtually every law affecting the interests of the states has to pass through the *Bundesrat*, the states' legislative assembly (Articles 50 ff. *Grundgesetz*) which, unlike the equivalent in other federations such as the United States, Canada or Australia, is a true states' House in the sense that its members are appointed by state governments, recalled by them, and are strictly bound to the directions of their respective governments (*imperatives Mandat*). The actual status of the *Bundesrat* in federal legislation has given the German states a strong position compared both to Germany's own past[44] and to other federations.

Particularly in the field of taxation and related fields is the influence of the states far-reaching, because the consent of the *Bundesrat* is required with respect to (i) all laws affecting the proceeds of taxes accruing entirely or in part to the states, (ii) federal laws on fiscal equalisation, and (iii) federal laws regulating the administration by fiscal authorities of the states (Articles 105 (3), 106 (4), 107 (2) and 108 (3) *Grundgesetz*).

In Germany the power to legislate on specific taxes has to be seen as being totally distinct from the right of each layer of government to appropriate the proceeds from these taxes. Tax assignment to specific levels of governments is guaranteed by the Constitution itself, with only minor adjustments to be made through federal legislation. Major revisions of federal financial arrangements – for instance as a consequence of German unification – can, hence, only be made through a change in the Constitution requiring a two-thirds majority in both Houses of the federal parliament.

3.3.3 Vertical Tax Assignment, Federal and State Taxes, and Joint Taxation

As mentioned before, joint or shared taxes cover all of the most important revenue sources in Germany. In 1989, the wage and income tax, the corporation tax and VAT – all joint taxes – yielded approximately three-quarters of total tax revenue in the Federal Republic.

These taxes are apportioned to the different layers of government as shown in the table overleaf. In addition to these taxes, the local business tax is also shared by all three levels of government – although it is not officially a joint tax.[45] From its share of VAT the federal government has to finance the contributions made to finance the EC Commission's budget.

The vertical distribution of income taxes is fixed by the Constitution (Article 106 (3) *Grundgesetz*) and, except for grants, any adjustments of the vertical distribution of public funds are exclusively effected through renegotiating the shares of turnover taxes (VAT). The result of the bargaining between the federal and the states governments is embodied in a federal law requiring the consent of the *Bundesrat*.

Distribution of joint taxes for each level of government in Germany
(in per cent)

Joint tax	Federal	Länder	Local
Personal income tax	42 ½	42 ½	15
Corporate income tax	50	50	0
Value-added tax	65	35	0

The regional distribution of income taxes follows the regional pattern of tax yields (according to the residence principle, with special rules for the apportionment of the corporation tax). The regional distribution of VAT is essentially on a per capita basis (which implies an implicit equalisation effect). A small share of VAT is used by the federal government for explicit equalisation purposes in the form of unconditional asymmetrical vertical grants (*Ergänzungszuweisungen*).

The main federal taxes (11.8 per cent of total taxes in 1989) are excise taxes,[46] the most important of which are those on mineral oil, tobacco and alcohol (except beer).[47] The main state taxes (4.7 per cent of total taxes) are the motor vehicle tax and the net wealth tax – a rather unimportant tax in Germany. Apart from the local business tax, municipalities employ a property tax and communal levies on public services (utilities). The vertical assignment of taxes in Germany is shown in Table 3.3.

Table 3.3   Sources of revenue for each level of government in Germany
(in per cent)

Revenue source	Federal	State	Local
Exclusive taxes	22	9	4
Shared taxes	70	64	30
Unconditional bloc grants	–	1	11
Specific purpose grants	–	14	11
Other	8	12	43
Total revenue	100	100	100

Totals do not add up correctly due to rounding.

3.3.4   Cooperative Federalism

The German federal machinery does not employ vertical general revenue grants.[48] They would make little sense within the tax-sharing arrangements, which allow vertical adjustments through the share of VAT. There are, however, specific vertical grants that imply federal cofinancing of state projects. These grants function within a complex network of interstate cooperation and monitoring, which is typical for 'cooperative federalism', the antagonistic approach to the 'independent layer-cake' model.

In addition to the joint federal legislation process, there are further instruments of policy coordination provided by the Constitution: an institutional joint-decision-making and responsibility-sharing machinery combined with joint planning and joint financing and/or grants-in-aid – which is a peculiarity of the German federal arrangements.[49]

These elements of cooperative federalism were introduced in 1969, when it had become clear that federal legislation alone was not sufficient to coordinate policies at the central level. The federal division of functions – with framework legislation assigned to the centre and the implementation of policies to the lower tiers of government – was deficient in view of the (then more important) goals of coordinated stabilisation policies.[50] The model also precluded the federal government from setting guidelines or prerogatives within those policy areas in which policies cannot be controlled by legislation – that is the provision of public goods and services, especially public infrastructure. It was in these policy areas ' . . that the planning and spending functions assigned to the *Länder* proved to be more important than the legislative functions assigned to the federal government' (Reissert 1978, pp. 24–5).

Two major coordinative instruments were therefore created in 1969: (i) the 'joint tasks' (*Gemeinschaftsaufgaben*) according to Articles 91a and 91b; and (ii) grants-in-aid (*Finanzhilfen*) according to Article 104 a (4) *Grundgesetz*.

Joint tasks were defined in the Constitution for five policy domains.[51] Grants-in-aid were given to the states for regional and local investments within certain areas to be defined by federal law or by federal-state agreement. Again, the uniformity-of-living-conditions principle is visible in these arrangements, since the Constitution stipulates that these grants are to be used only for equalising regional disparities, for stabilisation purposes, and for stimulating growth.

These constitutional rules have legalised anterior practices whereby the federal government had provided funds to the *Länder* on a bilateral basis. Instead of bilateralism the new instruments stress multilateral agreements

– at least for the joint tasks – within the so-called 'planning committees' (*Planungsausschüsse*), where the federation shares the votes with all of the states. There is joint planning and joint financing of all state projects adopted by the federal government and a majority of the states. These coordinative instruments have thus increased the scope for central government interference in many ways, not only through its impact on the planning process (in particular on the selection of projects), but also through the potential threat to withdraw federal cofinancing – that usually covers 50 per cent of the costs.[52]

The arrangements have therefore met criticism at the state level, and further attempts to centralise powers in Germany have been successfully resisted in the 1980s.[53] On the contrary: scepticism as regards the effectiveness of central stabilisation policies, as well as the high costs of coordination and administration – together with political constraints imposed on state governments and parliaments by the mixed financing arrangements[54] – have recently encouraged attempts to redecentralise powers. However, German unification, as well as the Gulf war, have contributed to reinvigorating the role of the federal government at the expense of state power.

3.3.5   Equalisation and Horizontal Grants

As noted before, one particular feature of German federalism is the existence of interstate equalisation, the *Finanzausgleich*. This is achieved through a specific set of rules governing a second-round redistribution of financial means among the states themselves (except for West Berlin which so far has received – and receives – a federal grant instead). These rules are set out by federal law based on Article 107 (2) *Grundgesetz*.[55] It should be noted in advance that this mechanism applies only to the Western states – even after unification. The process starts from

- definition of a state and local fiscal capacity measure for any one Land (*Steuerkraftmesszahl*), which is roughly the sum of state tax revenues corrected for special burdens and local tax revenues adjusted for population density, the degree of urbanisation and so on. This measure is then related to
- an equalisation yardstick for this *Land* (*Ausgleichsmesszahl*) derived from the average per capita fiscal capacity of all participating states multiplied by the population of this particular *Land*.

Any shortfall of fiscal capacity in relation to the yardstick is equalised in steps with graduated rates. A uniform average is not requested, yet there is a guarantee that fiscal capacity (including equalisation payments) should reach at least 95 per cent of the average for the states as a whole.

Equalisation payments are made by those states the fiscal capacity of which exceeds the yardstick, again in graduated contributions. The system works as a clearing mechanism, that means that payments made by the financially stronger states always equal the sum of receipts of the weaker states.

The financial settlement among states has had a fairly strong equalising effect in the past[56] – and, at the outset, the mechanism worked reasonably well. Yet the fact that the burden of the settlement has consistently shifted onto two states only – Baden-Wuerttemberg and Hesse – while all other states either benefited or were exempt from contributing, led to severe political tensions among the states, that are reflected in actions to amend the arrangement by appealing to the Constitutional Court.[57] This proves that the 'brotherly' financial-settlement arrangements among the states seem to have been stretched to their political limits in West Germany – even without the new problems created by German unification.

3.3.6 Constraints on Deficit Financing

The institutional limits on deficit financing are twofold in Germany.

*   Para. 20, *Bundesbankgesetz* restricts borrowing by all tiers of government from the Central Bank (local governments having no access to this form of deficit financing at all). There are fixed ceilings set for this type of borrowing by legislation – which are proportional to population for the *Länder*, and the amounts appear to be relatively low.
*   The Constitution – in its Article 115 – restricts federal government borrowing to the 'amount of projected outlays for investment purposes in the budget'. Similar rules apply to *Länder* budgeting in accordance with state constitutions or legislation. Local government borrowing is subject to state control.

Budget constraints thus appear to be rather tough in Germany. Notably, the 'quasi-constitutional' limitation of access to *Bundesbank* financing is often praised by German politicians as being at the origin of low inflation, a strong currency and the financial stability of the public sector. In principle this cannot be denied – especially since legislation has rendered the *Bundesbank* legally independent from the federal and state governments.

Yet one could argue that the system was not put to any severe test in the past, and that it has worked, largely, based on a consensus formed by all political parties and interest groups – trading partners, in particular. History shows, however, that the constraint may have been less binding than many people thought, and the test of German unification has made it definitely clear that judicial control of budget deficits is difficult to achieve – even with constitutional rules.

The public budget constraint has been 'softened' in many respects.

- First, it is far from clear what should be understood by 'investment purposes'. Events have shown that it is possible to redefine current outlays to represent investment outlays without much difficulty in some instances.
- An amendment to the Constitution, made in 1969, has permitted the federal government to raise loan money in order to combat 'disturbances of general economic equilibrium'. This rule is even more difficult to monitor in quantitative terms. The provision was introduced in the heydays of legislation sanctioning Keynesian demand-management policies (which are no longer applied as such in Germany). Application of this rule reached its climax only recently, however, when 'disturbance of general economic equilibrium' was interpreted as relating to the consequences of German unification.
- German unification, with its massive needs to transfer resources from one part of the country to the other (see below), has brought to the fore another strategy for dissimulating budget deficits and for softening legal budget constraint: a proliferation of 'off-budget' funding. Political developments have created the Fund 'German Unity', the *Treuhandanstalt* and the *Kreditabwicklungsfond*. All rely heavily on loan funding.[58]

Even as to the formal limitation of money creation in Germany, a few qualifications must be made.

- German Monetary Union, introduced on 1 July 1990, has lead to the monetisation of almost all the personal savings of East German citizens at a ratio of 1 Ostmark : 1 DM – against the will of the *Bundesbank*. This was not necessarily inflationary. Yet it has eased the budget constraint of German governments (and accentuated the financial situation of East German business firms) since money thus created was available to be invested in interest-bearing government bonds.
- Even under normal circumstances the *Bundesbank* had been indirectly

supportive of government debt financing by its open-market policies. It should be recognised, however, that this was mainly achieved without macroeconomic distortions and with the central bank responsibly following its main policy objective: price stability.

- Cost-push inflation mounting as a result of unification, and its financing through higher taxes as well as higher money wages, have increased money demand M3 far beyond its – admittedly unrealistic – targets set by the central bank for 1992. This has, however, led to strong reactions from monetary authorities with unprecedented high interest rates, a policy that runs counter to the government's intentions to stimulate growth.

Central bank independence is thus, in fact, the cornerstone for budgetary discipline in the German public sector. Yet it should also be clear that deficit financing is much 'softer' than it may appear at first sight. Restrictive constitutional rules and restrictive monetary policies have not been able to prevent the German public sector from running massive deficits that may amount to DM190 billion for 1991, or approximately 7 per cent of (total) German GNP.[59,60] As to federal and regional loan financing of public budgets in Germany, the effective constraints appear to be much softer than is indicated by existing legal provisions.

3.3.7 German Unification and the New Strain on Fiscal Federal Relations in Germany

On 3 October 1990 five new Eastern states[61] joined the Federal Republic of Germany that had formerly been administered centrally by a socialist government. The West German currency was adopted even before unification and the tax system was introduced, in rapid steps, almost fully – without any major amendment.

The effects on the German federal machinery were enormous: productivity levels are extremely low in the East compared to the West and markets for East German products almost instantaneously vanished as a result of the German Monetary Union: some products could no longer be sold to traditional former COMECON markets – since they were priced in convertible currency – and often they failed on Western markets. The consequences were closures of product lines and firms – with concomitant unemployment or short-time work. This rendered the taxable capacity of Eastern states lower than that of their Western counterparts.

On the other hand, there were large demands for government services. Some services have had to be created from scratch (for example, tax administration, unemployment insurance, the administration of welfare programmes, parts of public education and jurisdiction); and needs are most urgent in the area of public infrastructure – notably at the local level. Obviously, large public-sector deficits for Eastern state governments result from these imbalances, requiring particular solutions.

Germany is in the midst of this process of economic and fiscal adjustment (Krupp 1991). What had to be solved immediately was the distribution of joint taxes among the different states.

Politically, horizontal tax apportionment of shared income taxes did not pose major problems, since the residence (or tax yield) principle applies. Economically, however, income taxes are thus distributed very unevenly – through the progressivity of the tariff – as long as income levels are much lower in the East.[62]

On the other hand the distribution of VAT has caused a major political controversy, since it is apportioned on a per capita basis implying strong horizontal equalisation effects. Yet, in spite of initial resistance expressed by Western states, the system now applies fully to Eastern Germany – which lets the East implicitly benefit from the higher productivity levels in the West.

At present fiscal federal relations in the West continue to be governed by the old system. Yet political pressure is continuously mounting, given the threat of Eastern municipalities – and even states – becoming unable to finance their current outlays. Local governments may have to close certain operations (or threaten to do so). The most urgent problem is, however, unemployment. Employment may be thought to be left to the labour market to be settled; yet mass-unemployment has a political and social dimension calling for government intervention. It hence has a bearing on public budget – whether one likes it or not.

Solutions, proposed and applied, for dealing with the most urgent needs of the Eastern government are *ad hoc*, implying a great number of vertical and horizontal specific purpose payments. For 1991, public funds of approximately DM170 billion are being transferred from Western to Eastern Germany (Deutsche Bundesbank 1992, p. 16). This corresponds to approximately 80 per cent of East Germany's own GNP; it is one-and-a-half times the size of the EC budget – or, per capita, in relation to the constituencies concerned, roughly thirty times as much; and it amounts to approximately twice the amount the industrialised world as a whole gives to all LDCs in the form of official government aid[63] – or, per capita of the respective recipients, more than a ten-fold of what the North gives to the South per annum (discounted appropriately for GNP per capita). The German West-East transfer programme ought to be considered as the most massive regional redistribution scheme ever put into effect in the history of mankind.

The transfers take the following forms:

- specific purpose payments by the federal government (support for regional development, infrastructure, traffic, social expenditure, interest payments);
- transfers through a separate fund '*Aufschwung Ost*' (including an investment programme for communities, measures for job creation, as well as road and house building);
- direct transfers from the West German unemployment insurance scheme and other social security funds (in particular old-age pensions);
- equalising payments through the new states' full participation in the per capita distribution of VAT;
- payments from the old *Länder*, and
- contributions of the federal government and the old states through the 'German Unity Fund'.

The complex incidence pattern generated by the activities of the *Treuhandanstalt* cannot be considered here. Intentionally this institution was set up to privatise the business sector formerly under the control of the socialist government. It was hence expected to generate extra funds for the federal budget.[64] However, the threat of mass-unemployment contingent on decisions of the *Treuhandanstalt* is likely to force this institution more and more into advancing cash for salaries to be paid to the potentially unemployed[65] – which may not only force it to run down its own liquid assets, but may also require support from the federal and Western state governments. As far as the horizontal fiscal settlement scheme among states is concerned, the problems relating to German unification are not yet resolved or even touched upon. The inclusion of the East German *Länder* into the system of horizontal perequation would have meant a further considerable loss for Western states (Krupp 1991, pp. 375–6) and all of them (but Breme) would have had to contribute to the clearing mechanism – even those that are now at the receiving end. In view of this historic challenge, a radical review of German *Finanzausgleich* and fiscal federal relations in general may seem to be in order – with possible consequences for a constitutional reform.

A new system of fiscal federal relations is in fact scheduled to be introduced in 1995. So far, not even the shadow of any new principles governing future intergovernmental fiscal relations can be detected. It seems obvious though that the new arrangements will have to stress cost or even needs criteria – given that the costs of providing government services have started to vary widely in Germany. Cost elements are almost entirely missing from the present equalisation machinery. The work of the Australian Commonwealth Grants Commission may be useful in this regard.

Yet it seems almost certain that the uniformity-of-living-conditions principle will remain *the* cornerstone of German intergovernmental financial relations. As a basic constitutional right it is most likely to survive. Given new large regional discrepancies it is not easy to fulfil this mandate however. In order to preserve the principle, criteria based on it may have to be slightly amended – hopefully by taking economic cost elements more strongly into account. This reform remains on the agenda of German federal politics for the years to come.

3.3.8   Unitary Federalism or Cooperative Federalism? An Attempted Answer

It is in fact true that the German federal financial arrangements convey the impression of a rather unitary state: uniform tax legislation, extensive tax sharing and horizontal financial-settlement arrangements may be interpreted in this fashion. Yet this impression is essentially misleading. The role of the states' House – allowing the states to inject their voice into federal legislation, responsibility-sharing and cofinancing arrangements in important areas of state policy, and the horizontal design of the federal machinery, by which the centre coordinates through 'framework legislation', whereas the states are free to implement their policies within that framework, all constitute a complex *ensemble* of political checks and balances requiring a high degree of cooperation.

The German model of federalism can be seen as the antagonistic approach to the layer-cake view of the economist. The direct link between the taxpayer's bill and the provision of public goods is destroyed through tax sharing as well as implicit and explicit equalisation. Regional taxation powers are virtually non-existent. Standards for the provision of public goods are set at average levels – as a consequence of the uniformity-of-living-conditions principle.

In spite of all these features, the German economy – notwithstanding actual problems due to the integration of a formerly socialist economy – seems to be vigorous and robust. This may indicate that the failure to comply with the economists' prescriptions need not necessarily imply low productivity levels due to inefficiencies in the provision of public services.

The German model of federalism is highly cooperative – not unitary. As in Switzerland, it is based on a strong consensus to create a politically stable, socially pacified and economically robust environment for the further development of German society. It remains to be seen whether this model is capable of coping with the challenge of German unification. Despite possible amendments as regards specific aspects of the German federal machinery – notably horizontal perequation – the fundamental approach is most likely to survive, however.

It is questionable, though, whether the German federation could become a model for the further enhancement of the European Community in its relations with member states. Cohesion is a concept far from homogeneity, and national sovereignty is much stronger at the European level than among the German states. Nevertheless, German experience may impinge on the development of the institutional setting within the EC. Already the European Council is very similar to the German *Bundesrat*. A strong voice for regional governments within the central legislation process is a prerequisite for their handing over parts of their national sovereignties to the EC. However, centripetal forces are still relatively weak in Europe compared to Germany. This is for institutional reasons (restricted role of the European Parliament, lack of a democratically elected central government) as well as for political and cultural reasons.

3.4 THE EUROPEAN COMMUNITY: THE CENTRE AT THE MERCY OF STATES?

3.4.1 General Characteristics of EC Federal Arrangements

This is not the place to go into the details of actual financial federal arrangements between the EC and its member states. Yet a few remarks seem to be in order (Commission of the European Communities 1989).

Similar to the early days of the Swiss Confederation and the German *Reich*, the EC budget was initially financed through national contributions, yet this was supplanted – similarly to developments in other federations – by a system of own resources for the EC at a meeting of Heads of State in The Hague in 1969 – which came into force in 1971. The main features of this system have developed gradually and were stabilised in a major reform in 1988. The structure of the actual system is sketched in chapter 3.4.2. Although the Community disposes of own resources, and can manage these funds autonomously, there are a number of features in Community-state relations that may convey the impression – unlike the Australian case – of the centre still remaining at the mercy of member states financially.

- Tax discretion of the EC is extremely limited. Customs duties are relatively inelastic as a revenue source (notably as a consequence of the progress made in dismantling tariffs). As in other federations, their share of total EC revenue has been continuously eroded. Discretion for agricultural levies is with the Council – hence with member states – and they tend to be extremely volatile in response to non-budgetary developments outside the realm of the EC – supply reactions of farmers, for instance, or the fluctuating of the US dollar.

- The main elements of the revenue side of the EC budget, VAT and the GNP-based resource, may be characterised as general revenue grants – or tax sharing – similar to state financial assistance in Australia, yet going in the opposite direction. Although this provides stable funding to the centre it does not comprise the EC's right to vary the scope of these means through own tax discretion.

- The EC is virtually prohibited from access to loan finance that could ease its budget constraint.

The situation very much resembles the Australian approach but with opposite emphasis: all the major taxes remain at the state level and the EC's (comparably small) budget is financed with general financial assistance provided from the lower tier at its discretion, and with truly own tax instruments the bases of which are eroding and/or volatile.

Yet the EC budget exhibits a peculiarity that is hardly ever found in any other budgeting procedure: not only is the parliament's role in the budgeting process extremely limited – this may be true for other constituencies as well; but the budget distinguishes between so-called compulsory and non-compulsory expenditures, where only the latter can be controlled through traditional budgetary procedures. Compulsory expenditure, which is approximately two-thirds of total expenditure, is governed through a complex set of rules involving a number of elements: (i) market reactions, notably supply decisions of farmers; (ii) *ad hoc* decisions of the Council, notably on intervention prices; (iii) the interplay of world-market prices for agricultural products, EC levies and the vagaries of the US dollar, and (iv) the formula-flexibility and adjustment procedures concerning budgetary discipline introduced by the Council in 1988.[66] Although controlling the budget was modestly successful, notably after the 1988 decisions to constrain compulsory expenditures, it has to be stressed that, in economic terms, parts of the budget, those relating to compulsory expenditures, are virtually open-ended – in spite of all restricting measures – as long as the basic underlying supply processes determining such expenditures remain unchallenged. Hence, compulsory expenditures – which take precedence in the budget over other categories – tend to pre-empt the field for non-compulsory outlays. Its jeopardising other EC functions is also potentially a threat to EC autonomy. Yet does this all warrant speaking of the EC as being at the mercy of member states?

3.4.2 Tax Assignment and Revenue Sharing

Little has to be added to what has been said on the revenue side of the EC budget. Own resources of the Community were initially (from 1971 on):

- customs duties;
- agricultural levies, and
- one per cent of member states' VAT revenue (on a standardised tax base).

Yet, over the years, a growing fiscal imbalance between the Community's expenditure needs and its own resources on one hand, and horizontal imbalances on the other, led to a crisis in Community finance that accentuated more and more in the 1980s. The crisis was exacerbated by political issues relating to the operation of the annual budget procedure, and to a conflict between legislative and budgetary powers at the EC level.[67]

The problem of a growing inadequacy of own resources was finally attacked within a comprehensive reform of Community finances in 1988 ('Delors Package I', KOM 100). These are the main elements of the package.

- The total amount of own resources was related to total Community GNP – not just VAT; in addition the ceilings were gradually raised.
- Traditional own revenues (levies, customs duties) were 'rationalised', and a collection-cost-reimbursement scheme was introduced.
- VAT-based own resources were raised to 1.4 per cent of the standardised tax base, with a provision narrowing horizontal disparities for the tax base.
- A new category of own resources was introduced in the form of a fourth levy based on member states' GNP.

The increase – and restructuring – of the revenue side of the budget was supported by measures aimed at containing agricultural outlays on the expenditure side. These cannot be discussed here. Yet, as to the revenue structure of the EC budget, a few remarks should be added.

- First, the EC's own resources fall into two distinct types of revenue: (i) general financial assistance (in the form of VAT sharing and the 'fourth levy' – essentially a general revenue grant based on a comprehensive statistical indicator); and (ii) genuine tax instruments (customs duties and agricultural levies). The former stress the pure revenue effect of financial assistance; the latter exhibit a potential for EC tax policies – through the changing of relative prices – to be exerted by the Commission. If this potential is not fully exploited at present it hinges on the EC's role in financial legislation being extremely limited.
- The 1988 reform has not altered the philosophy of EC financial arrangements. In particular, it has avoided establishing new tax competences for the EC by according its independent taxation rights to the national tax bases of member states – either directly or indirectly through piggy-back levies.
- The intrinsic problems with the open-endedness of compulsory expenditures have not been solved. This would have required either setting a 'cap' on these outlay categories or – better – putting these outlays 'off budget', to be governed by their own constraining (or non-constraining) rules.[68]

The 1988 reform has, however, also brought adjustments as to the horizontal distribution of EC own funding, which will be addressed in the next chapter.

3.4.3   Equalisation and Horizontal Tax Coordination

The EC does not really attempt to install an explicit equalisation scheme similar to those found in Australia, Switzerland or Germany. In this respect it resembles much more the US. Equalisation is implicit in

- the regional incidence of CAP subsidies;
- the incidence of specific expenditure programmes – notably the three structural funds (ERDF, ESF, and EGGFA Guidance Section) and the integrated Mediterranean programmes. The former typically provide specific purpose grants (with matching requirements); the

latter provide unconditional specific purpose assistance to the regions concerned. These instruments are officially aimed at fostering 'social cohesion' within the Community;

* last but not least, the incidence pattern of public goods provided by the Community – through its policies in the areas of energy, industry, environment, technology and research, for instance. The latter aspect cannot be emphasised enough since these benefits are often neglected in the superficial *'juste-retour'* calculations that try to monitor contributions made and benefits received by each member state. The effects of the Community's budget *are different from zero-sum games*. With the scope for Community public services expanding in the future, the importance of this expenditure category – as the equalising effects of its incidence pattern – will also increase.

Yet the finance reforms of the EC in the 1980s have mainly focused on the regional distribution of contributions made to the EC budget. Some important regional tax concessions were accorded to EC member state governments bearing on the horizontal distribution of funds. These concessions have taken both explicit and implicit forms. An example of explicit regional tax concessions is associated with the preferential treatment of the United Kingdom and Germany; implicit regional tax concessions relate to the introduction of a GNP levy as well as to the planned reform of value-added taxation in the EC.

* This is not the place to give a full account of the history of regional tax concessions granted to the UK and German governments for their contributions to the EC budget.[69] At the origin of the UK problem was a major structural imbalance in the country's financial links with the Community, resulting from a relatively small agricultural sector – entailing small benefits from CAP – and large contributions to the financing of the Community budget through the country's relatively high VAT base. Political pressure to rectify this imbalance dates back to the 1975 referendum on the country's continued membership of the Community. Similarly, the German government – stressing its role as a major paymaster to the Community budget – was pressuring for relief on an *ad hoc* basis. The issues were (temporarily) resolved through direct compensation mechanisms agreed upon at the Fontainebleau European Council meeting in June 1984.
* As mentioned before, the 1988 reform of the Community budget has introduced a GNP-based additional resource, the so-called 'fourth levy' (Commission of the European Communities 1989, p. 59). This

is a variable 'topping-up' resource the character of which is more a general revenue grant (rather than a tax or a levy), since it is based on statistical indicators, not on bases defined by tax legislation. Its implicit impact on the horizontal distribution of financial burdens within the Community somewhat mitigates the regressive effects of VAT as a Community resource. Whereas VAT alleviates the burden for countries experiencing trade surpluses within the Community – through the tax credit given to net exporters – while burdening deficit countries disproportionately, the GNP-levy is more in line with the country's production – and hence general welfare – by imposing exports and exempting imports. The reform was meant to install an implicit equalisation effect for the financing of the Community budget, rendering the system 'more progressive' among regions by relating financial contributions to levels of prosperity.

- As mentioned before, the 1988 reform has also reduced the variance of financial contributions of member states by narrowing the scope of standardised VAT bases for the levy.
- Another problem of horizontal tax coordination will be related to the switch to a new system of VAT collection after the abolishing of internal tax barriers within the Community. This will be more fully addressed in chapter 4 of this book.

Generally speaking, it seems unlikely that the EC will embark on a fully-fledged equalisation scheme in the near future. As in Australia in the early days, 'compensation' (for relative disadvantages of various regions) may be a first step only; fiscal needs and fiscal equalisation are likely to be later-stage developments.

3.4.4   Constraints on Deficit Financing

It has been said that the EC budget has virtually no access to loan finance. This has to be qualified somewhat. Both the ECSC and Euratom are entitled to borrow funds provided they are used to grant loans or to make contributions to investments.[70] Although the EEC Treaty had made no provision for lending and borrowing, such activities were finally authorised in 1975 – yet to a very limited degree (Commission of the European Communities 1989, p. 35). Medium-term financial assistance for member states' balances of payments, and the NCI (New Community instrument for the promotion of investment in the Community) were set up and renewed consequently.

It is interesting to note that borrowing and lending operations do not appear in the respective budgets – which constitutes a breach in the principle of unity. This is for both technical and political reasons. As to technical aspects, these could easily be resolved by special provisions for a 'capital budget' to be combined with a 'current budget'. The Commission has consistently proposed such an inclusion of borrowing/lending operations in the budget. Yet the unwillingness of the Council to share powers with the parliament seems to have prevented any institutional reform so far.[71]

Yet an interesting observation can be made with regard to the binding nature of the extremely limited access to loan finance at the EC level: the constraints again appear much softer than it might seem at first sight. This can be illustrated by looking at the experience of the 1980s, with its continuous financial crises and the Community's ways of dealing with these crises. The EC budget essentially continued to operate despite a shortage of own resources. This was mainly resolved by supplementary and amended budgets, the payment of intergovernmental advances, the entry of a 'negative reserve', and by broad interpretations of budgetary rules. Eventually the crisis of the EC budget exerted political pressure on member states and the Council to readjust the vertical imbalance of financial resources. The EC's limited access to loan finance was thus instrumental in reaching a political solution – and it demonstrates EC power, not EC dependence.

3.4.5   The Centre at the Mercy of States? An Attempted Answer

As can be seen from this discussion, the EC budget largely depends on revenue raised at the national level – and transferred to the supranational level by member states. The EC is essentially restricted from levying its own taxes with full autonomy. Nevertheless the predominant type of general revenue assistance (or tax sharing of VAT) provides a firmly established and secure revenue source that was given to the Community as an 'own resource' based on a quasi-constitutional right.[72] Despite the fact that the Community has virtually no discretion to raise loan money, and that the budget continues to be subject to the vagaries of CAP revenues and outlays, it would be inappropriate to talk of the EC as being at the mercy of states – as it was inappropriate, for similar reasons, to hold the Australian states as being at the mercy of the Commonwealth. Limited access to the capital market even seems to enhance the EC's political standing *vis-à-vis* member states' governments.

Furthermore, the influence of a central government is not necessarily a function of financing arrangements – not even of the size of the budget. Firmly established rules, through international treaties, are increasingly being applied and rendered specific by both supranational and national executives and legislatures, and, in particular, by the European High Court. Framework legislation – as in the German (and Swiss) models of horizontal federalism – may lead to a structure in which general rules will establish policy guidelines that continue to be applied essentially at the national level. In this way, unity in diversity is realised with relatively small budgetary resources being engaged at the supranational level of government.

The international comparisons of existing federations have shown up another fact: that the EC has absorbed a number of important elements of Swiss and German federalism already. This applies not only to institutions (like the role of the Council); it also applies to basic ingredients of the EC federal financial machinery. Vertical fiscal relations seem to be governed more in accordance with German federalism. Notably, revenue sharing and the principle of subsidiarity must be stressed in this context.

Horizontal fiscal coordination and equalisation in the EC seem to be more in line with the Helvetian approach to federalism. It underlines fiscal responsibility at the regional level, restricted tax competition and effective fiscal coordination among provinces, with the central government exerting a *de facto* coordinating power in the area of cantonal taxation – even for income tax. It should be remembered that all federations apply some form of equalisation schemes – even the decentralised Swiss model of federalism. As it appears, the EC is likely to extend its responsibilities in the area of regional policies as well – which are designed to enhance regional economic and social cohesion within Europe. These policies should not be guided by uniformity and homogeneity considerations. They must lead to a more balanced provision of public goods throughout the EC however, for instance through the Commission's own expenditure programmes on public goods, through minimum standards to be set by the Commission (possibly combined with conforming guarantees to be given through cofinancing provisions).

If another conclusion can be drawn from the foregoing analysis – notably the Swiss and the German federal arrangements – it could be the following: a truly integrated European Community requires a much greater degree of cooperation, among regional governments and the centre, within the EC. As far as the budget of the EC is concerned this must lead to a strengthening of responsibility-sharing and cofinancing arrangements, respectively, and to a greater use of grants-in-aid programmes in the future.

Furthermore, comparisons with existing federations have made clear that the centre's role will probably increase – also in budgetary terms. This is, of course, contingent on a number of policy decisions to be taken conjointly by member state governments. The greater the realm for the central provision of public goods – notably defence, foreign policy, and general welfare – the more the centre's budget will have to expand. This is rendered extensively clear by a look at the US federal budget – to which the Constitution has assigned these three functions, and *only* these functions. The next chapter explores avenues toward moderately increasing the importance of the EC budget and redesigning its financial structure accordingly.

4 The Future of the Community Budget under EMU

4.1 EUROPEAN INTEGRATION AND FISCAL SYSTEMS

4.1.1 The Economic and Monetary Union

The 70s and early 80s were in fact difficult for the European Community: high rates of inflation combined with sluggish economic growth and persistently high unemployment. The process of European economic integration had almost come to a halt. The only major institutional reform was the creation, in 1979, of the European Monetary System (EMS) which was then regarded with suspicion by many analysts in particular by academics and central bankers. Concomitantly the United States, from 1982 on, experienced a strong expansion of their economy that brought about substantial employment growth and the reduction of inflation rates. The American experience was mainly attributed to three major economic policy measures: restrictive monetary policies, supply-side economics (mainly expressed through a lowering of tax rates), and deregulation, that is the reduction of state interference in the economy.[1]

Europeans reacted in a very similar vein: A 'White Paper' drafted under the responsibility of Lord Cockfield proposed about 300 separate pieces of legislation aiming at the achievement of a unified Single Market within the EC by 1992. Government interference and internal protectionism was to be reduced and all economic borders be abolished be they material, technical, or fiscal in nature. These policy objectives were endorsed by the Heads of Member States through the so-called 'Single European Act' that came into force on July 1st, 1987. It unleashed a great number of changes sweeping before it many obstacles which had hitherto prevented the EC from becoming a truly single market. By the end of 1992 European companies will share a home market potentially larger than any other in the free world. More recently, the creation of an economic zone in conjunction with EFTA – with some of their member having already applied for admission to the Community as full members – and the according by

76

the Community of an associated status to formerly communist States in Eastern Europe, Poland, Czechoslovakia and Hungary, have increased this potential even further.

The Single European Act and further agreements among Community Members culminating in the Maastricht accord of December 1991 have speeded-up the process of economic integration in Europe. The main elements were the following:

- There was first a clear time table for the implementation of legislation leading toward the Single Market: the end of 1992. This psychological factor cannot be stressed enough since it contributed to the change of basic attitudes of European businessmen who started asking themselves whether their traditional markets would remain uncontested under the new conditions, whether there were extending markets to be discovered and exploited, and what strategies they would have to develop in order to survive in a changing environment.
- There was second the complete comprehensiveness of the programme: essentially all internal frontiers will come down irrespective of the sector of economic activity, including services and even government procurements, nothwithstanding some exceptions of minor importance.
- There was third a new simplified decision-making machinery for collective decisions to be taken within the Community. Whereas before a strict unanimity rule was applied, Heads of States have now accepted a qualified majority-voting procedure for most – except a few, though important – policy areas. This has accelerated the pace of integration since minorities can no longer veto important joint decisions. Moreover the Maastricht summit has recognised the right of any one member to 'opt out' from specific coordinated policy areas notably from the European Monetary Union, or a group of members to 'opt in' for new joint responsibilities like social policy, which allows some Member States to go even faster than others. The accord has thus sanctioned the idea of a Europe at multiple speeds.
- Fourth a substantial change in the philosophy of economic integration could be observed during the 80s:
  As regards the *vertical relationship among governments*, the 'subsidiarity principle' was discovered and officially adopted. It requires to leave public decisions at the lowest government level possible. If policies can be exerted effectively by local, regional or national governments, no attempt should be made to transfer them onto higher levels of competence. Only policies requiring coordinated action at the supranational level should thus be handed over to the

Community. The latter should act, in the wording of the Maastricht accord, 'only if . . . the objective of the proposed action cannot be sufficiently achieved by the member states and can therefore, by reason of the scale or effects of the proposed action, be better achieved by the Community'. This severely restrains the scope for supranational policy action and it acts as a safeguard against the erosion of regional political power.

As regards the *horizontal relationship among governments*, another marked change in philosophy can be identified. Whereas the approach to integration was initially founded on the idea of harmonisation and standardisation, hence uniformity within the Community, the new philosophy stresses the idea of the mutual recognition of national standards in combination with home-based quality controls. Thus, if a product or a service can be supplied to customers under a given national rule for any one country of the EC, it automatically becomes accessible to *all* customers within the federation. This rule establishes the idea of national competition of policies and of economic and political unity with full respect to national diversity. It also abandons monolithic thinking in favour of more pluralistic attitudes, thus avoiding one of the key errors made in Eastern Europe under communist rule. It has also accelerated the process of integration by the very fact that agreeing on common standards is usually fraught with political frictions, whereas accepting each others standards is simpler – once the basic choice has been made.

Apart from these fundamental changes, EC governments have agreed on extending the Community's responsibilities significantly during the coming decade, and they have paved the way toward greater policy coordination in important domains, and even toward the forming of an economic and political union. Again, the Maastricht accord has certainly been the most spectacular step ahead since the initial Treaty of Rome.

As far as *economic policies* are concerned, several chapters of the accord have introduced new EC responsibilities.

- The treaty has established a clear timetable for the achievement of an Economic and Monetary Union in Europe (EMU), the creation of a coordinated central banking system and the introduction of a single European currency. Passage to EMU is scheduled for 1999 at the latest, and it would be 'irreversible'. Great Britain has, however, obtained the right to 'opt out' of the single European currency zone.
- The Community has obtained new responsibilities in the area of

consumer protection, supraregional aspects of health and education policies, and in 'trans-European' networking (telecommunication, transport and energy networks). Furthermore, environmental planning, industrial policy and culture have been opened up for EC policy action.[2]

- As to social policy, all countries (but the United Kingdom) have decided to embark on common policies regarding working conditions, information and consultation for workers, and on equal rights for men and women. Furthermore, they have agreed to develop common attitudes toward job protection, social security, third-country nationals from outside the EC working in the Community, as well as asylum-seekers and immigrants.
- 'Cohesion' among Member States of different economic standing will be enhanced by asymmetrical contributions to the financing of the EC budget and by the creation of a 'cohesion fund' in favour of the poorer regions of the Community.

As far as the road toward *political union* in Europe is concerned, the results are less striking but perhaps even further reaching.

- The chapter on common foreign policies may have been watered down by the proviso that policy decisions would have to be taken unanimously and that, even after agreement, countries would be allowed to act independently in the case of 'imperative need'. But the special foreign policy secretariat set up in Brussels may well become the nucleus of an EC foreign ministry in the longer run.
- Defence policies in Europe will be coordinated by the Western European Union (WEU), the defence wing of the Community, which has recently been revitalised, forming now, in the wording of the Maastricht accord, 'an integral part of the European Union'. At present it serves as a body for the framing of a common defence strategy but it may well lead to European defence policies in the longer run.
- The European Parliament has obtained greater power through its right to veto laws in certain EC policy domains, and EC citizens will be entitled to live anywhere in the Community, to stand and vote in local and European elections, and to obtain consular help from any EC government when outside the Community. This has sanctioned a split status of foreigners in the EC, those who benefit from EC citizenship and those who do not, and it will probably contribute to most – if not all – non-EC governments in Europe applying for full EC membership over the years.

Evaluating the general thrust of the Maastricht accord, a few observations seem to be in order.

Foreign and defence policies will continue to be the responsibility of national governments for the foreseeable future, yet common challenges – like the Gulf war, the dismal situation in Yugoslavia and potential unrest in Eastern Europe – will consistently move member governments into closer policy coordination, which may result in a common policy in the end. As regards Third World countries and development policies, this may even occur much faster than in other areas, since there are unwritten accords on 'regional competence' to be exerted by specific national governments within the EC, notably the ex-colonial powers *vis-à-vis* their former colonies. At least development policies will exhibit a greater degree of homogeneity and coordination, thus avoiding national competition and multiple financing of projects. The Community will achieve a full Union only in the long term. The central government will remain relatively weak, notably in comparison with its counterpart, the US federal government. Not only will it be based on distinct institutional pillars (the Commission for certain domains of economic policy-making, the European System of Central Banks (ESCB) for monetary and exchange-rate policies, the foreign policy secretariat and the WEU for foreign and defence policies); it will also be constrained by the subsidiarity principle as well as by a weak institutional setting (the Commission and European Parliament still being at the mercy of intergovernmental bodies like the Council). Yet one important integrating element inherent in the European institutional framework should be noted in passing: once an accord on EC policies has been struck by national governments, jurisdiction exerted by the European High Court will be consistently reducing the scope for national government intervention in the respective policy domain, according to past experiences, and this is likely to strengthen the role of European central institutions in the longer run.

For the immediate future, the accord on EMU has certainly the stronger bearing on EC economies and on the rest of the world. A single European money will immediately rival the US dollar, which is now the main means of payment in the world economy. This will affect financial flows for both international payments and portfolio investments. EMU is likely to weaken the dollar even further (given a certain monetary 'dollar overhang' in the world economy that is caused by extraterritorial flows-of-funds denominated in that currency). It will render the Community more attractive to international investors, both by the removal of 'internal' exchange-rate risks as well as by the reduction of transaction costs associated with hedging operations. It is also likely to be beneficial to more peripheral regions in the EC that will obtain easier access to world capital markets under a common currency. Investments in Europe will become less selective as to preferred regions, and this will enhance capital efficiency within the EC, rendering it even more attractive *vis-à-vis* other parts of the world.

4.1.2 EMU and National Fiscal Systems

EMU will have pervasive effects on the national fiscal systems of member states as it will impinge on European intergovernmental fiscal relations. The impact of EMU on national tax systems cannot be dealt with here in any detail. Only a few aspects, regarding necessary adjustments at national levels, will be touched upon at this point. They may identify potential risks both through the need to restructure national tax systems – due to the shortfall of traditional revenue – and through the need to coordinate national tax policies horizontally.

- The most obvious impact of EMU is on revenue raising through seigniorage – the right to issue national moneys. To the extent that member countries may have to refrain from accessing this revenue source they must exploit taxes more intensively.
- EMU may also render access to loan finance more difficult for some governments. Those countries that have relied more heavily on capital markets in the past may have to look for other revenue sources or to intensify the exploitation of existing tax instruments.
- EMU may cause a comprehensive revision of national tax codes and tax assessment rules as a consequence of rebasing the code on a new unit of account. Not only nominal values have to be redefined; real effects may result from revising statutory interest rates (that now exhibit various levels of price expectations) or index clauses, and they are related to resulting capital gains and losses and their tax treatment. This is likely to entail some revenue effects – although these may be considered of minor importance and appear to be once-and-for-all adjustments.
- National tax legislation may find itself increasingly subject to constraints set by the rulings of the High Court in Luxembourg – as more and more elements of national tax codes discriminating against EC nationals will be identified.[3] In the long run this may also contribute to forcing national tax legislators into a greater degree of tax coordination at the European level.
- Finally EMU may intensify national tax competition and thus impinge

heavily on revision of national tax codes in the longer run – with consistent shifts in the level and in the structure of revenue raising. Especially in the area of corporate and personal capital income taxation such adjustments are expected to be significant, calling for greater cooperation among governments.

Obviously adjustments in the structure of public revenue raising – where they are substantial – have to be anticipated *before* fixing the exchange rate of national moneys *vis-à-vis* the future common unit of account. In fact these adjustments would best be accommodated before any transition to EMU. If, for instance, a government benefiting strongly from large domestic capital markets at present finds access to these markets more difficult under EMU, and, as a consequence, has to raise tax rates, it may then be forced to plunge the region into a recession because it can no longer account on exchange-rate changes.

Moreover, EMU is likely to entail a change in the structure of taxation at national levels. Adjustments in the revenue structure may consistently fall onto direct taxes – since adjustments of indirect taxes are increasingly constrained by EC rules on horizontal tax coordination – for instance through narrower bands for tax rates or through tax competition. However, indirect taxation will remain a major revenue source to be exploited by the EC and national governments conjointly and in a coordinated fashion. On the other hand direct taxation – notably the taxation of volatile portfolio capital – will also become more and more constrained by horizontal tax competition. Hence the long-term structure of taxation must change under EMU. National tax autonomy will increasingly be asserted in the area of direct taxation.

Direct taxation will itself undergo transformation processes, finally stressing elements of personal income taxation under the residence principle and of corporate profit taxation under the origin principle. There may also result a strengthening of personal consumption tax elements in national tax legislation (Spahn 1989).

4.1.3 National Fiscal Systems and the EC Budget

EMU may also have a direct impact on the EC budget in its intergovernmental financial relations with member states' governments. We shall discuss this in more detail in the following subchapters. Yet a few general remarks seem to be in order.

* If tax coordination is indeed progressing more rapidly in the area of indirect taxation, forcing national governments into asserting their

tax autonomy more strongly in the area of direct taxation, it is most unlikely that the EC will penetrate into the area of direct taxation in the near future. Personal income tax is likely to remain sacrosanct to a supranational authority. The case of corporation tax is more complex. Nevertheless it is likely to remain a national tax for a number of reasons to be discussed below.

- The foregoing contentions are reinforced by the fact that the EC budget is largely based on vertical VAT sharing already. The Single Market will lead to a reform of VAT systems,[4] and the horizontal effects of such a reform still remain to be sorted out. Yet any revision of vertical imbalances resulting from a relative expansion of the EC budget are likely to be resolved by extending the share of VAT to be allocated to the centre government. Some excise taxes may also be centralised in the longer run.

- Also, the scope for new forms of taxation at the EC level is severely restricted. The most important sources of revenue are being exploited by national governments already, and often tax assignment at the national level is fixed by the Constitution – rendering it difficult for the EC to penetrate into existing areas of taxation. It seems possible, however, that the EC will be more successful in establishing own tax competences in those policy domains that are barely developed at national levels at present – notably in the field of ecotaxation which, as a rule, is not even mentioned in national Constitutions. If the Commission were to be successful in conquering this field, and ecotaxes should prove to be more lucrative than anticipated, the ensuing vertical imbalance could always be corrected by downward-oriented general revenue grants (or tax-reimbursement grants) as illustrated – for other taxes – by the examples of Australia and Switzerland.

- As was said before, regional integration under EMU may require the centralisation of payment or funding functions in Europe, respectively a clearing system to operate at the Community level. Regional clearing mechanisms and 'wind-up funds' will enhance the Commission's 'churning activities' and they will intensify its relationship with member state governments; it need not lead to a greater vertical transfer of resources to the central government though.

- As a final point it may be noted that the EC's impact on national tax legislation will grow over the years through its *de facto* coordinative powers and competences in resolving horizontal conflicts of tax competition among member states. This is clearly shown from the review of fiscal federal relations in Switzerland, where the Confederation has taken an active role in tax policy coordination.

Not only will EMU and the Single Market influence national fiscal systems and their relationship with the EC Budget, they are also likely to affect the scope for responsibilities at the central level as well. This hinges on a number of policy decisions to be taken. However, it may be appropriate to discuss some elements that may eventually lead to an expansion of the centre's role, before turning to the need to increase the relative share of resources to be allotted to the EC budget.

4.2   SCENARIO FOR EXPANDING RESPONSIBILITY AREAS IN THE EC BUDGET

4.2.1   Federal Theory and Centralising Tendencies

For the Community budget after 1992 and with regard to the implementation of the Maastricht accord it is essential to know which functions will have to be centralised and which functions are likely to remain at national levels under EMU. The literature on fiscal federalism offers some advice regarding this question. It is typical of this literature, however, that it tends to start from the unitary state, asking: why decentralise? At best it assumes an existing federal structure, asking whether its design is optimal in some sense. There is little attention given to the question: why centralise? – which is typical for the EC. And the dynamics of federalism are hardly ever addressed – apart from historical analyses.

As to the assignment of general government functions, there seems to be wide agreement among economists that macroeconomic stabilisation should be left to the central government, while distribution and allocation functions may eventually be exerted at lower levels. It is useful to discuss these aspects of public policy making in somewhat more detail.

4.2.1.1   Allocation and federalism

The strongest case for decentralisation, and hence national policies, is made for the allocation function. If there are various forms of public goods – which can be consumed only jointly and be provided uniformly – these goods should ideally be supplied at the level at which consumer preferences are relatively homogeneous. This is the essence of Oates's (1972) decentralisation theorem. Where preferences differ among regions, a decentralised provision of public goods entails efficiency gains; decentralisation would also allow the application of the benefit-pricing rule for public services, which is difficult to implement at higher government levels, since regional tax discrimination is typically prohibited by federal constitutions. Although the efficient provision of regional public goods could eventually be effected at the central level this would normally imply information requirements that are difficult to meet and it would entail costs relating to uncertainties (Tresch 1981).

The decentralised provision of government services also facilitates political decision-making, as it enhances the cost-effectiveness of supplying such services: political representation closer to voter-taxpayers can be expected to be both more responsive to demand, and more accountable for policy actions (Cornes and Sandler 1986). This would constitute welfare improvements for regional polities, as it would mobilise political resources through greater involvement of taxpayers. Organisational diversity, institutional competition, and experimentation would all contribute to stimulate innovation and creativity at the regional level.

The decentralisation theorem, put on its head, would recommend centralisation only for such public goods the benefits of which are general and supraregional in nature. Defence would be the typical candidate. For the EC, defence was not the main driving force behind regional integration. It was the improvement of economic welfare through the creation of a Single Market and through economic cooperation. Specific supraregional benefits can be expected to result from structural policies, energy policies (common energy carriers), transportation and communication, environmental protection, technology and research policies (and – to some extent – higher education), as well as from foreign trade policy.

Apart from public goods there are at least two further arguments in favour of a more centralised provision of public services: (i) increasing returns to scale in producing such services; and (ii) spillover effects between lower-level jurisdictions of the federation.

Although these arguments are often used in the literature, they may be challenged as to their importance for federal policy design. Increasing returns to scale had been overstressed by communist rulers in Eastern Europe – with disastrous economic and political results. While such cost-reducing effects cannot be denied in principle, it is likely for decentralisation to exhibit greater dynamic cost-reducing potentials than centralisation – through competition and process innovation. This may be true despite higher coordination costs.

Moreover, neither increasing returns to scale – where they exist – nor regional spillover effects would preclude regional governments from cooperating at the horizontal level, and there is empirical evidence for this happening on a voluntary basis. Cooperation does, however, entail coordination costs. And these costs may be sufficiently high to open up the way for central government intervention. Free-rider strategies and competition among governments may further complicate negotiations at subcentral levels, creating deadlocks in decision-making and leading to the suboptimal provision of regional services.

However, these arguments do not support the concentration of expenditure functions within a federation. All they indicate is some scope for regulatory action and a catalytic role of central government. An optimal institutional design would then seek to minimise organisational and coordination costs within such a framework.

From an economic point of view coordination costs – including political and organisational aspects – will be the clue to the centralisation problem, and there is large scope for further research in that area. Whereas there is a general presumption in favour of a decentralised provision of public services, and this not only for economic reasons,[5] managerial aspects may recommend some coordinated action, although not always centralisation. The principal-agent paradigm lends itself to the analysis of cost-minimising behaviour in multilevel government; also, regulatory federalism as well as questions relating to interjurisdictional competition seem to have found increasing attention in recent years (Oates 1991).

4.2.1.2 *Distribution and federalism*
Much of the work related to the analysis of distribution in a federation is tied to the Tiebout (1956) model, which investigates the optimality of the decentralised provision of public goods, hence its allocative aspects. Tiebout emphasises the role of the taxpayer as constraining local government by 'voting with his feet', each voter choosing that mix of local public goods and taxes that would best suit his particular preference function.

This is not the place to discuss Tiebout's hypothesis in full – which has sparked an extensive literature (see, for instance, attachment 1 in Walsh 1992). With regard to the distribution function, the main conclusions seem to be the following: in a world of free migration, movers create fiscal externalities to all members of the municipality they leave, as they would inflict externalities on residents of receiving jurisdictions. Such effects could eventually be corrected for by a system of unconditional transfers among jurisdictions to the point where they compensate for interregional externalities resulting from migration.

Migration would, however, effectively constrain regional governments to exert redistributional policies. This would result from an adverse selection process: the rich would leave municipalities using high redistributive taxation, as the poor would be attracted by such policies. Locational neutrality of taxation and – for that matter – of public assistance would thus point towards centralising the distribution function.

Despite this argument, many federations employ distribution policies at lower levels of government. This may be explained by various reasons: (i) altruistic behaviour; and (ii) a limited mobility of taxpayers. The former argument may have some bearing at the municipal level – in particular with regard to its 'own poor'; at the EC level the latter argument is more decisive: supposing social and economic cohesion to become reality, income differentials in the EC will narrow; cultural and language barriers are likely to restrict migration to a large extent. Furthermore, primary incomes and wealth are not independent from locational decisions, as implied by the Tiebout model. Migration can thus become rather costly for moving citizens.[6]

More recently analysts seem to agree that the scope for regional redistribution policies is wider than the traditional view would suggest (see, for instance, King 1984). This is particularly relevant for the EC, where distribution policy is likely to remain at national levels, especially with regard to interpersonal redistribution. Yet, in addition to that there may be scope for interregional redistribution, which could eventually be effected through horizontal grants – as in Germany – or through the EC budget. Distribution policies may thus become a shared task among different levels of government where some harmonisation of outcomes is achieved either by policy coordination or by compensating interregional grants.

4.2.1.3 Macroeconomic management and federalism

As mentioned before, the traditional view would assign the stabilisation function to a central government. There are a number of arguments supporting this view: (i) the openness of regional economies that would result in large spillout effects of a regional fiscal policy; (ii) the high degree of integration of a federation and the positive correlation of a national business cycle and regional economic development; (iii) the threat of excessive monetisation of regional budget deficits and an undue expansion of the money supply; and (iv) limited access of regional governments to capital markets.

As with other traditional views on federalism, the general presumption in favour of central stabilisation policies has been challenged in recent years. Apart from a general scepticism as to the usefulness of interventionist macroeconomic stabilisation policies, that was nurtured by monetarist and supply-side theoreticians alike, the literature on fiscal federalism has come to realise the importance of automatic stabilisers embodied in the federal machinery. Built-in stabilisers may, however, work at all levels of government. Furthermore, a federal system may establish a coordinative machinery for budget policies as for monetary and exchange-rate policies.

The European Monetary System (EMS) is an example in place. Hence, the transfer of exclusive competences for macroeconomic management onto the central government is by no means necessary for achieving stability in the federation. Yet the central government is typically setting the pace for stabilising policy actions either by its own budgetary policies or through coordination. For the EC the latter seems to be the only feasible option, given the largely restricted size of its budget. If the Community *in toto* is subject to an external shock, fiscal and monetary response must come from national policy actions, although these may have to be coordinated.

The case is more difficult for regionally asymmetric shocks: where these occur, markets should be allowed to react whenever those shocks are permanent. Migration and/or capital flows may then change relative prices in order to restore macroeconomic equilibrium. Where such shocks are temporary some authors believe that a regional policy response could achieve macroeconomic stabilisation more effectively than central government intervention (Gramlich 1987). While subcentral governments may have advantages in recognising the cause of economic disturbances, they may, however, have to be assisted when implementing stabilisation policies. This is a case for central government coordination.

More recently, however, stabilisation schemes have been proposed that may work at the centre level with little costs (Goodhart and Smith 1992; Pisani-Ferry and Italianer 1992). They are designed to absorb asymmetrical shocks only, and they seem to avoid moral-hazard problems to a large extent. At least these models challenge the traditional view that a large central budget is needed for implementing effective stabilisation policies.

4.2.1.4   The centralisation of functions in the EC

It is difficult to predict the expansion of outlay functions at the EC level as a function of the Single Market, of EMU and of the Political Union in quantitative terms. However, it is possible to identify certain existing trends that will transform intergovernmental relations in the coming decade and thereafter. Despite a number of political and economic uncertainties, these trends may be characterised as follows:

Centralising tendencies
- The Commission will continue to expand its role in economic policy making, and new political functions will be transferred to supranational authorities by national governments – with full respect to the subsidiarity principle. The philosophy expressed in the Single European Act of 1986 will further expand the size of the European Budget, which is now rather small (about one per cent of total GNP in the EC).

Among these functions of the centre are structural policies, energy policies (common energy carriers), transportation and communication, environmental protection, technology and research policies (and – to a minor extent – higher education), as well as foreign trade policy – once a monetary union has successfully been established. Also, the quest for moderate redistribution policies among member states – based on the notion of 'cohesion' – will mount, leading to the expansion of regional policies within the Community.

- With the creation of a monetary union, foreign-exchange operations with third countries will be centralised – through a European Federal Bank (ESCB). The same is true for seigniorage. As will be discussed later, there are strong reasons for attributing the profits from seigniorage to the European Commission as a new own resource after EMU.

- At the present time there is an enormous uncertainty on future defence policies in Europe and worldwide. It is useful to remember that most federations – if not all – have been formed, in the past, with the aim of combining mutual defence interests. If the Community were to embark on any joint European defence programme in the future – whether restricted in size and/or embodied in traditional or new defence treaties – this would remarkably strengthen the role of the centre in the long run – requiring more resources to be handed over to the Community. For the following discussion of the EC budget under EMU, the impact of greater centralisation of defence efforts is, however, neglected.

- Another uncertainty concerns general welfare policies. As can be demonstrated by looking at existing federations, there seems to be a tendency for these functions to become more centralised in the longer run. This would, again, require substantial increases in the proportion of public resources to be handed over to the EC.

- As for defence, it is assumed that there will be no large revision in the assignment of policies for macroeconomic stabilisation. While the Community budget may play some role in the case of asymmetrical shocks, it is likely to absorb little resources in accordance with proposals discussed before (for instance, Pisani-Ferry and Italianer 1992).

- Olson's argument in favour of a stronger central government[7] to contain the influence of private-interest groups at the regional level will also work to some extent. Yet, as stressed before, it warrants greater responsibilities for the Commission in the setting of a framework for national legislation; it does not necessarily entail a greater EC budget.

Decentralising tendencies

- Contrary to the centripetal forces, Europe will retain a decentralised political structure with strong regional governments at the national level. Centrifugal forces may even increase, leading to self-determination of subregions and devolution within nations according to the German or even the Swiss model of federalism. The quest for more cultural and economic autonomy of regions will notably hinge on the success of such claims in Eastern Europe, especially in the former Soviet Union, and national governments in Europe may also be pushed into conceding political self-rule to some of their regions – from Spain to Northern Ireland.
- Also, the role of local government will have to increase in most member states of the Community. Where local government is weak, local infrastructure is usually less developed or lacking, and economic regional imbalances result.[8] The model of decentralised economic decision making at the municipal level is likely to become more and more attractive to European governments.

It seems obvious that the structure of government finance in Europe will essentially remain decentralised – despite the increasing role of supranational policies and possible shifts of new functions onto the EC. However, if only some of the centralising trends identified continue to shape future EC politics, the need for restructuring and bolstering-up the EC budget cannot be denied.

4.2.2   The Present EC Budget and the Delors II Package

At present, the Community budget is rather small, totalling roughly 1.1 to 1.2 per cent of total Community GDP. The 1991 budget had a volume of 56 billion ECU; the projected 1992 budget is about 63 billion ECU, which is only slightly below the spending limit for the Community's own resources of 1.2 per cent of total GDP (Table 4.1). Yet spending at the Community level is still dominated by interventions securing guaranteed prices to farmers under CAP, although these outlays have been decreasing in recent years, following the measures taken under the Delors I package of 1988. More recent policy decisions indicate that guarantee payments are likely to be gradually phased out in favour of direct income subsidies, and that CAP may become redecentralised under the 'subsidiarity principle' and new policy objectives, notably those associating farming activities with the environment.

Leaving aside spending for agriculture and the structural funds, which

Table 4.1   The composition of the EC budget (1991 and 1992)[a]

Budgetary category	1991 million ECU	per cent	1992 million ECU	per cent
Expenditures				
Agriculture policy	32516	58.0	36039	57.4
Structural operations	14290	25.5	17619	28.0
External policy	2651	4.7	2269	3.6
Research policy	1745	3.1	1945	3.1
Administrative outlays	2690	4.8	2928	4.7
Other policies	2194	3.9	2027	3.2
Total	56086	100.0	62827	100.0
Revenue				
Agricultural levies	1621	2.9	1112	1.8
Sugar levies	1142	2.0	1216	1.9
Customs duties	11201	20.0	11600	18.5
Value-added tax	30269	54.0	34232	54.5
GNP-levy	7415	13.2	14281	22.7
Miscellaneous	4438	7.9	386	0.6
Total	56086	100.0	62827	100.0
In per cent of EC GDP	1.1		1.16	

[a] Source: *Official Journal of the European Communities*, 3 February 1992, pp. 103–7; own calculations.

are instruments of the EC's sectoral policies, little is left for allocation and regional redistribution. The principal instrument of European allocation policies still remains regulation, which is increasingly receiving negative publicity. A notable exception is R&D support, for which about 2 billion ECU were spent in 1991.

Although the EC has acquired important new responsibilities in other policy areas, such as infrastructure (transport and communication) and the environment, with large cross-border dimensions, the budgetary impact of such functions is hard to measure, since it is implied in various spending categories. Explicit budgetary support is still relatively small. However, a larger and increasing third-country component of the budget is noteworthy.

Also, the Community's redistributive capacities are weak. They result from various elements of the budgetary process, in particular from (i) a country's contribution to financing the budget, (ii) the importance of the agricultural sector in the national economy, and (iii) the impact of interventions through the structural fund, which has a strong geographical concentration.

The distributional aspects of the EC have lead, in the past, to various attempts to quantify the effective incidence or net benefits derived from EC budgetary processes. This indicates that redistribution through the EC budget is politically delicate and the scope for such policies likely to be limited. It also reveals that the nature of a supranational budget is ill-understood: since the emphasis of the budget still lies on allocation policies, with positive externalities to be expected for all participants, simple cashflows cannot reflect such incidence patterns of benefits. It is therefore vain to insist on corresponding '*juste retour*' exercises and/or to monitor regional budgetary flows as such.

Without any new policy measures, as foreseen under EMU, and despite the relative decline of spending on agriculture, the EC budget is likely to have hit its ceiling of 1.2 per cent of Community GDP even in 1992. In anticipation of such developments the Commission published another consolidation proposal at the beginning of 1992, the Delors II package. The package proposes an increase in the ceiling for own resources of the Community to 1.37 per cent until 1997. It also indicates major shifts in policies in order to increase the EC's competitiveness through transeuropean networking, research, professional training and retraining, as well as to achieve economic and social cohesion in the Community. Also, the area of external relations is emphasised in the Delors II package. Furthermore, the package includes a financial reserve of 0.03 of GNP for extraordinary expenditures in the realm of external policy.

As to the structure of own resources, the package proposes limiting the VAT base to 50 per cent of GNP (from the present 55 per cent) in order to mitigate the regressive impact of this revenue instrument, and increasing the relative contribution of the more proportional GNP-levy (compare ch. 3.4). Both measures would reduce the share of VAT from 55 per cent to 35 per cent of the Community's own resources.

It was perhaps unfortunate and politically adventurous to submit Delors II immediately after the Maastricht accord. The timely coincidence and various statements in Delors II suggest it to be the 'bill' for Maastricht – which is, of course, an oversimplification. As mentioned before, the EC budget will already have hit its ceiling in 1992, whereas most of the measures relating to EMU will develop their budgetary impact only in the longer run. Whether the increment of 0.17 of GDP above the present level of own resources, according to Delors II, will be sufficient to cope with the future requirements of the Community budget is certainly debatable. The figure is likely to reflect the present strong reluctance of

European governments to increase the Community budget, reflecting tight financial constraints at national levels.[9] It is, however, necessary to assess the validity of a budgetary target for EMU in more sober terms – and abstracting from political considerations.

4.2.3   The Scope for New EC Policies and the Community Budget

A more systematic analysis of the Community's extended role under EMU, which strictly applies the subsidiarity principle for the whole European federation, estimates the medium-term size of the EC budget to be in the order of 2–3 per cent of total GNP in order to secure the feasibility of EC policies under EMU (Courchène *et al.* 1992). It is hence approximately twice the rather modest Delors II target of 1.37 per cent. This is still a rather restrictive assumption, since it excludes the possibility of any major shift in responsibilities that may in fact be on the political agenda – notably in the areas of defence, general welfare, and equalisation.

Although this target means a doubling – or almost tripling – of the actual size of the EC budget, the revenue impact seems to be limited. In particular, it would not warrant the transfer of one of the major national tax sources entirely to the EC budget.

The study emphasises an enhanced Community role in resource allocation – environmental protection, R&D, public investment in infrastructure, and education – specifying, for each category, spending requirements on the basis of international comparisons and catch-up needs. Most of the expenditure functions have clear-cut public-goods characteristics and exhibit regional spillover effects with benefits for many – if not all – regions of the EC, for instance in technology and research. Other functions exhibit more specific – and potentially uneven – regional benefit patterns, for instance in the areas of transportation, telecommunication or higher education. It seems to be inconceivable to have the EC decide without state cooperation in these instances. Responsibilities may have to be shared among governments – with some horizontal decision-making or even institutionalised joint-tasks and cofinancing schemes to be developed in the longer run according to the German (and Swiss) approach(es).

A critical area of EC competence will be equalisation. As was stressed before, the EC is unlikely to embark on large-scale regional redistribution schemes, yet it has to be recognised that 'cohesion', as a policy goal, requires a moderate expansion of EC activities designed to establish the equality of opportunities among regions and their respective citizens. It is unlikely, however, that this will be achieved through an explicit general-revenue-grants system – either vertically or horizontally – as in most existing federations. The political constraints – notably the philosophy of *'juste retour'* – are still too strong, and central policies with widely recognised public-goods characteristics still remain to be developed (and *marketed* successfully).

Assessing past experiences, explicit equalisation will only be acceptable to member states for a system of specific or tied grants. The Community has adopted such an approach for most of its regional and sectoral policies, where matching grants have become the rule. There are a few exceptions to this however, for instance in the integrated Mediterranean programme, where G*-type grants are dominant (compare ch. 2.2.2). It is most likely, however, that the specific matching grant will continue to dominate developments in the area of explicit equalisation. Not incomes will be equalised in the Community, but the potential for creating such income through a better balancing of available public infrastructure and equal opportunities.

For the achievement of economic cohesion in the Community, the future role of the Structural Funds is essential. The study mentioned above (Courchène *et al.* 1992) analyses the present characteristics and redistributive effects of ERDF, ESF and EGGFA, which have doubled in real terms since the budgetary agreement of 1988, attaining about 25 to 30 per cent of the budget by 1993, or 0.3 per cent of GDP. A further expansion of structural adjustment programmes can be expected following a more intensive '"North-South" bargaining between the EC member states, to which the Maastricht protocol on cohesion and the prospect of the creation of a separate "cohesion fund" form a prelude' (Courchène *et al.* 1992, p. 79). The need to enhance the role of the Community budget in the area of redistribution is underlined by the necessity of providing economic assistance to third countries, notably to formerly socialist countries in Eastern Europe, and to developing economies in the Third World. It must be stressed that such aid should not be considered as simple redistributive side-payments; it also enhances the viability of those fragile economies, and strengthens their political and institutional structures, as it stimulates the emergence of mass purchasing power, internal savings and investment potentials. It thus contributes to improving trade relations between the EC and its partners in the longer run, besides securing political and social stability in Europe and fostering economic cohesion. It is thus far more than a simple redistributive device.

Within the EC itself, equalisation can also be achieved implicitly – through tax-sharing arrangements and/or new tax instruments – like the 'fourth levy', that is based on a statistical indicator of relative national economic well-being. The 'fourth' (and the projected 'fifth') 'levy(ies)' could indeed become the nucleus of implicit revenue equalisation schemes for the Community. Other implicit equalisation effects could stem from automatisms inherent in own tax instruments of the Community, an approach that hinges on the centre getting access to national tax bases beyond existing ones – that are supranational in nature (customs duties or agricultural levies), or shared taxes (VAT). A possible candidate would be a cashflow corporation tax on a standardised (origin-oriented) tax base with a flat rate. This tax and its resulting equalisation effects will be discussed in chapter 4.3.5.2.

4.3 CONSEQUENCES FOR THE REVENUE STRUCTURE OF THE EC BUDGET

4.3.1 General Remarks

4.3.1.1 Economic aspects
It has been stressed on several occasions that vertical imbalances in the assignment of revenue sources can *always* be corrected through devices implying pure revenue redistribution within the public sector. The increase in the relative size of the EC budget could thus be matched by a corresponding enlargement of the tax-sharing formula in favour of the central government, for instance. This has been realised in the past; it is likely to remain the first choice for politicians in the future. Yet this may not be the preferred option of the economist, who would usually strive to establish more visible links between taxation and the scope for EC outlay functions; or who would like the Commission to employ specific tax instruments in order to achieve its policy objectives more effectively. Exclusive EC taxation powers may thus be recommended for certain areas.

As mentioned before, the projected increase in the EC budget under EMU is relatively small; it is certainly not sizeable enough to warrant exclusive powers over any of the major national taxes to be transferred to the EC. Yet this argument by itself is not sufficient to reject such a transfer. As discussed more fully in chapter 2.2.1, there may be reasons for recommending the centralisation of taxation powers in spite of their leading to a vertical imbalance of resources – which could then be corrected by downward-oriented G-grants or revenue sharing.

For the scenario presented, the important *benefit-pricing argument* seems to be even weaker than previously stated – since, for any of the more important national taxes, volumes transferred would exceed the increase in

EC expenditure. Yet the principle would have to be reassessed if either (i) a partial transfer of a given tax is envisaged (for instance through revenue sharing or a piggy-back levy), or (ii) a more substantial increase in EC responsibilities – such as defence – would occur (which is excluded from this scenario). We therefore retain the argument for more detailed analyses regarding specific tax instruments.

As to the *instrumental-approach argument*, it has been stressed several times that this may win importance in certain areas of EC competence – notably for energy and transportation policies, and for environmental control. Establishing EC tax competences in these areas may be dictated by noticeable gains in policy effectiveness pursuant to the availability of corresponding tax instruments at the central level. In contrast to the pure revenue-raising aspect, the case for central taxes based on the instrumental approach is rather strong.

The *regional-arbitrariness argument* may have to be investigated more thoroughly in connection with possible clearing mechanisms that may become necessary in order to correct the regional incidence pattern of certain forms of taxation – notably in the area of VAT, and of corporate taxation.

4.3.1.2   Administrative aspects

The residual argument of the economist largely rests on *economies of scale in collecting taxes* or *transaction costs*. As discussed before, the argument is mainly related to administrative aspects. Central tax collection does not need to mean a central appropriation of the proceeds from taxes. Administrative matters are only marginal to the subject of this study. Yet a few remarks should be made before entering into a more specific discussion of EC taxation.

Obviously it will be difficult to dismantle national tax administrations, even though this may be commendable on transaction-cost arguments. This is mainly for political reasons. Furthermore, it is questionable whether a *Euro Tax Office* would in fact exhibit economies of scale in tax collection. National tax laws are still extremely heterogeneous – especially in the area of direct taxes; they apply different philosophies and they have adopted specific legal concepts, established firm judicial rules, as they reflect national priorities that are all difficult to handle administratively at the European level – despite progress made in standardising certain tax-related areas (for instance accounting). To this is added a severe language problem for the central administrator, which is exacerbated by the fact that the similarity of expressions may hide – rather than clarify – the variety of legal, administrative and other concepts governing the operation of national tax systems. Direct tax administration, is thus almost certain to remain at the national level for ever.

The argument is less convincing for indirect taxes, notably for VAT, where progress has been made in harmonising tax bases – although not on administrative procedures and on tax jurisdiction. In fact there may be a much stronger case for the EC getting involved in VAT administration (or at least co-administration) under the new scheme reasserted recently (Ecofin Council of 24 June 1991).

The case for centralised VAT collection is stronger than one might at first think. It should be noted that the system implies (i) the need for a regional clearing mechanism. This clearing mechanism could be administered (ia) multilaterally or (ib) by charging a central agency. (ii) The agency could act (iia) on behalf of the states, or (iib) on its own.

The optimal design of the tax collection system will hinge on solving an inherent principal-agent problem: institution (ia), apart from being extremely costly because of communication costs,[10] would require each state to have full confidence in the administrative capability and honesty of all other tax administrations (since their revenue will depend on successful intergovernmental cooperation in administering VAT). Institution (ib) seems to be more effective in this regard – since confidence may be established more easily because of the lower costs of monitoring and auditing this agency. Moreover, special competences to be formed centring on the clearing mechanism, and this mechanism alone, will be more effective than overburdening national tax collectors with yet another dimension of administration.[11] Institution (iia) could work effectively based on control and auditing procedures alone. Institution (iib) seems to be even more effective, though, since it is supported by the self-interests of the collecting body, the EC, as long as it participates – through VAT sharing – in the proceeds from the taxes administered.

A similar case for a clearing mechanism can be made for corporate taxes (after equivalent reforms under pressure from horizontal tax competition, as discussed below). It will be argued, however, that reformed corporate taxation does not necessarily imply revenue sharing of these taxes between the EC and its member states. The incentive to adopt solution (iib) is less pronounced in this case. For corporate taxation, opting for solution (iia) under a joint-taxation scheme – involving both national tax administrations and a central clearing office – would seem to be more appropriate.

4.3.1.3   Regional tax progressivity

In addition to the economic and administrative aspects of EC taxation, a further argument has to be discussed that is of a distributive nature: regional tax progressivity. Analogously to personal income tax progressivity – individual relative tax burdens increasing with income – it is sometimes stipulated that richer regions should contribute relatively more to the financing of the EC budget than poorer ones. It is not sufficient that regions pay in accordance with per capita levels of regional production; progressivity implies differentiated contribution rates, the level of which is positively related to production.

First, it ought to be stressed that the argument is wholly normative – implying political value judgements. Attempts at basing the notion of progressivity on positive theoretical foundations – such as falling marginal utility of income – have all been unsuccessful. Even assuming problems of interpersonal and – even more critical – interregional comparisons of individual utility to have been resolved, it still remains to be decided whether progressivity – or regional equality in sacrificing utility – should be defined in absolute, in relative or in marginal terms – which is intrinsically a normative question.

Second, personal tax progressivity may be warranted on ability-to-pay or social-justice arguments. Under the residence principle the incentives to avoid taxes may be small (although there may be some Tiebout migration where progressivity is excessive); distortive allocation effects are therefore likely to be limited. Regional progressivity, however, would impose a heavier tax burden on economic activities in certain areas – which could eventually deter investment in that particular region (unless there are regional rents to be reaped). This could entail severe regional distortions, and it runs counter to the idea of regional tax neutrality within a Single European Market.

Third, looking at existing federations, there is no example of explicit regional progressivity in regional contributions to the financing of central budgets. The exception is through the implicit effects of a uniform income tax that operates at the federal level (US, Australia, Switzerland for the confederal income tax) or under revenue sharing (as in Germany). To the extent that such taxes exhibit *personal income progressivity*, the working of this tax element is also reflected at the regional level if taxable capacities vary among provinces. Proponents of regional progressivity would therefore often propose centralising the proceeds from income taxes or allowing for central piggy-back taxation on the proceeds of these taxes. We shall argue below that this is unlikely to be operational for the financing of the EC budget – because another requirement would be uniformity of tax rules, a requirement difficult to meet within the EC.

Fourth, looking at the past history of federal financial relations in the EC, it is obvious that regional progressivity has little support among politicians. Neglecting the regional incidence pattern of customs duties and of agricultural levies, the incidence of VAT sharing is clearly *regressive* with respect to income (but essentially proportional to private consumption).[12] As was argued in chapter 3.4, the introduction of the GNP-levy has mitigated this regressivity to some extent – although not fully. The political trends seem to be towards proportional contributions, not towards regional progressivity.[13]

Based on pure personal judgement and on a subjective interpretation of trends, it is our contention that explicit regional progressivity for financing the EC budget will not become an issue in the near future. Equalisation is more likely to be effected explicitly on the expenditure side of the budget.

A last point should be made with regard to regional tax progressivity: if our proposal to implement a cashflow corporate tax were to be adopted (ch. 4.3.5.2), such a tax would exhibit implicit regional tax progressivity which is not based on normative arguments, but on firm economic criteria: regional windfall profits or economic rents. As will be more fully discussed below, the effective cashflow tax rate is zero on normal profits. It is positive on excess profits, and it subsidises regions that have not yet come to full maturity – where short-term profits are below normal.[14] Furthermore, the effects of such a definition of regional tax progressivity would not lead to allocative distortions through capital flight – since windfall profits and regional economic rents have a clear-cut regional incidence pattern, attracting capital as long as they are not taxed away fully.

4.3.1.4   Uniform taxation or tax coordination

A last general issue to be discussed before embarking on specific taxes relates to the question of tax uniformity.

Uniformity of taxation in a federation is sometimes praised as avoiding possible tax distortions, as being regionally equitable and as being administratively cheaper than a system of concurrent taxation powers with unhomogeneous tax legislation. It is, in particular, the idea of regional 'fairness' or equitable treatment of all citizens in a federation that has given support to the idea of uniform taxation. Yet the case for tax harmonisation and centralisation of tax policies in federations may also be made on efficiency grounds – based on traditional externality arguments or game-theoretic analyses of tax competition (Gordon 1983, 1990; Wilson

1986). The model case for a uniform tax system operating in a federation is in fact Germany; it essentially applies to Australia as well.

Opponents of this view stress the remarkable differences between member states, both in absolute per capita tax revenue and in tax revenue as a percentage of GDP, as reflecting varying preferences of voters and hence underlying policies regarding the level and, presumably, the structure of government spending. This view – based on Oates's (1972) decentralisation theorem or Brennan/Buchanan's (1980) public-choice arguments – contends that regional differences in taxation are not only inevitable, they are also desirable for economic efficiency. The favourite models for these scholars are of course Switzerland and – to some extent – the US.

At first glance there seems to be a basic dilemma here: if, on one hand, it is considered *inequitable* to base the financing of the central budget on varying regional taxes (respectively the proceeds from these taxes) – because these reflect basic choices regarding the provision of *regional* public goods, *not* of centrally provided public services – and if, on the other hand, regional tax diversity is needed for reasons of *efficiency*, distributive and allocative policy objectives seem to be in contradiction.

Taking a finalistic view, proponents of uniform taxation would then try to resolve the issue as follows: if financing the EC budget through a variety of rules governing regional taxation is not acceptable, these rules should be harmonised when transferring taxes to the central government.[15] This was indeed what happened to Australian income tax; it may be the eventual outcome for European VAT.

Indeed, historical evidence tells that, where 'tax jungles' – meaning a lack of uniformity or insufficient tax coordination – may be identified at lower levels of government, at least central taxes are uniform throughout a federation. This is true whether taxes are own instruments or shared with subregional jurisdictions, because federal Constitutions, as a rule, put a strict ban on regional tax discrimination. This is even valid for the Swiss and for US federal income taxes.[16] It applies to the EC as well, where customs duties and agricultural levies are uniform and the VAT-levy – *nucleus* of a tax-sharing scheme – is calculated on a standardised base.

The question is whether *central taxation* – or revenue sharing – would always result in uniform – or standardised – taxation. The answer is yes – since a discriminatory treatment of regions by the EC government is politically unacceptable, legally unjustifiable, and counterproductive as to the idea of a Single Market.[17] Only if a tax – at least in its base – can be fully harmonised would this tax qualify for financing the central budget. This is likely to exclude quite a number of taxes from being considered to form potential future revenue sources for the EC budget.

However, the result is *not* at odds with the economist's predilection for tax diversity at the horizontal level. It is not warranted to stress any dilemma between efficiency and equity in this context. Although uniformity (or standardisation) may be dictated by federal Constitutions with regard to taxes used for financing the *central* government's budget, a case for harmonising *regional* taxation, at the horizontal level and on a broader scale, would *not* follow from such a presumption. Cutting the weed of an alleged 'tax jungle' would be neither desirable nor acceptable for a number of *economic* reasons – leaving aside political constraints.

- *Preferences* with regard to taxation *differ* across member states – for cultural, social and political reasons. Actual differences in the tax systems may better reflect *individual* or *local* – that is, country-specific – preferences than uniform rates (see, also, Helm and Smith 1989, pp. 2ff, and Cnossen 1990).
- Furthermore, existing taxes are heavily intertwined with a country's set of production functions. Hence there is a strong preference for the *status quo* in taxation, particularly if the structure of tax rates has influenced business organisation or locational decisions of firms. Inertia in the productive sector will entail inertia in tax legislation – through the political pressure of interest groups – and this works against any attempt toward harmonisation.
- Moreover, there may be economic arguments for choosing different rates of taxation in different EC countries even for indirect taxes. If the pattern of demand for goods and services differs across member states, goods which appear as necessities in some parts of the Community may have the characteristics of luxuries in other states; an optimal structure of indirect taxes following the *Ramsey rules* would then assign different goods to higher and lower tax rates, depending on the characteristics of demand in each member state.[18]
- Whilst a completely uniform tax system could possibly eliminate certain *tax-induced distortions* – like cross-border shopping – within a Single Market, this conclusion is questionable from a policy point of view. As Smith has emphasised, 'the question is not how to avoid all sources of tax-induced distortion within the Community, but to identify those areas where different tax systems and tax rates have the greatest impact, across countries, on the pattern of activity, and to seek to minimise those distortionary effects whilst causing the least disturbance to member states' revenue raising powers' (Smith 1990, p. 9).
- And, 'tax rate alignment need not prove welfare enhancing as long

as public expenditure measures and non-tariff barriers distort trade activities' (Genser 1992) – which is the ultimate destructive counter -argument based on second-best theorising.

We thus fully accept the case for tax diversity, and would still have to admit tendencies toward more tax coordination and uniformity within the EC. This would notably be the case if

- a totally new EC tax were to be introduced for the financing of the EC budget. Such a tax would of course have to comply with the principle of regional non-discrimination – setting its own rules uniformly throughout the federation; and
- if central tax coordination becomes more effective in certain areas – such as VAT or excises – where *de facto* harmonisation must be achieved, at least on the definition of tax bases (whilst tax rates may continue to diverge).

If this contention is acceptable, it will constitute a powerful decision rule that greatly facilitates our examination of the appropriateness of various tax instruments for the financing of the EC budget. In order to discard possible sources of EC finance, it simply has to be shown either that the tax is unlikely to become an exclusive (or joint) tax for the EC budget, or that it is not conducive to tax-base harmonisation.

4.3.2   The Scope for EC Intervention in Areas of National Tax Competence

4.3.2.1   EC value-added taxation?

The present VAT system in the European Community. Today all member states of the European Community operate systems of VAT as the principal indirect tax on goods and services. By zero-rating exports[19] and taxing imports at the rate applied to domestic sales, the present VAT system guarantees full tax neutrality for international trade: zero-rating of exports ensures that goods sold to another country bear no VAT of the origin country; the corresponding import tax will generally raise the price of imports to the consumer price level of the country of destination (*destination principle*).[20] Hence French material sold in West Germany, for instance, bears the German (standard) VAT rate of 14 per cent, *not* the French rate – which is 18.6 per cent.

In addition, this treatment of international trade ensures, for intra-Community fiscal relations, that revenue from VAT is assigned to that member state where goods are actually being consumed.[21] It should therefore be stressed that the present regime realises the destination principle in a *double sense*: (i) as regards the allocation of tax burdens, or *(formal) regional tax incidence*; and (ii) as regards the allocation of tax revenue among the fiscs of member states, or *regional fiscal assignment*. This is important to keep in mind for the discussion of VAT-reform proposals below.

Currently, fiscal frontiers form an integral part of VAT systems. They are necessary to ascertain that zero-rated exports have in fact left the country. And, as goods enter the country, VAT has to be paid to revenue authorities of the importing country which again requires fiscal controls. Without these controls companies might use goods for untaxed sales on the domestic market – pretending to have exported them – or they might simply import goods tax-free.

The present VAT system is to be reformed for intra-Community trade after the completion of the Single Market by 1993, when internal border posts will have been removed. First, it seems that, without border controls, the EC would have to adopt the *origin principle* for its intra-regional trade – for both regional tax incidence and fiscal assignment. Second, this system would seem to call for *uniform* tax rates throughout the EC – since differentiated rates would invite consumers to realise gains from tax arbitrage by shopping in low-tax countries – with the consumption in high-tax countries remaining free of additional charges. Third, it would also lead to a massive redirection of tax revenue, to be reassigned to member state governments horizontally.

As Cnossen (1981, pp. 223ff; 1983, pp. 242ff; 1991) has pointed out, border controls are, however, *not* absolutely essential for fiscal neutrality to be achieved while retaining the destination principle. He discusses essentially two proposals in this context.

- *Deferred payment scheme* – Under this scheme, exports are free of tax, and no import tax is levied at borders. In order to bring the value of the imported goods to the domestic price level, the credit mechanism of VAT is relied upon – ensuring that the first taxable unit in the importing country implicitly pays the tax. This occurs because there is no offsetting credit for imported goods unless imports are declared. The recipient of the goods – not necessarily the importer himself – reports and computes the compensatory import tax, but may take credit for that tax at the same time. Since – as a rule – the import tax is not paid until the product is resold, import taxes are *deferred*, hence the name of the scheme. This system has been operating in the

Benelux states under the name of PAS since 1966; it was also used in the UK until November 1984.[22]

A few remarks regarding this system may be appropriate.

- The destination principle can only be realised for trading among firms liable to VAT. It cannot be applied for direct imports by consumers. Thus, for direct imports, the origin principle applies – as to both regional fiscal assignment and regional tax incidence.
- Documentation still has to be provided at customs posts – in order to ensure that tax-free exports have in fact left the country. The main advantage of the scheme seems to be that border formalities due to the levying of import-VAT are reduced.
- Adopted at the Community level *without* border controls, the scheme seems to exhibit incentives to cheat on import-tax credits – through collusion between exporters and importers – where the tax rate of the importing country is higher than that of the exporting country.[23] In order to avoid this collusion, bureaucratic administrative procedures would have to be put in place.[24]

It seems obvious that the deferred payment scheme would not be operational under the Single Market – although the method had been proposed by the Commission in Article 23 of the Sixth Directive.[25]

- *Tax credit clearance system* – Under this scheme, exporters to other EC countries would pay full VAT to their own governments – that is, exports would no longer be zero-taxed. However, the importing firm would receive a tax credit for out-of-state taxes paid from its own fisc. Border tax adjustments would simply be shifted to books of account of firms residing in importing member states. The EC-wide VAT system would thus work in the same way as national VAT systems do now; the EC would form a truly Single Market for VAT.

Again, a few remarks regarding this system may be appropriate.

- Although the system would continue to secure the destination principle for regional tax incidence, it would apply the origin principle for regional fiscal assignment. Net-exporter nations would levy *more* taxes – since they would no longer have to exempt exports, as net-importer nations would *lose* tax revenue through the tax credit given on out-of-state taxes. In order to correct for the resulting horizontal fiscal imbalances, the system would have to install a *clearing mechanism* by which exporter countries would reimburse importer countries for tax credits accorded to their importing firms. Such a mechanism might prove to be very cumbersome administratively.[26]

- As under the deferred payment scheme, the destination principle can only be realised for trading among firms liable to VAT. It cannot be applied for direct imports by consumers, where the origin principle would work for both regional tax incidence and regional fiscal assignment.[27]

- Apart from the problem of revenue allocation among member states, the system might create severe regional distortions if tax rates varied widely across regions: the 'mixed tax principle' would encourage consumers to arbitrage on tax differentials through direct purchases of high-value goods (like cars, yachts, antiques, jewellery) in low-VAT countries. Cross-border shopping would thus lead to tax competition among member states, with the danger of beggar-thy-neighbour policies that might drive tax rates below efficient levels.[28]

The potential for tax competition among EC member states, based on existing VAT rates, is illustrated by the diversity expressed in Table 4.2.[29]

It seems obvious that the tax credit clearance system *is* an interesting option for post-1993 VAT systems in the Community, yet it requires supplementary rules – apart from the clearing mechanism – 'that exempt or regulate intracommunity imports by nontaxable persons such as individuals and exempt organizations and institutions, including governments.' (Cnossen 1991)

Special provisions would also have to apply to mail-order firms, that could otherwise exploit the potential for tax arbitrage inherent in differential tax rates. Furthermore, it requires central coordination of tax-rate policies in order to avoid horizontal tax competition induced by the effects of cross-border shopping. This could effectively be achieved by negotiating a price floor for VAT rates.

Summarising the discussion of present VAT and its alternatives, it is obvious that both the existing system as well as the deferred payment scheme would impede the realisation of a Single European Market. Both systems zero-rate exports, and, for such systems, extensive controls will have to remain in place. These controls are costly in several ways. They

Table 4.2   *VAT rates applicable in EC member states as of 1 April 1991*
(in per cent)

Member state	Reduced rate	Intermediate rate	Increased rate
Belgium	1/6	17/19	25/25+8
Denmark	–	22	–
France	2.1/5.5/13	18.6	22
Germany	7	14	–
Greece	4/8	18	36
Ireland	0/2.3/10/12.5	21	–
Italy	4/9	19	38
Luxembourg	3/6	12	–
Netherlands	6	18.5	–
Portugal	8	17	30
Spain	6	12	33
United Kingdom	0	17.5	–

Source: EC Commission, internal document II-B-1, EC/dc, of 1 October 1991.

cause delays in transporting goods across frontiers, and national authorities have to utilise resources to maintain frontier posts. Moreover, costs are imposed on companies when complying with border formalities.[30] Even if alternative administrative procedures without border controls were applied, they would entail large transaction costs that would discourage potential trade and market integration.

The tax credit clearance system would, in fact, eliminate the need for fiscal border controls, yet it would either lead to the adoption of the origin principle for regional fiscal assignment – with consequential regional imbalances in tax collection – or require the setting-up of a clearing mechanism by which the actual destination principle for fiscal assignment could be preserved. Moreover, regional tax incidence is affected through cross-border direct purchases by consumers, for which the origin principle applies. This entails the need for greater horizontal cooperation among member states, with tax arbitrage forcing governments to harmonise tax rates down to the price floor to be set by the Community.

The Commission's proposals on a VAT system for intra-Community trade. The Commission has made several proposals for tailoring VAT to the needs of a Single Market without border controls. The more relevant later models can be summarised as follows.

- *Proposal of 1987 (KOM (87) 320)* – This proposal resembles the tax clearance system sketched above. The destination principle for regional tax incidence is preserved for the taxable sector (companies); the destination principle for regional fiscal assignment is achieved through a budget-neutral clearing mechanism based on individual accounts of traders (*microeconomic clearing*) – a procedure that would involve large administrative costs.

For direct purchases the switch to the origin principle is accepted. The proposal thus exhibits a 'mixed tax principle'; the emphasis is on destination however. In order to reduce horizontal tax competition resulting from cross-border shopping, the Commission proposes a narrower band of VAT rates – where the standard rate is between 14 and 20 per cent, the reduced rate is between 4 and 9 per cent. Furthermore, the range of products for which each rate applies is defined in a harmonised fashion.

The proposal was criticised mainly for the heavy administrative burden of the clearing mechanism, and for its disallowing domestic sales under zero-rating.

- *Proposal of 1989 (KOM (89) 260)* – This proposal basically acknowledges the origin principle for regional tax incidence on intra-Community trade. Yet the scope for horizontal tax competition that may result is reduced by continuing the application of the destination principle for a number of important intra-Community transactions, notably for the purchase of cars, for mail-order firms, for transborder trading among firms belonging to the same supraregional concern, and for tax-exempt public corporations and financial institutions. Again, the proposal exhibits a 'mixed tax principle' where the emphasis is on origin however.

For fiscal assignment, the destination principle is preserved – that is, the relative position of member states regarding VAT collection is maintained. This requires, again, a clearing mechanism. However, the number of transactions is substantially reduced by basing tax clearing on macroeconomic indicators (trade statistics), *not* on individual accounts of traders (*macroeconomic clearing*).

As far as tax competition is concerned, the Commission proposes to announce floors for standard and reduced VAT rates. As a compromise, zero-rating is allowed for a 'very reduced number of products' (KOM (89) 260, no. 11).

- *Proposal of 1990/91 (ECO/FIN 3 and 10 June 1990, and 24 June 1991)* – The Ecofin Council reached a – non-binding – political agreement on introducing a VAT system in accordance with the Commissions philosophy adopted in the 1989 proposal – hence a *hybrid system* with 'mixed tax principles' for tax incidence (emphasising, however, the origin principle), and the destination principle for fiscal assignment (to be achieved by a macroeconomic clearing system). This system is to be introduced on 1 January 1996 – subject to revision before the end of 1995.

From 1 January 1993 on, an *intermediate system* will be put into operation that preserves the destination principle in both regards. With border controls removed, companies will be required to submit the amounts of intra-EC purchases and sales on their quarterly VAT returns, which puts most of the administrative burden on private firms. In order to monitor tax-exempt exports effectively, firms have to exchange their registered VAT numbers, and numbers of trading partners will have to be reported in VAT returns. This allows verification of returns through normal commercial documents (invoices). The largest firms will have to submit statistical returns which can be used for cross-checking. The transitory scheme is scheduled to end in 1995.[31]

As from 1993 on, a minimum standard VAT rate of 15 per cent is to be applied. Concessions have been made to different member states as regards reduced (or zero) rates.

The future development of VAT, and the chances of an EC VAT. Given that a basic agreement has been reached on a definitive EC VAT system, future trends seem to be pointing in the following direction.

- Despite the special provisions made to preserve the destination principle for tax incidence on car sales, mail-order sales and long-distance sales, the origin principle will finally dominate European VAT systems. Tax competition and/or the informal tax leadership of important economies within the EC are likely to harmonise tax rates in the longer term according to the Swiss experience of formal guidance by a central government. There will be a tendency toward more uniformity in value-added taxation – national tax autonomy being increasingly sought in the realm of direct taxation, where effective constraints on policy-making are less pronounced. The 15 per cent line will mark a floor, but it will not be necessary for tax rates to be driven down to that level by tax competition under all circumstances. Tax leadership, as well as horizontal tax coordination, may well allow other rates – although not substantially higher.
- The continuing governance of the destination principle with regard to

fiscal assignment (or the apportionment of VAT proceeds) will require a clearing mechanism that is likely to be based on macroeconomic indicators. The (budget-neutral) flows of funds resulting from such a scheme may be incorporated in the EC budget; they may also be operated under a separate fund. According to our analysis of administrative costs for the corresponding principal-agent problem to be resolved, the more effective solution would be to centralise such clearing functions under the (interested) supervision of the EC. The interest of the EC in operating this scheme effectively is warranted by the EC budget's participation in the proceeds from VAT through revenue sharing.

In the longer run, European national VAT systems are not only likely to converge to uniform taxation under the origin principle (which would then allow the abolition of the special provisions made for mail-order firms, car sales and so on); they are also likely to be transformed into a full-fledged tax-sharing scheme with horizontal perequation effects. Two options seem to be open to the Community:

- decentralised tax collection with horizontal tax cooperation through the clearing mechanism – with the central government participating in the proceeds from taxes; and
- centralised tax collection with vertical tax sharing – according to the German arrangements for sharing VAT among the federal government and the *Länder* – together with an apportionment formula for the regional distribution of proceeds from VAT.

It is not unlikely that the German model of VAT sharing will shape fiscal federal relations between the EC and its member states in the longer term – especially if EC functions expand more rapidly, with a greater share of VAT to be handed to the central government. It is unlikely, however, that governments will accept a per capita distribution formula – as in the German case – which would exhibit far-reaching perequation effects; if existing political intentions regarding the future macroeconomic clearing mechanism are interpreted correctly, the horizontal distribution formula is likely to be based on criteria of general economic well-being – such as GNP – or, eventually, needs.

Summarising the discussion on VAT as a possible future revenue source for the EC budget, it is absolutely certain that VAT will continue to shape EC finance in the future; it is likely that VAT sharing will become even more important for the EC budget after the completion of the Single

Market, because the EC will be regarded as a neutral arbiter, and still an effective – because interested – administrator of the clearing fund.[32]

Furthermore, VAT is likely to become more uniform under EMU, rendering it suitable to become an own EC tax in the longer run – possibly even subject to EC legislation. VAT is, however, likely to remain a shared tax – similar to the German system – with some regional perequation embodied in the distribution formula governing horizontal fiscal relations. The perequation element will be rather weak initially; it may, however, become stronger as regional economies move toward greater economic cohesion under EMU.

4.3.2.2   EC excise taxation?

Excise taxation in the European Community. At present there is a broad variety of excise taxes levied in EC member states. Some of them – like the salt tax, or taxes on hunting and fishing – are as old as taxation itself, recalling ancient *regalia*, formerly usurped privileges of princes. Others are degenerated luxury taxes – like taxes on coffee and tea, or the German (progressive!) tax on light bulbs. Others again are associated with specific expenditure functions and their financing according to an intended *quid pro quo* – taxes on mineral oil, for instance, that were initially attributed to road-building programmes. Others, finally, simply reflect the ingenuity of national governments in raising money.

Many of these taxes have a bad record as to their distorting effects on the allocation of resources; they are criticised for their income-regressive distribution effects; and most of them are poor revenue raisers.

Revenue elasticities with regard to GNP are indeed low – because tax bases are usually defined in quantities (not *ad valorem*); revenue elasticities with regard to rate increases are often high, however, because of low price-elasticities of demand for the taxed goods. Thus taxes on alcohol may be levied on quantities consumed (in *hl*), entailing only small increases in revenue resulting from the expansion of consumption; yet, since consumption of alcohol is relatively price-inelastic, legislators may easily raise more revenue by increasing tax rates.

Most federations in the world – except in North America – have transferred excise taxation to the central government. This raises the question of whether excises could also become instruments to finance the EC budget in the future. Before discussing this hypothesis, a few remarks regarding the future of excise taxation in the EC may seem to be appropriate.

The Commission's proposals on excise taxation in the EC. According to the Commission, excises contributing only little to the financing of government budgets (*bagatelle* taxes) should all be abolished. What had been prevented at national levels by resistance of tax bureaucrats and legislative inertia is expected to be accommodated by an EC directive of the Council. Only a very restricted number of more important excises should be retained: those on tobacco, on alcoholic beverages, and on hydrocarbon oils.

Furthermore, the destination principle will be applied at the consuming stage. Goods will be transported to the country of destination tax-free, whilst being taxed when taken from inventories for sale to the consumer. Since excise rates diverge widely among regions within the Community, the Commission aims for greater tax coordination through the setting of minimum and target rates; the Ecofin Council of June 1991 has set tax floors, abandoning the idea of target rates. This is intended to reduce the scope for potential tax competition among member states through cross-border shopping.

Table 4.3 gives a survey of existing tax rates for some of the excises to be retained in the Community.[33]

The chances for EC excise taxation. Despite the fact that excise taxation is centralised in Australia, in Germany and in Switzerland, the chances for EC excises are generally ambiguous. This is because philosophies governing the remaining excises under EMU have changed since the fiscal constitutions of the former federations were drafted. Until very recently, excises were considered to be mainly revenue instruments. However, modern theory of public finance has stressed their instrumental qualities as to achieving certain allocative objectives. Two major strands may be distinguished.

- *Taxation of demerit goods* – This applies to excises on tobacco and alcohol, the consumption of which exhibits substantial health risks to the population. Taxing these demerit goods is expected to curtail consumption of the respective goods, thus diminishing the health hazard and related costs.
- *Energy conservation and environmental control* – This applies to excises on hydrocarbon oils, the consumption of which leads to pollution, to congestion costs through traffic jams, to health hazards through accidents and nervous stress, and – last but not least – to climatic changes (global warming). Furthermore, the consumption of mineral oil has a negative effect on the balance of payments for most of the EC countries, which reinforces the general quest for energy conservation.

As far as taxation of demerit goods is concerned, the large variety of

Table 4.3   *Excise rates applicable in EC member states as of 1 January 1990 (in ECU)*

Member state	Cigarettes[a]	Spirits[b]	Petrol (unleaded)[c]
Belgium	4.55	1489.50	290.93
Denmark	77.00	1814.50	442.60
France	2.67	1127.90	396.87
Germany	35.02	1258.86	403.19
Greece	0.99	134.70	135.69
Ireland	52.93	2612.07	358.55
Italy	2.26	291.05	538.23
Luxembourg	1.95	891.55	139.83
Netherlands	26.57	1388.97	341.87
Portugal	2.52	281.00	379.76
Spain	1.14	555.54	316.15
United Kingdom	47.53	2362.28	265.37
Commission's proposal of February 1991			
Minimum rate	15.00	1118.50	287.00
Target rate	21.50	1398.10	445.00
Ecofin proposal of June 1991[d]	57 per cent of sale price	1118.50	287.00

[a] Per 1000; [b] per *hl*; [c] per 1000 *hl*; the Commission's proposals have been accepted by the Council in 1992 with only minimum changes.

tax rates existing in the Community indicates very different attitudes among member states with regard to the corresponding policy goals. The vehemence with which national governments have so far striven for greater taxation autonomy in the area of excises signals their being severely reluctant to cede national sovereignty in these policy domains. Indeed, a strong case can be made for health policies, for instance, to remain at national levels; the subsidiarity principle is likely to prevent these domains from becoming centralised. This also applies to the corresponding excise taxes.

Moreover, it can be expected that cross-border sales will not necessarily lead to strong tax competition for demerit-goods taxation – forcing tax rates to be coordinated to more uniform levels. As can be seen from the US experience, tax competition will be a function of relative transaction costs which may create problems closer to fiscal borders, but not within the EC in general. Thus, Greece and Portugal may continue to tax cigarettes or alcohol lightly without this policy significantly affecting local consumption in high-tax Ireland, Denmark or the United Kingdom. Harmonising tax rates through price floors does not even seem to be necessary here.

Energy taxation is more complex however. With falling economic rents in the transportation sector – as a consequence of deregulation and greater competition after the completion of the Single Market – and with prices for transportation services becoming more responsive to cost differentials, energy costs are likely to be subject to severe regional competition in the future. Governments of high-tax member states will then come under stronger pressure to harmonise tax rates down to the tax floor set by central coordination. Floors *are* therefore essential for that policy domain, yet tax rates within member states appear to be much closer together already compared with those for demerit goods. Coordination should thus prove to be easier in this matter.

Assuming that mineral-oil taxation will become more and more uniform under EMU – fulfilling an important criterion for centralising the tax – it still remains uncertain whether this tax could – and should – be assigned to the EC budget.

In principle, control of energy taxation ought to be attributed to that level of government that is in charge of energy policies, according to the instrumental approach. Without access to *the* basic instrument for influencing prices in this domain, policies may not achieve their objectives. And energy policy *is* an EC responsibility – although shared with national governments. It can therefore be expected that the EC budget will eventually get access to this important revenue source in the longer run.

The major obstacle to centralising energy taxes is the loss of national tax revenue – hence fiscal considerations. In order to mitigate resistance against EC participation in energy taxation, the Commission should opt for a surcharge, or piggy-back tax, on national energy consumption (to be collected by national tax administrations). This is technically feasible because tax bases may easily be standardised. And it should be acceptable to national governments as long as tax revenue is earmarked for financing specific functions in corresponding policy domains – for instance, research relating to alternative energies or energy conservation, or intra-Community public-transportation projects.[34] Surcharge financing on national energy taxes is also likely to establish the tax/benefit link that is expected to enhance efficiency for EC policies, and, it is hoped, to create solidarity and cohesion across nation states within the Community.

4.3.2.3   EC personal income taxation?

Personal income taxes constitute a main revenue source of national and subnational governments in all industrialised countries. As was discussed in chapter 2, these taxes are usually assigned to lower levels of government or administered jointly in existing federations – with the notable exceptions of the US, where state (and local) income taxes play only a secondary role, and Canada, where the provinces (except Quebec) levy subfederal personal income taxes as fixed percentages of the federal income tax. The EC budget has no access to national income tax bases so far.

Income taxes – although now widely based on a uniform Schanz-Haig-Simons definition of comprehensive income – exhibit a very large variety as to their concrete forms embodied in national legislation. Generally they are levied 'on the income of individuals and of unincorporated enterprises (for example the self-employed, small businesses, farmers and the liberal professions), as well as income taxes earmarked for social security expenditures and, when integrated with the income tax, capital gains taxes' (OECD 1986, p. 8).

This definition points to a number of problems relating to the delineation of income taxes: (i) they are intertwined with the corporation tax (since income of unincorporated enterprises is assessed under income tax); (ii) the borderline between social security contributions and income taxes is not clearly drawn; (iii) income tax policy may be affected by structural policies relating to specific sectors of the economy that are often subsidised indirectly through income tax (or even excluded from taxation, for example owner-occupied housing); (iv) the tax base is affected by the variety of national rules governing the assessment of capital gains for taxation.

Apart from problems relating to the differentiation of 'taxable income' from non-taxable revenue or revenue taxed under separate schemes, there are large differences in the definition of the tax base itself. Since income is a net concept, there are problems as to the delineation of costs attributable to income-generation, as against private expenditures to be borne out of taxed income – notably various forms of income-in-kind, so-called 'fringe benefits'. Similar problems may arise when drawing a borderline between interest paid against income-generating assets and interest against privately used assets. And finally, there are problems associated with income as to its periodicity – where large-scale differences exist for depreciation allowances, for the attribution of multiperiod income, and for the treatment of old-age pension schemes, for instance.

But income tax legislation varies not only as to the definition of the tax base, and administrative rules governing the delineation of taxable and non-taxable income, it is also subject to normative judgements that vary widely among member states' governments. As a rule, income taxation is loaded with (sometimes contradictory) legal provisions relating to non-fiscal objectives from other policy domains.[35]

- *Redistribution policies* – All countries use direct personal income tax for the purpose of income redistribution to varying degrees. For reasons of horizontal equity, a number of specific deductions and exemptions are granted; for reasons of vertical equity, the average tax rates usually increase with income – according to a presumed mounting ability to pay taxes. Minimum and top tax rates vary enormously across countries, as does the tax schedule itself.

  Distributional justice is, however, often difficult to ascertain through progressive rate structures where tax loopholes exist and/or tax bases can be reduced to nil through legal tax arbitrage (not to speak of tax fraud). Some countries therefore consider introducing minimum taxes – according to the US example – or supplementary gross income taxes, moving the tax base closer to a personal consumption tax base, and rendering the income tax more and more complex. Compromises of that sort are already widely accepted to varying degrees, which has encouraged some authors to dub personal income tax a 'hybrid' (Aaron/Galper/Pechman 1988).

- *Allocation policies* – Income tax usually exhibits a great number of overt and hidden preferences given to certain sectors of the economy (notably farming, the housing sector, and ailing industries like coal mining, steel and shipbuilding) and to specific groups of taxpayers, affecting their marginal tax rates to varying degrees.

  Recent tax reforms in European countries (and throughout the Western world) have tended to stress allocative goals in response to the objectives of the 1986 US tax reform (Pechman 1988, Spahn 1988, Cnossen/Messere 1990). It has notably been the incentive to work and to save that has guided tax reformers throughout the world. Yet a severe allocation problem will remain on the reform agenda: the taxation of capital income. Since the various forms of income exhibit a wide variety in the mobility of their tax bases, with the price-elasticity of portfolio capital being almost infinite, optimal income tax rates would ideally have to be differentiated – with the effective marginal tax rate on portfolio capital being zero. This is, of course, in contradiction to the idea of a comprehensive income tax – which would tax all forms of income indiscriminately.

  Some countries have been reacting to this challenge by imposing a flat rate for capital income with progressive rates only on labour income (Denmark); others are about to exempt large parts of interest income from taxation (Germany). Yet the issue is severely complicated by problems of international tax competition (where preferential treatment is often given to foreigners) and it remains largely unresolved (Wilson 1986, Genser 1992, Sinn 1990, Spahn/Kaiser 1991).

- *Stabilisation and inflation policies* – Income tax is also being used for stabilisation purposes – using tax rebates or surcharges in order to influence global demand. Recently an income tax surcharge has been used to finance government expenditures related to German unification. Moreover, the income tax itself is subject to the business cycle through a so-called 'built-in flexibility' of the tax. This flexibility is also a function of the varying rules governing the indexation of the tax schedule, of tax exemptions and deductions, and of certain forms of income. Indexation is, however, far from comprehensive, especially with regard to business income and capital gains, and it is disallowed by law in some instances (Germany).

- *Social policies* – Some countries integrate employers' and employees' social security contributions with the personal income tax (Denmark, the Netherlands). Some (notably the Scandinavian countries) pay their social security expenditures almost entirely out of tax moneys, whereas others insist on PAYE systems or even capital-based funding.

All countries concede basic exemptions to their taxpayers at varying degrees – leaving a living allowance untaxed. Yet, while most taxpayers – for instance in France – are exempt from paying income taxes at all, they are all subject to a proportional payroll tax – where no basic allowances exist.

Contributions for income-maintenance purposes are often excluded from taxable income (although usually provided with a cap), with the benefits drawn sometimes being tax free (health insurance, interest on some pension rights), sometimes being taxed at normal or preferential rates (pensions). Income tax treatment of life insurance premiums and accumulated interest differs widely from country to country.

Where there are tax benefits related to private life insurance schemes, countries often impose strict regulations on the investment policies of private pension and superannuation funds.

- *Housing policies* – Most countries provide preferential treatment of imputed rental income from owner-occupied housing – in addition to other forms of indirect subsidies. Although imputed income may not be taxable (or be taxed at prices below market values), some expenditures – notably interest payments – may be deductible against this income. Commercial housing may also benefit considerably through tax benefits ranging from tax credits for special forms of investment (for example related to energy saving) to accelerated depreciation schemes. Housing may also benefit – to varying degrees – from the exclusion from taxation of capital gains (even when realised).

- *Environmental policies* – Sometimes income tax is used to create incentives for measures to protect the environment – for instance through the deductibility of expenditure on devices for energy saving (modern heating systems, insulation).

- *Education policies* – Although education is regularly provided free of charge in European countries, remaining private expenditures are sometimes allowed to be deductible for tax purposes (although usually provided with a cap).

- *Family policies* – Mainly based on normative judgements, tax policies exhibit a great variety as to the treatment of the family in EC member states (Cnossen/Messere, 1990, pp. 44–9). Some countries apply strict individual taxation (with some relief in the form of allowances or credits); this is true for Belgium, Denmark, Greece, Italy and the Netherlands. Others apply joint or family taxation, notably France, Germany, Ireland, Luxembourg and Spain. Some countries use income-splitting which may be limited to spouses only (Germany) or extended to dependent children as well (France, Luxembourg).

It is obvious – given the wide variety of tax rules governing personal income taxes in EC member states – that there is also a wide dispersion of effective tax rates in these countries. This is depicted in Table 4.4.

Although the effective tax contributions of personal income tax have been converging in recent years – and tax-reform policies have been coordinated by the *de facto* leadership of the 1986 *Tax Reform Act* in the United States – remaining discrepancies are large within EC member states. There is a clear-cut North-South bias: Southern European countries have traditionally shied away from direct taxation, exploiting indirect taxes more intensively. Among the bigger countries, France remains a low-income-tax country – exempting about half of its population, yet taxing the other half all the more heavily.

As has been discussed before personal income tax is likely to become more internationalised as there is a need for greater intra-Community tax coordination – especially in the field of taxing capital incomes. Yet the income tax will undoubtedly remain the cornerstone of national tax policies. It will become the 'core' of member states' taxation autonomy

Table 4.4 Taxes on personal income in EC member states, the US
and Japan[a] (in per cent of GDP)

Member state	1965	1975	1987
Belgium	6.3	13.1	15.1
Denmark	12.4	23.1	25.6
France	3.7	4.5	5.7
Germany	8.2	10.8	10.9
Greece	1.5	2.3	4.6
Ireland	4.3	7.9	13.8
Italy	2.8	4.0	9.5
Luxembourg	7.6	10.9	11.1
Netherlands	9.2	11.8	9.5
Spain	2.1	2.8	7.0
United Kingdom	9.1	13.5	10.0
EC Average	6.1	9.5	11.2
Standard Deviation	3.3	5.9	5.5
United States	7.9	9.5	10.9
Japan	4.0	5.0	7.3

[a] *Source*: *OECD* 1989, table 10; own calculations.

given that indirect taxation is likely to be harmonised more strongly within
the EC.

This renders personal income tax most inappropriate as an own resource
for the EC budget – either by direct access to national tax bases or through
tax sharing. Differential treatment by taxing authorities at national levels –
that might be warranted on the grounds of well-defined policy objectives
– would become regionally 'unfair' if applied uniformly at the EC level.
Since tax bases are most unlikely to become standardised in the near future,
any attempt by the EC to tap these bases is inherently inequitable, favouring
those nations that rely more heavily on indirect taxation. It is thus most
unlikely that the EC will penetrate into the area of personal direct taxation
in the near future.

4.3.2.4 EC corporate taxation?

Basic forms of corporate taxation. There are two basic philosophies
concerning the taxing of corporations: (i) corporations may be regarded as
separate and independent (legal) subjects with their own taxable capacity;
(ii) corporations may be regarded as being owned by taxable (natural) subjects, the personal taxable capacity of whom should ultimately determine
tax liabilities. In the first case, corporation tax is imposed in addition to

personal income tax – leading to the double-taxation of corporate income (classical system); in the second, the corporation tax is levied as a source tax on corporate income that should ideally be fully credited against the personal income tax of the owners (integrated systems).

Model (i) is implemented in the United States, in Switzerland, in Luxembourg and in the Netherlands. Model (ii) is nowhere applied consistently, since all variants would disallow credits for taxes paid on retained earnings. As to the variants themselves, there is full tax crediting on dividends in Germany and in Italy; tax crediting on distributed profits is only partial in Belgium, Denmark, France and the UK.

The corporation tax base is usually determined by rules similar (and to a large extent identical) to those governing personal income tax – especially for integrated systems; the tax rate is usually proportional, although differentiated as to retained earnings and dividends paid.[36]

Corporate taxes are either centralised or shared. Only in the United States, in Switzerland and in Canada are corporation taxes being levied at subnational levels.[37] The degree of subfederal fiscal autonomy for corporate income taxes seems to be somewhat lower empirically than for personal income tax. It remains to be seen whether this is an indication for centralising taxation powers for corporation taxes within the EC.

Locational non-neutrality of corporation tax and tax competition. In a sense corporation tax is less complex than personal income tax – since there are no adjustments to be made relating to the personal situation of taxpayers; in another sense, however, it is even more complicated, since all problems relating to the international taxation of capital income have a prominent bearing on this tax.

In a federal setting where regional capital mobility is high – which would be the case under EMU – independent taxing of capital income at the regional level is likely to induce horizontal regional differences in the marginal productivity of capital. This causes inefficiencies in national investment. Regional differences in consumers' marginal rates of time preference may cause inefficiencies in national savings. Such horizontal differences in marginal tax rates would lead to international capital flight – and to resulting tax competition among member states. Hence, small open economies would choose to tax neither income generated by the physical capital located within the country (Diamond/Mirrlees 1971) nor national saving (Razin/Sadka 1989).

A first approach toward assessing the potential of tax competition for international capital is expressed in the differences between statutory marginal rates for taxing capital income. Table 4.5 gives on overview on those rates applying in EC countries, the US, Japan and Switzerland.

Table 4.5   Capital income taxes on interest and dividends for 1988: the EC, Switzerland, the USA and Japan (tax rates in per cent)[1]

Country	On Interest[2] to		On Dividends to	
	Local	Foreign	Local	Foreign
	Capital Owners		Capital Owners	
Belgium	25[b]	25	25[a,b]	25
Denmark	–[c]	–	30[a,c]	30
France	–[c,d]	25[e,k]	–[a,c]	25
Germany	–	–	25[a]	25
Greece	25[f]	56 ½[f]	45[g]	45[g]
Ireland	35	35	–[a]	–
Italy	12 ½[h]	30[e]	10[a]	30
Luxembourg	–	–	15	15
Netherlands	–[c]	–[c]	25	25
Portugal	10[i,j]	10[i,j]	12[i]	12[i]
Spain	20	20	20	20
United Kingdom	25	25[k]	–[a]	–
Japan	20	20	20[a]	20
Switzerland	35	35	35	35
USA	–[c]	30[c,k]	–[c]	30[c]

Source: Bundesministerium der Finanzen (1988).

Notes:

[1]   General rates (without special provisions and exemptions).

[2]   Fixed interest payments on bonds.

[a]   Partial or full credit system of corporation tax for the shareholder to his personal income tax.

[b]   Definitive tax on capital yields (with surcharges for higher income), as long as personal tax assessment is not opted for.

[c]   Control statements are sent to the tax office.

[d]   Under certain circumstances, a definitive source tax of 52 per cent can be opted for, which dispenses from personal income tax.

[e]   Several rates and exemptions exist for certain types of interest.

[f]   For debt-holding corporations; for individuals the rate is the personal-income-tax rate.

[g]   For owner-shares traded in the stock exchange; other types of shares may be taxed at rates between 42 and 53 per cent.

[h]   Definitive tax.

[i]   May be increased by other source taxes from non-registered owner-shares the proceed of which are not assessed.

[j]   Special surcharge of 6 per cent in 1988.

[k]   Exemptions of interest-bearing assets geared to foreign portfolio holders.

As can be seen from the table, Denmark, Germany, Luxembourg and the Netherlands did not apply source taxes on interest income (although this income would have to be declared under the personal income tax). Some governments even discriminate against foreign interest income (France, Greece, and Italy). As to the taxing of dividends, there is a source tax for foreigners in all countries but Ireland and the United Kingdom. Yet one should be aware of the fact that these rates may not necessarily be decisive for international capital flows. The issue of tax competition is more complex

- because there is a potential for a source-based capital income tax where there are excess profits tied to a geographical location; we argue, however, that a source-based corporation tax should be avoided; if there is scope for skimming off local pure profits this should, rather, be achieved through a cashflow corporate tax to be administered at the European level (see below);
- because corporation taxes may be equivalent to services derived from regional public goods accruing to factors of production of the corporation; yet it would then be more appropriate to tax the immobile factors of production rather than income derived from it;
- because statutory rates are not decisive where legal provisions allow a reduction of the tax base – leading to a reduction of *effective marginal tax rates* for capital income; as King and Fullerton (1984) have shown, these hinge on a number of factors to be influenced by investors (like the structure of assets and liabilities, specific tax benefits for investment and so on);[38]
- because international double-taxation treaties may mitigate the impact of corporate taxation at source by according (partial or full) credit for taxes paid abroad,
- because the EC has recently decided to abolish withholding taxes for certain forms of dividends distributed.[39]

The issue is, indeed, complicated by existing rules governing the international treatment of corporate profits for tax purposes. These rules form the nucleus of an effective coordination of capital income taxation at the international level. They are designed to strike a balance between a source country's interest in taxing capital income generated by its resident firms – whether appropriated by foreigners or not – and the desire of the individual taxpayer's residence country to tax the income of its citizens comprehensively. Double-taxation conventions, together with national tax legislation, have created a hybrid system of capital taxation where both criteria, the residence and the source principles, coexist.

It is obvious that tax coordination on corporation tax will have to progress under EMU, and there is hardly any subject that has found more attention in recent years than the taxation of capital income and corporate taxation in a global world economy (Devereux and Pearson 1989, Vanheukelen 1991, IFS Capital Taxes Group 1991, OECD 1991, US Department of the Treasury 1992, and the Ruding Committee 1992). A full discussion of tax competition and coordination in the area of company taxation cannot be given here. In order to assess the possibility of the EC obtaining access to national corporation taxes, the following considerations may be useful however.

Tax coordination and harmonisation. Efficiency arguments – Under an integrated system, where full tax credit is given to individual taxpayers, and is accorded to foreigners by their respective governments, capital will not be discriminated against as a function of locational investment decisions within the Community. Wherever an individual places his capital in the world, the same personal tax rate as in his home country will apply. Under such a rule – the *residence principle* – there is no tax competition, although tax rates may diverge among member states.[40] This is analogous to the destination principle for VAT.

If, however, capital income is taxed only in the country where it is produced – applying the *source principle* to income taxation – differences in tax rates may become a matter of concern. In this case capital will seek the location with the lowest tax rate, where the net-of-tax return is highest *ceteris paribus*. This will impose a constraint on all other countries, which will be inclined to compete for international capital by reducing tax rates competitively. In this case, lowering tax rates may become a beggar-thy-neighbour policy, and the equilibrium outcome of the Nash-game is undertaxation of capital (Giovannini 1989). But, as long as gross rates of return are the same in all regions, tax competition does not entail efficiency losses other than that. Investors would locate their capital in the lowest tax region, other regions would forego tax yields, yet production efficiency is unaffected by this relocation. The pure residence principle seems to be superior to the source principle, since it tends to avoid tax competition and the resulting underprovision of public goods; thus, the basic choice of European countries seems to be in order.

However, the argument is not as straightforward as that. With respect to economic efficiency for the EC as a whole, both systems may be distorting locational decisions of direct investors. This is true whenever differing economic rents are observed (Devereux/Pearson 1989).

- If all countries were offering equal economic rents, different tax rates under the *source principle* would *not distort* investment decisions; if, however, one country offers locational rents higher than those of others – either because consumers exhibit specific preferences or the country has comparative advantages in production – for example natural resources, skilled labour, better infrastructure – one would want investors to exploit these advantages by investing capital in that country. Yet the country may be a high-tax country, and therefore the net return on capital may be lower in comparison with other locations that finally end up attracting investments. Hence, the source principle entails inefficiencies whenever there are rents based on the specific characteristics of a high-tax producer country.

- Conversely, if all companies were equally efficient, different tax rates under the *residence principle* would not distort investment decisions; if, however, one company were more efficient than all others – say, because of a patent on an advanced technology – one would want this company to get the contract, wherever in Europe it was. Yet the company might reside in a high tax-country, and hence the price of its products might exceed that of its inefficient competitors that will finally get the contract. Hence, also the residence principle entails inefficiencies whenever there are rents based on the specific advantages of an investor residing in a high-tax country. One may argue that this distortion is less important than the first one, since differences in company efficiency are limited – because of increased competition in the Single Market. Nevertheless one should note that the net present value of the existing stock of a company also depends on the level of the corporation tax and, to the extent that a tax credit cannot fully be transferred to foreign investors, this must reduce the attractiveness of the high-tax country for foreign portfolio investors.

EC countries generally adhere to the philosophy of comprehensive income taxation which implies the residence principle.[41] But important qualifications have to be made: as to the *income receiving countries*, tax administrators will have difficulties in assessing the total world income of their taxpayers – as long as there is no provision for controlling income flows on a worldwide basis. Even though European tax administrations may in fact continue to develop new forms of international cooperation, there will always be smaller jurisdictions – within or outside the EC – that are tempted to exploit the benefits of non-cooperative games, thus forming tax havens for European investors.

On the other hand, *income producing countries* are inclined to tax foreigners on the grounds of interjurisdictional equity or fairness: if there are local rents that can be exploited by foreigners, why should local governments not participate in the proceeds from regional activities? This argument is supported by allocative considerations, since those tax yields may in fact be used to provide government services from which investors will benefit. However, source countries are aware of the fact that source taxation is limited by the size of local rents, and that they risk deterring foreign investment when taxes are too high.

Coordination strategies – One way out of this dilemma is, in fact, tax coordination. There seem to be several options here (Vanheukelen 1991, p. 348).

- *Pure residence principle with intra-Community tax coordination* – Since all countries may be both income receiving and income producing[42] there is room for a compromise that allows withholding taxes at source in combination with credits given to foreigners for taxes paid to source countries. Withholding taxes allow source countries to have a fair share of the cake that is produced in their jurisdiction; and the tax credit mitigates tax competition since – in principle – residence taxation is still applied.[43] If all source countries were to impose a proportional tax on capital income – with full credit against personal income of foreigners – tax competition could be avoided (and the comprehensive income tax eventually be saved). Yet, ideally, the proportional source tax rate should be equivalent to the highest marginal tax rate in the Community, since otherwise some investors would still pay lower taxes under such a regime by not declaring parts of their income earned abroad. Residence countries with low tax rates would thus subsidise the rest of the Community, and this is politically unacceptable.

- *European unitary taxation* – Another solution would be corporate tax harmonisation at the EC level. If all countries were to apply the same corporate tax rules (or, alternatively, all corporate income in the EC were to be lumped together in single units for tax purposes), all forms of tax competition within the Community would immediately vanish. Groups of companies would then be taxed on their Europe-wide profits. Withholding taxes could be abolished. There would be no problem of transfer pricing and thin capitalisation within the Community, nor of startup-losses – as long as they occurred within the EC – which could be offset against profits, and hence a major tax obstacle to mergers and acquisitions would disappear. Corporation taxes could be fully credited to shareholders in an imputation system, and thus most distorting elements would be removed within the EC.[44]

• *The European corporation tax* – Finally there could be a uniform European corporation tax to be levied on the same definition of taxable income and with the same tax rates. This would eliminate intra-EC tax competition instantaneously, since intra-regional 'loopholes' would no longer exist that could be used for the derouting and cross-hauling of capital in order to reduce the tax burden.

Political and administrative constraints – The latter two options are variants of a unitary approach – one decentralised, the other centralised. It was argued, above, that the appropriateness of various tax instruments for the financing of the EC budget can be tested against the uniformity criterion: since the tax should not be discriminatory at the supraregional level, it must be conducive to tax-base harmonisation.

Despite several proposals of the Commission to harmonise direct taxes, dating back as early as 1967 and, for corporation tax, 1975,[45] little has been achieved in this matter so far. Important decisions have been made recently regarding the fiscal treatment of companies operating in more than one member state,[46] yet the verdict remains valid that the 'national *general* corporate tax regime is not subject to any constraints as the various harmonizing proposals put forward by the Commission in the last twenty years always failed to obtain the necessary unanimous approval of the member states' (Vanheukelen 1991, p. 344). Whether the recommendations of the Ruding Committee will lead to fresh policy initiatives remains to be seen, in particular since many of the suggestions made are open to debate.[47]

The question is why there is so little progress in harmonising the corporation tax within the EC.

• First, there are still differing basic philosophies as to the degree of integration of the corporation tax with national income taxation. In the longer run, however, tax competition is likely to reduce the scope for taxing corporate profits on top of personal income taxes. If there are regional pure profits these could better be skimmed off by a corporate cashflow tax (see below). This would force national governments to integrate corporate and personal income taxes more and more, adopting in the end the full imputation of taxes paid on dividends. The corporation tax will thus become an income tax levied at source and credited against the residence-based personal income tax.

• Second, corporation taxes are most likely to continue being used as instruments for achieving national policy objectives in the realm of income taxation (see chapter 4.3.2.3). Since these taxes will become even more fully integrated with personal income tax, national rules governing national income tax bases are unlikely to be harmonised. Most countries will be loathe to give up their national discretion over the design of an important element of their direct tax structure.

- Third, even if the tax could be harmonised there is likely to be further political resistance to unitary taxation – either centralised or decentralised – because it would lead to a redistribution of fiscal means among member states. Tax credits to be given to shareholders within EC member states would reduce the proceeds from national personal income taxes. In order to restore the regional fiscal impact, parts of the corporation tax – that on dividends paid to EC citizens – would have to be reimbursed to national governments. This is not impossible; it would require yet another clearing mechanism within the EC however. Only the proceeds of the corporation tax on retained earnings – to the extent that it is not credited – and the tax on dividends paid to non-EC residents would remain a 'central' revenue, or 'joint' revenue, to be apportioned by a regional distribution formula. If the EC were accorded discretion for the setting of tax rates, it would be in a position to tap national personal income taxes through tax credit – unless this were neutralised through vertical clearing.

- Fourth, even with some clearing mechanism for redistributing tax proceeds within the Community, the problem of foreigners being taxed at higher rates on their source income than the domestic taxpayer in low tax jurisdictions would remain, since even the low tax source country would have to apply the uniform and maximum tax rate prevalent in the whole Community. This again seems to be unfeasible, given large psychological barriers against the supposed discrimination against foreigners, apart from the resistance against redistributing tax proceeds through a clearing house.

- And last, the application of a uniform tax rates on source income with full tax credit, in combination with a clearing house, is subject to a further constraint: although the proceeds from portfolio investment are caught within the EC, the EC *in toto* will have to compete with the rest of the world. Portfolio investors may still find tax havens outside the Community, and – unless member governments want to go for a 'fortress Europe', installing capital controls with third countries – arbitrage will still force portfolio capital out of the Community. The administrative response would be to create a worldwide network of source taxation with full crediting – which seems to imply a world tax office. This does not seem to be a feasible solution.

These arguments are mainly in favour of continuing national control for corporation taxes. However, national corporate taxation is equally under severe pressure from tax competition. The question is whether horizontal tax coordination, perhaps involving the Community as an arbiter, will be sufficient to solve these problems or whether capital income taxes, and hence the corporation tax, will end up being used by small open economies.

This question largely remains unresolved. It is interesting to note, however, that capital taxes have survived in the past – despite existing pressures of tax competition. This may be attributable to various influences such as the existence of capital controls or of a leading capital exporter not directly vulnerable to individual portfolio flows; more recent research on tax coordination seems to indicate, however, that there are avenues to preserving the possibility to tax capital – and hence, corporate income through policy coordination (Gordon 1990, Genser 1992). This may be achieved more effectively under existing double-taxation agreements, with the elimination of double-taxation 'at arm's length' through the rulings of an intra-European 'arbitration panel' – called an 'advisory commission' (Vanheukelen 1991, p. 347). It may also be more successful if the EC starts to combine its efforts, negotiating on capital income taxation on a world scale – within a largely tripolar system – and imposing constraints on potential joiners – such as Austria and Switzerland. It may, however, prove to be insufficient in view of a truly Single European Market where regional profit shifting and arbitrage on corporation tax should be avoided.

This is not the place to discuss corporate tax coordination within the EC in full (Devereux/Pearson 1989, Vanheukelen 1991, IFS Capital Taxes Group 1991, OECD 1991, US Department of the Treasury 1992, and the Ruding Committee 1992). It is likely to lead to substantial reforms in the area of national capital-income taxation. The reformed corporate tax does not necessarily imply revenue sharing of these taxes between the EC and its member states however. Despite an increasing need for international coordination, the tax itself may well remain a national revenue source.

Whatever the final outcome of this process, there is a potential risk of a regional redistribution of tax proceeds from these taxes even under a coordinated approach. Under existing rules, horizontal interstate tax credits are relatively limited. If the corporation tax were indeed moving in the direction of a source-based company tax to be credited fully against the residence-based individual income tax, this might again entail the need for a horizontal clearing mechanism – if tax relativities are to be maintained. As was argued before (chapter 4.3.1.3), to involve both national tax administrations and a central clearing office seems to be appropriate in this case.

4.3.2.5   EC wealth taxation?

A direct tax on personal net wealth is sometimes considered to enhance the equity and the efficiency of the tax system – even though it would not raise a great deal of tax moneys. In the EC, the tax is presently used in Denmark, Germany, Luxembourg, the Netherlands – and in some potential joiners like Norway, Sweden and Switzerland. It is not used in Anglo-Saxon countries – notably the United Kingdom – where there are specific property taxes (such as the land tax or the local rate); Germany uses both a (state) net wealth tax and a (municipal) tax on real property. Their contributions to national tax money are usually small – below 5 per cent (with the exception of the United States where the property tax is more important).

Net wealth taxes are usually discussed in conjunction with personal income taxes: their function is to supplement the charge on capital income on the grounds that the taxable capacity of an individual with a given income is greater for income derived from property than for income from personal economic activity, since property income is obtained with less effort and is usually permanent. Furthermore, with imperfect capital markets, property serves as a reserve of spending powers for emergencies, and it provides security for old age; it gives readier access to credit, and it confers social status. All this would warrant a separate net wealth tax, which would also strike at income that is not being taxed under the national income tax (services of consumer durables, jewellery, works of art, and unrealised capital gains). Furthermore, a net wealth tax is sometimes seen as preventing an undue concentration of individual wealth. Finally wealth taxes are said to foster economic growth by creating incentives for individuals to discard taxed assets with low or no returns on capital, entailing a switch in favour of higher-yielding portfolios.

It may be questionable whether some of the alleged advantages of a net wealth tax would stand the test in view of the changing conditions in capital markets – notably the high volatility of portfolio capital. An EC-wide wealth tax is likely to create severe locational distortions for the capital investors of the world – notwithstanding remaining excess profits that could eventually be taxed without distortions. Moreover, a net wealth tax penalises saving. net additions to capital, as it charges the proceeds from accumulated savings. It is likely to have an unfavourable effect on private capital formation, and the overall effects on economic growth would thus seem to be ambiguous – if not negative.

Applied at the EC level such a tax would meet insurmountable administrative difficulties: (i) net wealth would have to be assessed in monetary terms for all assets (and liabilities) irrespective of the existence of a market for the assets; (ii) net wealth would have to be assessed across regions, allowing for corresponding adjustments in costs and 'regional preferences'; (iii) application of assessment criteria would have to be administered uniformly in order to avoid regional inequities and locational distortions within the EC.

All these requirements are difficult – if not impossible – to meet. Assessing net wealth in monetary terms for all assets typically involves large problems. In Germany, for instance, net wealth assessed for specific assets like agricultural land and forestry is only a small percentage (sometimes even less than 1 per cent) of monetary assets such as bonds and shares (Andel 1990, p. 350, Wissenschaftlicher Beirat 1989). Moreover, the administrative burden for assessing net wealth is rather cumbersome, and – for certain assets like land – values are updated only at long intervals (of about 30 years). Recently there have been strong political trends in Germany to abolish the net wealth tax – at least for business firms, where it leads to double-taxation (net wealth of share-owning individuals being subject to the tax a second time). Administrative costs do not encourage the introduction of a wealth tax in East Germany, where assessment would have to be made from scratch and on a comprehensive scale – with many assets (and liabilities) remaining non-marketable.[48]

The regional dimension of the problem is even trickier: would it be equitable to consider – for tax purposes – a person owning a small apartment in Paris, Frankfurt or London to be 'richer' than someone owning a prestigious villa in Portugal, simply because the price of the metropolitan shelter is higher? Net wealth assessed for tax purposes is thus likely to exhibit severe regional inequities even if market values could be established for each asset. It would seem to be unwise for the EC to embark on net wealth taxes, both on equity and efficiency considerations. If inequities were to become too severe, the tax would be likely to antagonise citizens towards their European government.

Lastly, there is a strong case for subregional tax administration of the wealth tax – since administrators are closer to the objects assessed. Yet regional administrators can also be expected to perform poorly as agents of an eventual EC taxing authority – since the principal-agent problem to be resolved would indicate potential for collusion between taxpayers and local tax officers – at least in some parts of Southern Europe.

4.3.2.6   EC user charges?

User charges – as a compensation for specific government services – are usually discussed in the context of quasi-market transactions involving certain public goods. They are implemented for realising the *quid pro quo* principle in the provision of public services. Government services that are experienced as such by potential users – warranting user charges rather than unspecific taxes – are usually distributed at lower levels, notably at the municipal level of government. According to the layer-cake model, a supranational government would have to engage in activities exhibiting the largest possible regional impact of government services. It is, thus, hard to see what user charges could contribute to enhance efficiency at the Community level. Therefore user charges are likely to be an inappropriate means to financing the EC budget. They are not considered any further here.

4.3.3   Clearing Functions for the EC Budget

It has been noted on several occasions that the future EC budget is likely to perform certain clearing functions within horizontal (or vertically asymmetrical) fiscal federal relations among member states. These clearing functions could be incorporated into the normal EC budget; they are likely to be run more effectively *off-budget* however.

It seems to be appropriate to summarise those functions that – for the more important schemes – are more fully discussed in the respective chapters.

- *VAT clearing* – It has been noted that the future EC VAT system would require a clearing mechanism in order to preserve existing relativities in the horizontal distribution of revenues according to the destination principle for fiscal assignment – which is *not* up for review at present. VAT clearing is more fully discussed in chapter 4.3.2.1 of this book.
- *Corporate tax clearing* – If member-state governments were to opt to coordinate tax policies in the area of corporate taxation, the tax would be likely to become a more standardised source-based tax on specific forms of capital income, to be credited against residence-based national income taxes. This could lead to a horizontal redirection of tax proceeds within the EC, with some need for clearing in the longer run.
- *EFTS clearing* – In order to compensate regional governments for the loss of exchange-rate flexibility under EMU, a budget-neutral

system of horizontal specific assistance grants has been proposed for combating regional structural unemployment. Although the author remains sceptical as to the need for such a scheme, a proposal is made in chapter 4.3.5.2 (under the heading 'asymmetrical shocks, regional stabilisation policies, and the need for regional redistribution') to operate such a fund in conjunction with a corporate cashflow tax that exhibits full regional neutrality in fostering regional developments and economic growth within the EC. EFTS clearing could assist such a tax, not simply as a social-policy device – that might risk externalising regional structural unemployment – but as an instrument to enhance regional mobility and vocational training.

- *EC pension fund* – Old-age pension rights still remain a source of substantial regional immobility of the labour force, despite the early attempts of the Commission to resolve some of the related problems. It appears that the incentives inherent in coordinated national pension schemes work in an asymmetrical fashion – encouraging mainly South-North migration – and they are selective as to specific groups within the workforce. Hence, low-skilled labour under private contracts seems to be more mobile than high-skilled labour – especially if working for public employers. In the long run, an institutionalised 'EC Pension Scheme' (EPS) would therefore be desirable, funded by national pension schemes for those of their members that opt for the EPS. In order to guarantee uniformity in defining EC pension entitlements, some regional perequation is likely to become necessary – which would involve Community assistance.

- *EC CAP fund* – Similar to an eventual EC pension fund operating *off-balance* under its own rules, the workings of CAP could be enhanced – and control be enforced more effectively – by segmenting the price-guarantee section out of the EC budget and heaping it onto a separate fund (Spaventa, Koopmans, Salmon, Smith, Spahn 1986). Agricultural levies would form an important part of own finance for this fund according to the instrumental approach. Additional revenue might be warranted however – in order to maintain the existing level of benefits. This could be achieved through general revenue grants to be given to the fund. Not only would the amount of budget subsidies become more visible under such arrangements – stressing the tax/benefit link; the European Parliament would be put in a position to exert effective budgetary control through the limitation of this expenditure category. Other outlay functions of the EC budget would be safeguarded against automatic increases in 'compulsory' expenditures, that warrant priority over 'non-compulsory' functions, and the CAP fund would be forced to develop its own rules for effective budgetary control.

- *EMU wind-up funds* – EMU and the founding of ESCB, the European central banking system, is likely to entail wind-up funds for existing national government debt. Given that rules for accessing soft finance through money creation and through capital markets vary widely among member states, with resulting large regional imbalances in the distribution of government debt, it is most unlikely that existing commitments will simply be pooled when forming a monetary union. It is likely that existing government liabilities *vis-à-vis* national central banks will be transferred to the consolidated balance sheet of ESCB in well-determined proportions. Remaining liabilities will have to be swapped for marketable debt. This marketable debt of national governments – together with existing debt to the public – may be effectively transferred onto national (or EC) wind-up funds, to be served in accordance with longer-term financial planning, once a set of harmonised rules governing budgetary deficits has been put in place. It is most likely that the responsibility for debt redemption – and eventually even the administration of these funds – will remain at the national level. At least administering of these funds could eventually become an EC responsibility – in order to preserve the political independence of ESCB – with, possibly, EC aid toward debt redemption to be given through ESCB seigniorage revenue for instance.

4.3.4   The Scope for EC Surcharges on National Taxes

As has been discussed more fully in chapters 2 and 3, some federations employ surcharges, or piggy-back taxes, on taxes levied at other levels of government, in order to restore vertical fiscal balance. In Canada, for instance, all provinces and territories (except Quebec) levy a subfederal income tax in the form of a fixed-percentage surcharge on the federal income tax. Helvetian communes levy communal income tax in much the same way by piggy-backing onto cantonal taxes. In Germany the churches are allowed to levy surcharges on the federal income tax.

In all these cases, lower tiers piggy-back on tax instruments employed by higher tiers of government. It would thus seem to rule out an EC surcharge on national tax bases from the outset – if the historical evidence of existing federations is relied upon. The argument is not convincing however. The fact that surcharges are regularly applied by lower tiers of government relates to the very fact that a *standard* tax base is needed for vertical readjustments of fiscal needs under all circumstances. Such a standard base is usually formed by taxes levied at *higher levels* of government, which are being controlled – for the supraregional jurisdiction – in accordance with uniform rules. Piggy-backing on differing tax bases at *lower levels* of government would entail existing horizontal inequities being reflected in varying contributions toward the financing of the central government's budget. Moreover, regional governments would be encouraged to reduce their revenue-raising efforts in favour of taxes subject to central surcharges to the detriment of other regions – entailing regional tax competition within the federation. This is not acceptable politically, and it would be rejected as discriminatory by EC jurisdiction.

If, however, such a standard tax base could be defined at subregional levels across jurisdictions, the central government would not be inhibited from levying a surcharge on this base. This is true for the proposal for an EC piggy-back tax on national energy consumption made in chapter 4.3.2.2 of this book.

Recently Biehl (1985, 1990) has proposed a new EC revenue source in the form of a progressive surcharge on national (personal and/or corporate) income taxes. Having discussed the large regional variety in direct taxation – likely to become even greater under EMU – the proposal may have to be discarded on the grounds of regional inequities, and federal tax competition, which would be accentuated by this approach. Yet Biehl's proposal is more subtle than a straightforward surcharge on national direct taxes. He would proceed in two steps: (i) member states are 'assessed' on the basis of their GDP and GDP per capita; this way the amount to be paid by each state 'according to the principle of fair burden sharing' (Biehl 1990, p. 98) is fixed. (ii) Member states then transform this share into a progressive surcharge to be applied to each taxpayer – either individual or individual and corporate. The main objective of this proposal seems to be to 'directly confront European decision-makers and their electorate' (Biehl 1990, p. 98); hence, the famous tax/outlay-link argument reappears.

Stage (i) of Biehl's proposal does not seem to pose any problem. It is essentially equivalent to the existing GDP-based additional resource ('fourth levy') introduced through the Delors I package in 1988. Economically speaking it is a general revenue grant accorded by member states on the basis of a statistical indicator. Whether Biehl wants to incorporate further perequation effects when stressing the importance of per capita GNP and 'the principle of fair burden sharing' – whether, in fact, he wants the levy to become regionally 'progressive' – seems to be unclear. However, doubts have been expressed already regarding politicians' willingness to go beyond regional proportionality and to accept greater progressivity in horizontal fiscal federal relations within the EC (chapter 4.3.1.2).

Greater problems loom large when considering stage (ii) of Biehl's proposal.

- First, it seems to contradict the subsidiarity principle for vertical fiscal relations. National governments *must* reject strings attached to general revenue grants to be given to the EC budget. They may decide to render the contribution rate visible in the form of a surcharge on *any* tax; they may opt for proportional (rather than progressive) surcharges, or they may decide to transfer the grant from general budgetary means, without any earmarking according to the principle of universality. This should, in fact, be left to the discretion of national governments.

- Even though governments may agree conjointly to impose such progressive surcharges, there may be constraints on doing so at national levels – since the large variety in the area of direct taxation may prevent them from implementing the proposal. Germany, for instance, has a much broader individual income-tax base than France – where family allowances are much more important. Also, the relative share of individuals subject to the income tax is much higher in Germany than it is in France – a country that relies more heavily on (proportional) payroll taxes. If a similar proportion of GNP per capita had to be transformed into a progressive surcharge on income taxes in both countries, it would be likely to be twice as high in France as in Germany. This would be resented as highly inequitable, it would not enhance EC budget efficiency in spite of the tax/outlay link. It would simply alienate French taxpayers from the Community.

- A third criticism is related to the progressive nature of the surcharge. Individual tax progressivity is *very* different according to national tax codes. Progressivity is not only a question of the tax schedule (or rates), it also hinges on indirectly progressive effects introduced by exemptions and deductions, the treatment of capital gains, inflation accounting and other specificities of national tax laws. How could anyone hope to implement a progressive EC surcharge on national income taxes in an equitable, and regionally just – that is, standardised – fashion according to 'the principle of fair burden sharing'?

- And finally, given the present weakness of parliamentary influence at the EC level, and the decisions of the Council remaining subject to *national* control, much lesser so to EC politics, it is difficult to see what would be gained from 'confront(ing) European decision-makers and their electorate' through such a surcharge.

Summarising the discussion of this chapter, it would seem that there *is* scope for EC surcharges on national tax bases. But these tax bases must be uniformly defined (like the consumption of mineral oil in *hl*) if regional inequities in financing the EC budget, as well as regional tax competition, is to be avoided. Furthermore, these surcharges are likely to be proportional (and not progressive). Any surcharge on direct national taxation seems to be ruled out for decades to come – as long as national direct tax systems continue to exhibit wide varieties in policy and legislation.

4.3.5   The Scope for New Tax Instruments of the EC Budget

This chapter looks more fully into the possibilities (and eventual necessities) of creating new forms of taxation at the EC level that could contribute to the financing of the EC budget. This may seem to be extremely pretentious given the vast number of existing proposals to introduce new, and to reform or discard old taxes. Some of these proposals are being discussed intensively in academic circles (for example, Kaldor's 1955 personal expenditure tax and its modern derivatives, proposed by Meade 1978, Bradford 1986 or Kay/King 1986) – without even being noticed by tax politicians; others – like Tobin's capital transaction tax or Friedman's once popular negative income tax – have come to live more quietly these days.

Although some of these proposals deal explicitly with problems of international tax coordination, it would be vain to try discussing them systematically with regard to EC budget financing. The following sections must therefore be considered as a very limited, subjective selection of tax instruments, where the emphasis is placed essentially on two proposals: (1) ecotaxation (especially the use of a carbon tax); and (2) cashflow taxation for the corporate sector.[49]

4.3.5.1   Ecotaxes
General characteristics of ecotaxes and alternative instruments. Although ecotaxes form a relatively new area of public policy, their theoretical foundations date back to Pigou's early recommendations in the 1920s to use specific taxes as a corrective for externalities in the production and consumption of private goods. If an economic activity entails social costs, pollution for instance, that are *not* incorporated in private costs (and

pricing rules), it leads to an inefficient overactivity in the respective domain – and the social costs incurred continue to impose excessive damage on the environment. *One* means of correcting such inefficiencies would be Pigovian taxation, with the total tax amount corresponding to the cost of removing the damage incurred. Social costs would thus be internalised, and the activity would be reduced to efficient levels – where the damage done to the environment corresponds to society's willingness to pay for it. Government intervention is warranted in this case because externalities – like public goods – tend to encourage free-rider behaviour of economic agents if left to the market.

This is not the place to go into a full discussion of ecotaxes (see, for instance, Pearson/Smith 1990, Poterba 1990). Yet a number of important problems relating to such forms of taxation may be put forward.

- Ideally, ecotaxes should be designed so as to reduce pollution, at all levels of economic activity, to efficient levels. The aim is to internalise all externalities resulting from production and consumption. This seems to embody a definitional problem: if a strict *quid pro quo* rule applies, taxes are the *price* of removing the damage; one would rather speak of specific *levies* or even *user charges* – not of taxes. Taxes are usually defined as implying no *specific* benefit. Although this distinction is somewhat punctured by the economist's predilection for benefit-taxes, it will prove to be useful when discussing ecotaxation in a federal setting. We shall talk of environmental *levies* whenever its revenue is either assigned to removing the damage incurred or, if it is not, could be used for that purpose in principle. In the first case, *quid pro quo* is strictly applied; in the second, it is potentially effective yet society accepts the damage for a financial compensation. An *ecotax* is in fact non-specific as to the assignment of its revenue – because removing the damage is technically unfeasible, as in the case of global warming or damage to the ozone layer.
- Ecotaxes and ecolevies are both instrumental in reducing pollution indirectly through market forces. They do not remove pollution fully. They merely force producers to incorporate hitherto neglected marginal social costs into market prices, and consumers to take notice of the full costs of consumption. To the extent that consumers are willing to bear such costs, the activities concerned will continue – albeit, most likely, at lower levels.
- The net burden of levies (compensations paid minus the costs of removing the damage) would ideally become zero.[50] Revenue would thus vanish for an environmental levy that is successful in reaching

its objectives.[51] This does not seem to render ecolevies great revenue raisers. Ecotaxes, however, may prove to be successful in yielding net revenue – since it is impossible to remove the damage directly. The costs of any remaining damage have to be borne by society.

- For ecotaxes and levies to reach their objectives, it is necessary that the taxed activity is highly price-elastic (strong substitution effects). Unlike income tax or VAT, the revenue elasticities of these taxes must thus be fairly low. If an economic activity exhibits a low price-elasticity however – like energy consumption, where substitution is more difficult to achieve – ecotaxes may raise substantial revenue. But in this case they could be considered inappropriate for achieving their respective environmental objectives. It should be noted, however, that ecotaxation usually has a short-term and a longer-term perspective. Although energy consumption may not react substantially in the short term, it is likely to respond more fully over a long period – through greater incentives for substitution, encouraging technological change and rendering the consumer more aware of the costs incurred.

- Ecotaxation would largely hinge on the public's concern about the environment, and its awareness of it. There is strong evidence that worries about the environment are positively related to income levels. Poorer regions are likely to be less concerned about environmental policy objectives than richer nations. Regionally varying concern about the environment also poses a policy dilemma for the EC: the question arises as to whether to accept such diversity among member states, or to impose standard rules based on merit-goods arguments.

- Even with identical regional preferences, ecotax rates would have to be differentiated regionally according to the differential regional impact of activities on the environment as a consequence of differences in geography, climate, agglomeration effects, as well as the locational pattern of production, the industrial structure, and the production technologies applied.

- Technically speaking, ecotaxes and levies are inherently impractical because they would (i) require exact knowledge on the environmental damage of specific economic activities, and of technical developments; (ii) require a concise measurement of environmental damage and its costs for a large variety of activities and emissions; (iii) require measurements of differential regional impacts; (iv) require a correct attribution of environmental costs to a great number of economic activities.

This seems to lead to a very complex taxing system with a very large number of different taxes and tax rates. Monitoring such taxes and their economic effects would soon become unfeasible, and administrative costs are likely to be unbearable.

One should further note that ecotaxes and levies are not the only instruments for environmental control. Often their effects would be considered to be too uncertain, since they rest on market reactions to price changes that are largely unknown. More direct measures for environmental control seem to be appropriate in the following cases.

- To the extent that economic activities produce harmful *mass risks* (for example, health hazards through toxic substances), taxation is *not* appropriate to correct such processes through the market. Since it is impossible to price mass health risks, there is a strong case for outright bans on producing certain products (like DDT and FCCs), or for other forms of legal intervention and policing – such as specific ceilings set on certain emissions, with corresponding penalties on violations. Such bans should be universal, and policies on these matters should be attributed to the central government or coordinated on a large (if not worldwide) scale.

- To the extent that economic activities produce harmful *individual risks* (like alcohol consumption), risk reduction would, in principle, be possible through market processes, by requiring individuals or firms to pay a levy or user charge, or a corresponding insurance premium. Yet this poses severe ethical questions, which are sometimes responded to by reference to the market, through pricing (alcohol and tobacco consumption, traffic accidents), sometimes by reference to social merit-goods concepts, through legal interdiction and sanctions (drug consumption). Policy on these matters is value-laden and should be left to national choice.

- To the extent that environmental control would want to impose firm quantitative limitations to emissions, pollution rights (certificates) might be issued, for a fixed amount, that would be negotiable among the agents concerned (emissions trading). This would not *reduce* pollution, yet it could contribute to enhancing production at a given level of pollution by a market transfer of such rights to lesser polluting producers. Again, this is an area for national environmental policy.

- To the extent that the problem consists in removing *existing* damage to the environment, ecotaxes and levies are again inappropriate, since nothing can be gained *ex post* by relying on substitution effects.

For this kind of policy, private liabilities or, eventually, national (or regional) tax moneys are required for financing the removal of damage.

Ecotaxation in a federal structure. Ecotaxation in a federation would have to be based on the 'layer cake' concept, where larger constituencies supersede smaller regions, forming higher layers of government responsibility whenever this is warranted by regional spillovers of external effects (see chapter 2.1.1). Efficiency considerations recommend that lower governments take care of externalities produced within their own jurisdictions as long as spillover effects are negligible. Thus certain traditional environmental services – like garbage collection and disposal, or sewerage – are best provided at the local and subregional levels. Uniform standards and rules set at higher levels of government responsibility would entail Pareto-inefficiencies in these cases. For most of these services the *quid pro quo* principle can be applied; environmental instruments are thus, preferably, levies and user charges.

A further argument for assigning environmental levies to the local or regional level is experimentation. Since ecotaxes and levies are relatively new policy instruments, the effects of which are still unclear and have to be monitored closely, a great deal of experimentation at the subnational level is still needed in order to establish knowledge on the effective use of such policy levers. This is best achieved by encouraging diverse policy approaches at lower levels of government. Tax competition will then select the most promising instruments.

Where regional spillover effects on externalities are considerable, there are essentially two options.

- *Horizontal cooperation* – This is commendable where neighbouring regions are mutually being affected by externalities produced in other regions. Cooperation among governments and/or financial compensation for regional spillovers can then be based on mutual benefits. Pollution control of the river Rhine, for instance, may thus become an issue to be negotiated among the states directly concerned. If some regions are being affected unilaterally, however, and log-rolling potentials are low, bargaining processes among regions may become 'unfair'. In this case the central government may have to play a role as an impartial arbiter. In order to forestall ruinous regional tax competition where environmental damages can be 'exported' to other regions, there is a strong case for the setting of minimum standards by the EC. These may always be considered to be too low by environmentalists, and national standards may often be set at higher levels; yet it should be clear that harmonising EC standards to the highest national level is likely to entail inefficiencies.

- *Centralisation* – This is commendable where environmental damage is global, in that it affects the whole federation, the EC, or even the world. The benefits of environmental control are then consumed conjointly as a public good provided at the supranational level. Strengthening the central government, in this case, is also appropriate with regard to the bargaining position of the EC as a whole when negotiating environmental issues at the world level. Policies for combating global warming or reducing the damage to the ozone layer would thus appear to be typical responsibilities for the EC.

If this is accepted, the EC should also be equipped with the instruments needed to achieve its policy goals in the corresponding areas.

There seems to be a very broad range for ecotaxation: taxes are being discussed – or have been introduced – on sulfur emissions, on sulfur dioxide and NOx, on chlorofluorocarbons (FCCs), on heavy metals, on organic fertilisers, on pesticides and herbicides, on phosphates, on methane – apart from the 'classical' taxes on mineral oil, natural gas and coal. There are proposals to use taxes on specific forms of industrial and agricultural waste, on rubbish produced by the construction industry, on tropical wood, on plastic bags and aluminium foils, on cans, on the consumption of water, on batteries and light bulbs – sometimes combined with proposals for obligatory consumer deposits in order to foster the recycling of these materials. Most of these proposals would seem to qualify as environmental instruments at the national and subnational level however.[52]

Apart from energy taxation – which has been addressed in chapter 4.3.2.2 – there is a strong case for one specific European ecotax: a tax on carbon emissions.[53]

The case for an EC carbon tax. Carbon taxes seem to be en vogue. Finland, Sweden, Norway and the Netherlands have introduced small carbon taxes already. Even Germany – usually sceptical *vis-à-vis* ecotaxation – is considering such taxes.

Carbon emission is indeed a severe problem for the whole world. Climatic models hold these emissions to be responsible for a global warming ('greenhouse') effect by which temperatures on earth are expected to increase by from 0.2° to 0.5° C per decade.[54] Most – if not all – of it results from the combustion of fossil fuels – coal, gas and oil – the consumption of which continues at high and increasing levels (about 6 billion tons per year; Hoeller/Wallin 1991, p. 8).

Table 4.6   *Carbon dioxide emissions in EC member states,
the US and Japan*[a]

Member state	Per cent of world emissions	Emissions per unit of GDP	Price per ton of emissions
Belgium	0.5	0.19	319
Denmark	0.3	0.15	391
France	1.8	0.11	556
Germany	3.4	0.16	351
Greece	0.3	0.34	n.a.
Ireland	0.1	0.24	446
Italy	1.8	0.13	506
Luxembourg	0.1	0.39	n.a.
Netherlands	0.7	0.18	359
Portugal	0.2	0.23	441
Spain	0.9	0.16	373
United Kingdom	2.8	0.19	399
EC Total	12.9	0.17	418
United States	24.6	0.29	208
Japan	4.6	0.09	431

[a] *Source*: IEA 1991 (according to Hoeller/Wallin 1991); own calculations.

This substantiates the need for a noticeable reduction of carbon emissions during the next decades. Most OECD governments have expressed their willingness to reduce CO_2 emissions, with the reductions announced being in the range of the targets set by the 1988 World Climate Change Conference in Toronto: by 2005, carbon emissions are scheduled to be lowered by 20 per cent of the 1988 level, with a reduction of 50 per cent in the longer run. Most of the governments have not yet started to legislate the means for reducing emissions however.

Some data concerning carbon emissions in EC member states, the United States, and Japan are given in Table 4.6.

Quantitative rationing does not seem to be the appropriate answer to this challenge. Although emissions trading may be used in some instances, a comprehensive policy approach would imply limiting the consumption of energy at the micro level – households and industrial plants – which could exhibit inefficiencies (where across-the-board cuts are applied), and entail large administrative costs in policing consumers' compliance. It might also contradict basic philosophies of Western democracies underscoring the importance of individual freedom of choice.

A glance at the table above indicates that the relative emission of

Table 4.7   *Implicit carbon taxes in 1988 in EC member states,
the US and Japan*[a] *(dollar per ton of carbon)*

Member state	Implicit carbon tax			Implicit subsidies for coal industry		Exchange rate of $
	Oil	*Gas*	*Coal*	*Subsidy*	*Price support*	
Belgium	162	35	0	24	–	36.8
Denmark	297	110	0	–	–	6.7
France	351	38	0	25	–	6.0
Germany	212	23	0	28	49	1.8
Ireland	277	4	0	–	–	0.7
Italy	317	80	0	–	–	1302
Netherlands	221	27	0	–	–	2.0
Portugal	205	131	0	–	–	143.9
Spain	176	19	0	25	5	116.5
UK	297	0	0	10	36	0.6
US	65	0	0	–	–	1.0
Japan	130	2	0	2	15	128.0

[a] *Source*: Hoeller/Wallin (1991, table 4).

carbon is inversely related to the price. With prices twice as high in Europe and Japan compared with the US, carbon emission per unit of GDP in Europe is approximately half that of US emissions, and a third in Japan. A regression of emission intensities on prices per ton of emission implies a price elasticity of –1.04 (Hoeller/Wallin 1991, p. 9). A carbon tax would automatically affect energy consumption, rendering consumers and producers more aware of the global externalities associated with the setting free of carbon emissions related to their activities. It is thus likely to entail substantial substitution effects in the longer term, through a change in demand patterns and technology toward energy saving, and a change in the mix of fuels by encouraging a switch from high-emission fuels (like coal) to lower-emission gas, or from fossil to non-fossil fuels. It should be noted, in particular, that energy policies in Europe entail largely diverging implicit taxes on carbon emissions, and they often involve subsidies in the case of coal. The latter is true for Belgium, France, Germany, Spain and – to a lesser extent – the United Kingdom (Table 4.7).

Such a tax would have all the qualities needed for being levied at the supranational level: (i) externalities are global, requiring policy instruments that operate at the general level; unilateral use of carbon taxes by a single country would affect global warming only negligibly; (ii) the benefits of taxation accrue to all regions jointly (supranational public-good character-istics); (iii) there is a case for uniform taxation – since regional tax variety would lead to inefficient cross-border shopping and tax competition among member states, and hence entail suboptimal levels of taxation; uniform taxes would 'give each energy user the same incentive to abate, and leave the least-cost abatement decision to the individual' (Hoeller/Wallin 1991, p. 8); (iv) there is even a case for EC involvement in administering the tax, through the setting of common rules with regard to the definition and measurement of tax bases within the EC. This would guarantee equal opportunities for producers as to potential cost differentials among regions resulting from varying national standards. And (v) finally, it would enhance the EC's bargaining power *vis-à-vis* other industrialised nations – and some LDCs – for achieving global policy goals.

Revenue effects and potential vertical imbalances. At first the EC would have to introduce such a European-wide carbon tax very cautiously and tentatively – since it would compete with national energy taxes and the quantitative reactions are relatively unclear. Implicit carbon taxes, through the taxing of oil, gas and coal (the latter being sometimes subsidised), are relatively high already, and would have to be brought in line at the EC level (compare Table 4.7). Response to tax-rate changes would have to be monitored in a trial-and-error process, a policy *tâtonnement*. Since price elasticities of energy consumption are relatively low in the short run, however, the EC may have to increase tax rates more considerably if the initial response is unsatisfactory. This may render the carbon tax a potentially strong revenue source in the medium term, through higher tax rates combined with initially inelastic demand responses. In the longer run, however, the proceeds from this tax can be expected to become less buoyant.

Calculations by the OECD demonstrate that carbon taxes could raise substantial revenue in the future (compare the estimates in Table 4.8). If a 20 per cent cut is to be achieved by 2010 – with stabilisation of emissions thereafter – a tax rate of $200 per ton of carbon is required on average for Europe. This implies tax revenues of approximately 4 per cent of GDP at factor cost (Hoeller/Wallin 1991, pp. 12–13).

Applied at the EC level and with revenues assigned to the Commission's budget, the carbon tax would thus lead to substantial vertical fiscal imbal-ances favouring the budget of the Commission over member states. This would immediately call for compensatory provisions in order to rebalance budgets within the EC.

One proposal could be a per capita ecobonus, in the form of a downward-oriented general revenue grant to be given to the financing of member

*Table 4.8   Tax revenue of a $100 tax per ton of carbon at 1988
emission levels in EC member states, the US and Japan*[a]

Member state	Revenue raised by a $100 per ton carbon tax	Carbon tax revenue as a per cent of 1988	
	bill. dollar	*GDP*	*Total taxes*
Belgium	2.9	1.9	4.2
Denmark	1.7	1.5	3.0
France	10.1	1.1	2.4
Germany	19.6	1.6	4.4
Ireland	0.8	2.4	5.9
Italy	10.5	1.3	3.4
Netherlands	4.2	1.8	3.8
Portugal	1.0	2.3	6.7
Spain	5.4	1.6	4.8
United Kingdom	16.1	1.9	5.3
EC Total	72.3	1.6	3.7
United States	141.8	2.9	10.1
Japan	26.8	0.9	3.0

[a] *Source*: OECD, Revenue Statistics of OECD member Countries cited in Hoeller/Wallin (1991, table 4); own calculations.

states' budgets by the EC. According to the subsidiarity principle, national governments would be free to decide how to adjust their own taxation policies: by handing down the grant as a (neutral) lump-sum payment to individuals, by reducing other individual taxes (such as income tax), or by using the grant for additional spending (or a combination of such options). Alternatively a lump-sum per capita ecobonus could be considered, to be paid directly to EC citizens by the Commission. This is likely to be regarded as a personal reward by those individuals whose energy consumption is below average, and it would offer an encouragement to lower energy consumption individually (although not collectively). Furthermore, it is likely to enhance citizens' solidarity with EC environmental policies in general.

4.3.5.2   An origin-based corporate cashflow tax
General characteristics of the corporate cashflow tax. As was discussed earlier, it is most unlikely that personal income tax will be handed over to the EC government in the immediate future. The fact that corporate taxes based on the residence principle are often intertwined with personal

income taxation through tax credits, renders it difficult to separate those taxes from comprehensive income taxation. Traditional corporate taxes do *not* form independent tax instruments that could easily be transferred to the Commission.

On the other hand, the corporation tax has often been considered to be a potential EC tax, and – although the Commission seems to have abandoned the idea of harmonising and centralising this tax in the near future – it continues to keep an ogling eye on it – as proved by a recent statement of Christiane Scrivener, according to which 'the idea of a single European corporation tax is the expression of a European will, . . . which is necessary to build a strong Community'.[55]

The arguments put forward in support of *decentralised* corporate taxation and tax coordination do not have to be reiterated here. It is our conviction that they will indeed prevent the EC budget from obtaining access to this tax for the foreseeable future. Yet – as has been said before – there is at least one strong economic argument in favour of the EC participating in the gains from corporate activities in Europe: to the extent that European corporate law and EC policy measures lead to extra benefits for the business sector,[56] regional fairness would recommend assigning a corresponding tax base to the central government; and, to the extent that these profits are 'pure' – that is, above world-market profits – taxation may not even entail regional distortions, either within Europe or with regard to extra-European investment opportunities.

If traditional corporate taxes based on the Schanz/Haig/Simons comprehensive definition of income are not accessible to the EC, a possible candidate for EC taxation could be a cashflow corporation tax with a standardised tax base and a flat rate. Such a tax has been proposed in the literature in conjunction with a personal expenditure or consumption tax (for instance, Meade 1978, Sinn 1987 and Kay/King 1986). There is no space to go into the details of personal consumption taxation here (see, for instance, Bradford 1980a, 1980b, 1986, and Spahn 1990). As far as capital income is concerned, one should note, however, that the marginal effective tax rate applied to income from capital is zero under a consumption tax (McLure/Mutti/Thuronyi/Zodrow 1988). This would exclude the proceeds of portfolio investment from the tax base – except for unexpected *ex post* profits in excess of normal rates, that can always be taxed without distorting investment decisions; and it would include the proceeds of direct investment to the extent that there are inframarginal rates of return in excess of the cost of financing, and/or economic rents.[57] This guarantees the full neutrality of the tax with regard to the problem of international tax competition for mobile capital resources.

One model of taxing the 'consumption' of companies on a cashflow basis accords full expensing of investment[58] but disallows the deductibility of interest payments and dividends.[59] Such a tax would have a number of advantages: first, it would be neutral as to the sources of finance; it would avoid the discrimination of investment and savings inherent in the comprehensive income tax; it would render complex write-off procedures for capital amortisation superfluous; there would be problems neither of inflation-accounting nor of tax avoidance through unrealised capital gains; with a personal consumption tax,[60] the system would even become more equitable.[61]

In the international context, multilateral adoption of company taxation on a cashflow basis would eliminate nearly all of the problems of corporate income tax. This is true even though tax rates may differ between countries: as a source-oriented tax on excess profits the cashflow corporate tax is non-discriminatory as to locational decisions – because normal profits go untaxed. The latter applies in particular to portfolio investments. Nothing would thus be gained from routing capital through tax havens, swapping capital through 'cross hauling' – since there would be no high-tax residence country to circumvent – and many tax loopholes would effectively be closed instantaneously.

Adopted at the level of the Community – as an own source tax – it should *not* be credited against national personal income tax liabilities, since it would be on windfall profits or rents that might warrant separate tax treatment. This would avoid vertical tax competition between national governments and the EC. Furthermore, no country employs such a cashflow corporation tax at present. This may be regarded as representing an additional advantage – since it avoids possible conflicts with national tax legislators on existing tax bases – and vertical tax competition among the Commission and member states. Tax bases of the cashflow corporate tax and corporate income taxes are economically distinct and intrinsically non-competing – a message that could even be conveyed to constitutional lawyers.

The cashflow-tax solution is particularly interesting for the EC inasmuch as it must worry about potential capital flight in the future. The ambitious project of 1992, as well as the reconstruction of East Germany within a newly enlarged EC, will require enormous amounts of capital. On the other hand, world savings rates outside Europe – especially in the US – have tended to decline. One big world capital supplier, Germany, will drop out in the future – having to reorient direct investment to the new German states. New member states in Eastern Europe may join the EC – with typically low savings rates and high capital requirements. An income tax that discriminates against savings and induces highly distorting effects on the flow of capital worldwide – not to speak of the accentuation of inequities among jurisdictions and taxpayers – does not seem to be the appropriate answer for dealing with these challenges.

Revenue effects of the corporate cashflow tax. As pointed out earlier, tax proceeds from such a tax are most likely to be limited – since the effective marginal rate on profits is zero. Positive revenues collected in more mature regions (with a positive cashflow) are counterbalanced by negative revenues[62] in developing regions (with high private investment and hence negative cash flow). Net tax receipts follow the realisation of excess (or windfall) profits within the EC. It therefore reflects the competitive position of the EC economy as a whole *vis-à-vis* the rest of the world. It would therefore not distract international capital from the Community.

The fact that net receipts from the cashflow tax are automatically tied to the existence of inframarginal and excess profits, and hence limited, may render this tax attractive to public-sector minimalists – who tend to worry about a Leviathan government at the centre. This may reduce again political resistance to the assigning of such a new tax to the Community budget.

Administering the corporate cashflow tax. Administratively the cashflow corporation tax could easily be levied at the national level, starting from existing assessment procedures for corporate income (that is taxed in all EC countries). Traditional corporate income would have to be corrected, for instance for depreciation allowances (to be added in) and investment expenses (to be deducted). Similarly, interest payments – that are usually deductible – would have to be included in the tax base. These corrections are relatively easy to make on the basis of existing information and they would automatically do away with all variations in national tax legislation concerning the differential treatment of various sources of finance, of capital allowances, of inflation-accounting and the taxation of capital gains. Cashflow is indeed a much more homogeneous concept than comprehensive corporate income, with its national variety in valuation rules and effective taxation. Corporate cashflow taxation could operate under existing administrative procedures for corporate taxes – that secure diversity at the national level – and still produce a standard tax base for EC taxation. Administering the new tax appears to be fairly cheap. All it requires is some coordinated tax administration at national and EC levels.

Implicit regional reallocation effects of the corporate cashflow tax. A further advantage of the corporate cashflow tax seems to lie in its impact on regional policies at the EC level. It would act as an implicit regional reallocation scheme, since relatively strong private investment in developing regions entails low or even negative tax bases, whereas more mature economic regions – where rents can be skimmed off – would generate larger tax revenue. The tax would thus automatically induce implicit regional redistribution effects, through the EC budget, that hinge on the intensity of private investment activities. Without having to make discretionary decisions on the usefulness of the private investment proposals to be subsidised, and without interfering in price relativities, the Community would automatically foster all projects of private capital formation that were initiated and sustained by market processes. The tax would again be neutral as to investment decisions and as to financing, and it would not discriminate against portfolio investment, while skimming off any extra profits that might accrue to international direct investors.

Public investment activities cannot, however, be treated like private investment under this tax, since they do not generate taxable cashflow. In order to foster an even development of public infrastructure within the EC, the central government's budget would therefore still have to have recourse to specific purpose (matching) grants. These grants – together with the corporate cashflow tax – would form an appropriate arsenal of policy instruments to allow it to pursue the objective of 'cohesion' through stimulating both *public and private investment activities* within the EC.

Asymmetrical shocks, regional stabilisation policies, and the need for regional redistribution. The cashflow tax may worry those concerned with asymmetrical shocks within a system of regional economies operating under a monetary union with less than perfect mobility of factors of production. It is true that EMU – together with low labour mobility – tends to lead to regional under- (or over-)employment whenever there are asymmetrical shifts of regional demand in the federation disfavouring (or favouring) regional production. The same may result from supply-side effects leading to a relative increase (or decrease) in unit-labour cost for regional economies (for instance, Kenen 1987, van der Ploeg 1989).

In order to compensate for such asymmetrical country-specific shocks, the establishment of a European Federal Transfer Scheme (EFTS) has been proposed in the literature (van der Ploeg 1991, pp. 143ff). The loss of exchange-rate flexibility under EMU is made up through this scheme, which operates 'by transferring income from individuals of one nation to individuals of another nation' (van der Ploeg 1991, p. 144). A *budget-neutral* EC-wide tax is proposed that would work as an automatic stabiliser in this sense, skimming off resources in high-employment areas and shifting them into depressed areas – 'replac[ing], to a certain extent, the national unemployment compensation schemes' (van der Ploeg 1991,

p. 144). It seems to resemble a horizontal grants system according to the model of the German *Finanzausgleich*, yet the rationale would be different: whereas *Finanzausgleich* is used to equalise regional income in Germany, EFTS would act as a compensatory device for regional cyclical employment effects.

The EFTS seems to counteract the regional effects of the corporate cashflow tax. The latter would foster developing (investing) regions, and it would draw resources from regions where investment was sluggish. Thus an argument against the corporate cashflow tax seems to emerge from its implicit pro-cyclical effects. This superficial impression does not stand the test of a more thorough analysis however.

- First, regional production cycles need not fully correspond with regional investment. Investment in region A may support jobs in region B – for example, if A produces consumer goods, and B produces investment goods.
- Second, regional production cycles are more generally determined by export demand – not by local fixed capital formation, which may follow in order to expand capacities accordingly.
- Third, asymmetrical country-specific shocks – notably those related to the supply-side – may be desirable on the grounds of a more balanced growth in a federation. In other words: the *common* supply shock as an alleged 'neutral' reference point is only acceptable as long as economic welfare is distributed evenly within the federation. If not, developing (backward) regions should be encouraged to grow faster than the more advanced regions.
- Fourth, strongly investing regions in the EC may in fact be those where existing capital stocks are comparably low – and hence marginal returns on capital relatively high – once country-specific risks relating to the exchange rate have been removed under EMU. The corporate cashflow tax would foster such developments, whereas EFTS seems to retard it.
- Fifth, the EFTS may contribute to perpetuating high regional unemployment, especially if regional unemployment rates differ in the introductory phase of EFTS, because it would counteract the effects mentioned in the foregoing point, by which developing regions – with possibly high unemployment – attempt to grow out of the poverty trap. EFTS would constitute a disincentive for such policies – since it would lead to a loss of financial support – whereas the corporate cashflow tax would support it. To this may be added that 'an EFTS signals to the bargaining process that real wages can be

kept high, provides an invitation for free riding on European funds, and gives a fiscal incentive for government failure' (van der Ploeg 1991, p. 144).

This criticism is more in favour of corporate cashflow taxation than of a competing redistributive scheme in accordance with EFTS. The regional effects of the cashflow tax would favour developing regions such as Spain or Portugal, as they would favour a subregion like East Germany – provided these regions succeeded in reaping the benefits of potentially high marginal rates of return on capital under EMU – which is more a question of administrative red-tape and potential regional policy risks that are unrelated to EC policies.

Despite this criticism, concern about country-specific shocks leading to unemployment (overemployment) under EMU *is* founded. It is difficult to imagine, though, that politicians would embark on regional compensation schemes for *cyclical* unemployment where this unemployment was likely to become *structural* under EMU – because of imperfect market reactions (low regional and job mobility, lack of qualification and training and so on). EFTS may not only become very costly and lead to inefficiencies; it may also lead to consistent decifits within the scheme – failing to equate horizontal financial flows.

It is our feeling that policies aimed at combating structural unemployment should be left to regional governments, not be given to the EC. The former are not only 'closer to the problem', they also control the instruments needed to achieve desired employment targets – from sectoral or industrial policies, to education and retraining. The EC government may still want to support member states in these areas under EMU; yet the policies then look more like a horizontal income-redistribution scheme, *not* a compensatory device for regional cyclical unemployment. This, once again, will imply value judgements.

If – contrary to our expectations – national politicians do want to engage in horizontal income redistribution, the setting-up of an EFTS-like scheme would not be in conflict with the regional effects of the corporate cashflow tax. It could be established in conjunction with this tax. One should be aware that a centrally administered corporate cashflow tax would alleviate the burden of member states' budgets in expanding (investing) areas. There, the tax would not only have a positive liquidity effect; it might also generate regional tax revenue and reduce the need for government intervention on the expenditure side. If a centrally-run EFTS is desired, regional governments could be required to supplement any tax rebate given to firms in the regions by matching contributions, the collateral of which would be assigned to the EFTS; *vice versa*, governments of those regions would benefit from a transfer from the fund that would pay positive corporate cashflow taxes. The net surplus of the fund[63] could then be used to combat structural unemployment within the EC as the EC thinks fit.

This is not to stipulate that such a fund *should* be put into operation; it is just an illustration for both schemes working together without any policy conflict. The corporate cashflow tax would secure allocative neutrality and stimulate growth, the EFTS would perform a redistributive role – correcting for regional imbalances in the distribution of incomes and thus securing cohesion within the EC.

Corporate cashflow taxation and international tax coordination. A final comment may be made with regard to corporate cashflow tax within the international setting of tax coordination – notably through double-taxation treaties.

As has been said before, the corporate cashflow tax does not concede any tax credit to domestic corporations – since the tax base is 'pure' or 'windfall' profits that are considered to form a separate source of taxation. The EC's right to tap that source was derived from its providing public services to corporations operating in the EC under EMU – public goods, institutional framework legislation (European corporate law, European legislation relating to financial operations like banking and insurance and so on) and, not least, EMU itself, with its effects on lowering transaction costs and exchange-rate risks.

It is obvious that foreign investors would also forego any tax credit on the corporate cashflow tax. As said before, the tax would not deter foreign capital since foreign direct investment in the EC is likely to exhibit excess profits, that can be taxed without entailing regional distortions. If profits are below normal they are even supported by the scheme – leading to negative tax 'burdens'.

Finally, corporate cashflow taxation is not in conflict with existing double-taxation agreements, mainly for two reasons: (i) legally and economically the tax is not on income (which could then be subject to taxation of the foreign investor's home country); and (ii) if cashflow were considered to be equivalent to income of the foreign investor's home country, it could always be declared tax-exempt under existing agreements. If a capital-exporting country were to try to double-tax cashflow generated within the EC – and subject to EC corporate cashflow taxation – it would not only risk violating the rules of GATT; it would also hinder its capital exporters from investing in a region where returns are highest – and hence reduce its own welfare.

4.3.6   The EC Budget and Monetary Policy under EMU

National monetary policies will essentially disappear under EMU. Even if the statutes for a future 'Eurofed' foresee a largely decentralised system of central banking (ESCB) – with assets remaining at the national level – monetary policies will have to be strongly coordinated by the board of governors – that is, independent national monetary policies will no longer be feasible. This is likely to have repercussions on fiscal federal relations, since all national governments rely so far – to varying extents – on central banks' 'profits' resulting from seigniorage. Next, the general question is posed as to how far the EC budget should obtain direct access to capital markets for the financing of its budget, under new budgetary rules to be set for the budget, operating under the new conditions.

4.3.6.1   Financial benefits from seigniorage
The scope for seigniorage revenue. Seigniorage revenue stems from a central bank's monopoly power to issue money. Traditional, paper moneys (bank notes) were issued in exchange for gold, and, to the extent people were willing to hold these notes, the issuer could use the corresponding revenue for purchases of goods and services (and eventually go bankrupt on the paper certificates distributed). Under these circumstances, seigniorage could be identified as the gold equivalent of the nominal amount of certificates placed with the public in any one year. In a more modern interpretation it would correspond to the change in base money issued by the central bank.

This is an unsatisfactory definition however. Once an initial desire to hold notes has been satisfied, seigniorage is only possible in a growing economy – or, more precisely, with increasing demand for *fiat* money. And it neglects the benefits drawn on base money issued in *previous* periods: so long as a government is in a position to avoid redeeming existing debentures, it shirks opportunity costs on the stock of debt at the going market interest rate. A comprehensive measure of total annual benefits from seigniorage would therefore correspond to the stock of base money at the beginning of the period multiplied by a 'representative' market rate of interest, plus newly issued base money – which could be negative.

This approach has a number of drawbacks however. First, it is unclear what the 'representative' rate would be. Second, not all liabilities of a central bank constitute 'base money', and the delineation is often unclear – notably if there is substantial international demand for the currency concerned. Third, seigniorage, according to this definition, may be reduced by other central bank operations – equally relating to its monopoly power for monetary policies – notably real losses in exchange money through a necessary devaluation of foreign reserves to be kept on the balance sheet.[64]

The following discussion takes a holistic view of central bank operations under state monopoly – although some may want to separate out 'commercial' operations (or even privatise central banks *in toto*).[65] We shall adopt a broader view on seigniorage, including all profits of a central bank relating to its monopoly power. Since it is impossible to distinguish 'commercial' operations of a central bank from its operations relating to monetary policy, we simply refer to the 'profits' of a central bank (excluding the normal return on capital for its shareholders) as corresponding to seigniorage revenue.

A central banking system has a number of privileges and obligations. Its privilege is to issue non-(or low-)interest bearing debt – banknotes and compulsory minimum-reserve requirements of commercial banks – by acquiring interest-bearing assets in order to satisfy the demand for money of the economy. Some of these assets may be compulsory and non-interest bearing as well – foreign reserves[66] for instance. Others are interest-bearing but with rates below market prices (certain forms of loans to commercial banks). Furthermore, there are losses and gains due to a revaluation of assets (and, eventually, of liabilities).

The amount of seigniorage depends – apart from valuation effects – on a number of economic variables, notably the demand for money, portfolio decisions regarding the share in cash holdings of individuals and firms, the minimum-reserve requirements for commercial banks (and, possibly, the rate of interest to be paid on these reserves), and the interest-rate spread for central bank assets with regard to comparable market instruments. Many of these factors hinge on monetary policy decisions – notably the level of minimum reserves required; the higher these are, the higher is compulsory demand for base money – and hence seigniorage. Furthermore, there seems to be a strong positive correlation between the inflation rate – influencing the demand for transaction moneys – and the share of seigniorage income. Countries where both inflation rates and reserve requirements are high – like Portugal, Greece, Spain,[67] and Italy – seem to have generated higher shares of government revenue from seigniorage; the UK – which was a high-inflation country during the 80s – did not benefit much from seigniorage, probably because of lower reserve requirements. If 1990 seigniorage is regressed on reserve requirements and average inflation rates for the EC countries, the impact of these factors can be statistically validated.

The relationship between the level of reserve requirements, inflation rates and seigniorage revenues as a share of GDP is illustrated in Table

Table 4.9   *Reserve requirements in per cent of demand deposits,*
average inflation rates, and the evolution of seigniorage
income measured implicitly, in per cent of GDP
(1990 estimations in parentheses)

Member state	Reserve requirements mid-1988	Inflation rate in per cent 1980–1990	Seigniorage 1990	Steady-state seigniorage 1997 and after
Belgium	0	4.5	0.75 (0.30)	0.46
Denmark	0	5.8	0.46 (0.50)	0.22
France	5	6.3	0.55 (0.76)	0.28
Germany	6.6 to 12.1	2.9	0.86 (0.40)	0.39
Greece	7.5	18.5	2.33 (2.69)	0.67
Ireland	10	7.8	0.58 (1.17)	0.34
Italy	25	8.7	1.29 (1.84)	0.36
Luxembourg	0	4.8	0.11 (0.35)	0.16
Netherlands	15	2.0	0.79 (0.48)	0.46
Portugal	15	18.4	3.57 (2.95)	0.50
Spain	18.5	9.6	1.88 (1.75)	0.54
UK	0.5	6.2	0.34 (0.58)	0.23

Regression results:	Intercept	Reserve requirements	Average inflation rate
Coefficients	-0.358	0.0365	0.1460
Standard deviation	(0.450)	(0.017)	(0.027)
$R^2 = 0.83$			

Source: See note 68.

4.9.[68] Apart from the data, the table includes the regression results as well as seigniorage estimated on the basis of independent variables as predictors.

It is obvious that an independent ESCB will generate price stability for above-average-inflation countries under EMS and later EMU. This will not only reduce seigniorage income for these countries in the longer run; it will also bring the shares much closer together – as can be seen from the model calculation in Table 4.9.

Although the variation-reducing effect of greater monetary coordination on seigniorage seems to be out of doubt, it should be noted that the *level* of seigniorage revenue shown in the table above hinges on a number of assumptions that may indeed be questioned.

- Seigniorage revenue may be further *reduced* under EMU – apart from more price stability – if the following conditions hold. (i)

The relative share of transaction demand for money declines with regard to nominal GNP. This follows from standard theory on the demand for money, assuming optimising behaviour of transactors.[69] (ii) Transaction technologies may lead to a continuing erosion of relative cash holdings and hence of central bank monopoly power (Giovannini 1991, p. 95). (iii) Revenue may also suffer from the need to reduce reserve requirements under competition. If Europe-wide reserve ratios are being reduced to 1.5 per cent, for instance, the shrinkage in the stock of high-powered money may range from 22 per cent in France to 62 per cent in Italy (Giovannini 1991, p. 98) – with corresponding effects on the level of seigniorage.

- Seigniorage revenue may also be *increased* by a number of factors that may become relevant under EMU. (i) The need to hold idle foreign exchange in the ESCB may be considerably lower than the amount corresponding to the sum of foreign reserves actually held by national central banks. (ii) There is likely to be an important portfolio effect on the holdings of international reserves by non-EC central banks and the non-EC private sector. This may lead to a further reduction in holdings of US dollars (and Japanese yen) to the benefit of the single European currency. (iii) As open-market policies become more important at the European scale, the relative share of lower-interest-bearing assets – like papers accepted at the discount window – may decline. And (iv) international competition on reserve requirements for commercial banks may become less acute under EMU than many economists might think under the pressure of existing competitive forces.[70] This could then increase the scope for seigniorage revenue on an international scale.

- Seigniorage is also subject to the consolidated budget constraint of the ESCB. It is most likely that this budget will not be arrived at by simply adding assets and liabilities of national central banks under EMU. The initial structure will probably have to be adjusted by splitting off a number of wind-up funds (to be run separately from EC monetary policies). Moreover, assets and liabilities of the ESCB will have to be aligned to policy needs in a coordinated fashion.

For instance, if the relative share of foreign exchange assets is to be reduced, this must lead to a corresponding reduction in liabilities. This could be achieved for instance by simultaneously lowering reserve requirements for commercial banks – with possibly neutral effects on seigniorage revenue. If, however, international demand for ECU is mounting this could eventually be satisfied by the ESCB accepting interest-bearing assets at its open-market window (and the

EC accepting trade deficits *vis-à-vis* the rest of the world). Both effects would increase seigniorage revenue. Yet such a policy could also be resisted by monetary authorities leading (as was true for the US dollar in the initial phase of the Bretton Woods system) to a shortage of ECU on international markets – with corresponding effects on interest rates and exchange-rate developments.

Given these perspectives and inherent uncertainties, it is impossible to predict the quantitative role of seigniorage under EMU. Assessing the arguments subjectively, however, it seems to be reasonable that seigniorage revenues will indeed become less important under a system of monetary cooperation. If the model calculations presented in the table above are taken as a proxy, the revenue at stake (to be eventually assigned to the EC budget) is in the order of 0.4 per cent of GDP – which seems to be an acceptable level with regard to our previous assumptions on future developments of EC outlay functions.

Seigniorage revenue as an EC resource. There are strong economic and political arguments for ESCB seigniorage to be 'pooled' rather than administered at national levels. Whether this is a sufficient reason for handing it over to the Community as an own resource is yet another question. The following factors seem to be important in this regard.

- With the entry into stage three of EMU, the Community's monetary basis will have become an indissoluble whole. Monitoring the intra-EC distribution of ESCB liabilities will have no economic meaning, and it will be technically unfeasible – especially with regard to cash holdings. Since reserve requirements for commercial banks will have to be standardised under EMU (in order to avoid regional intra-EC arbitrage), the regional distribution of base money will essentially be determined by the incidence of private deposits with commercial banks – and by cash holdings. The locational pattern of intra-EC deposits is, however, totally arbitrary, since a common currency has no regional 'strings' attached – as under the present system, where currencies are only imperfect substitutes.
- Although ESCB is a rather decentralised system – with national central banks continuing to operate – it is no longer possible to split central banking operations into 'national' parts. It is, again, essentially arbitrary on which money market monetary interventions would be carried out for instance, and what forms of assets national central banks would acquire or sell in doing so. Therefore 'profits' of national central banks would cease to reflect the

pattern of national monopoly rents existing under present conditions.

- In particular, revaluations of ESCB assets – for instance, as a consequence of changes in the ECU exchange rate – will affect member states conjointly – although these reserves may continue to be held by regional central banks. To the extent that resulting losses and gains will have to be included in a broader definition of seigniorage, the regional pattern of seigniorage revenue is again arbitrary.

As in the case of customs duties – where the locational pattern of exports and imports may be totally unrelated to local production ('Rotterdam phenomenon') – the regional-arbitrariness criterion should also apply to seigniorage revenue. Customs duties have in fact been centralised within the EC; this is likely to become the longer-term future of seigniorage as well.

Yet, although the reasons to 'pool' seigniorage revenue of the ESCB are strong, it may still be questioned whether this revenue should in fact contribute to the financing of the EC budget. National governments may be tempted to distribute seigniorage among themselves – using some straightforward horizontal apportionment formula. Sharing global public revenue in such a manner is of course always possible;[71] yet it is questionable as to its basic philosophy – since seigniorage (because of its global revenue characteristics) *will have to become a Community resource* in the longer run.

Moreover, any attempt to redistribute seigniorage revenue onto national budgets must encounter the following dilemmas.

- Distribution on the basis of *existing* relativities of seigniorage revenue is not acceptable. It would favour countries with historically high inflation rates, and it would reflect policy-induced factors, like high reserve requirements – to name just one. Furthermore, these relativities will change under EMU, especially in stage three, when regional inflation rates will converge.
- Distribution on an *ad hoc* basis is also unsatisfactory because seigniorage – in our definition as central bank 'profits' – is likely to remain a rather volatile revenue source. This would render all implicit redistribution effects inherently unstable.
- If, for instance, seigniorage is redistributed on a per capita basis, it will entail strong regional equalisation effects in periods of high ESCB seigniorage, and negative effects in periods of monetary contraction or – more likely – losses due to a devaluation of foreign exchange.

- If seigniorage is redistributed on the basis of GNP, it is equivalent to handing it over to the EC whilst reducing the GNP-oriented 'fourth levy' accordingly – which would then become the more appropriate budget-neutral solution.

The final outcome on eventual horizontal-*cum*-vertical redistribution of ESCB seigniorage will largely depend on political bargaining processes. The position of the EC in this political game seems to be fairly strong however. It will hinge on (i) the agreed-upon expansion of EC outlay functions; (ii) the relative proportion of seigniorage revenue to additional EC expenditures; and (iii) the EC's readiness to compromise on eventual corrections in the sharing formula for VAT or on the GNP levy – in order to mitigate potential vertical imbalances through revenue reassignments.

The order of magnitude of ESCB seigniorage revenue would suit well the Community's prospective public finance needs. If this resource were indeed to settle at 0.4 per cent of Community GNP, it would still fall short of the revenue needs corresponding to the assumed expansion of EC responsibilities under EMU (see chapter 4.2.2 above). In qualitative terms, the EC's position could even be enhanced by the earmarking of parts (or all) of seigniorage revenue to certain EMU-related functions. For instance, the EC could offer to contribute a substantial part of this revenue to the serving of national governments' debt, swapped onto so-called 'wind-up funds' (see chapter 4.3.3). In doing so, the Commission would serve a double purpose: (i) it would temporarily ease regional inequities stemming from monetary regimes *prior* to EMU; and (ii) it would obtain the full control on seigniorage revenue in the longer run.

Lastly there could always be a compromise on the vertical sharing formula for other main Community resources such as VAT. This would exhibit long-term risks for the Community budget however. Whereas VAT seems to be a relatively stable and secure revenue source, seigniorage is likely to be volatile in the short run, and it is almost certain to lose importance in quantitative terms in the longer run. It is therefore preferable to look for a compromise that combines the transfer of seigniorage revenue to the Commission with temporary central functions to be exerted during or shortly after transition to EMU.

4.3.6.2   *Access to capital markets and deficit financing*

As was discussed earlier (see chapter 3.4.4), access to capital markets for financing the EC budget is severely limited. Balanced-budget requirements are indeed a strong institutional and legal constraint in order to secure 'sound financing' and fiscal responsibility. Whether it makes sense in economic terms is yet another question.

- First, a balanced-budget requirement seems absurd where more than half of the expenditures are not even subject to parliamentary control and are being partly determined by external market response – compulsory expenditures.
- Second, government responsibilities would normally include longer-term oriented public investment programmes – which are only feasible by borrowing against the necessary fixed capital formation.

As discussed more fully above, the problem of compulsory expenditures should be resolved by abolishing this category entirely. It remains the problem of EC capital formation and its financing.

It is obvious that allowing the EC budget access to capital markets may be resisted by national governments on fears of opening up avenues toward fiscal irresponsibility. This contention may be all the more justified as EC member countries exhibit very different attitudes toward loan finance, which renders it difficult to achieve a consensus on 'sound financing' procedures (as they may exist in Switzerland, and existed in the US before president Reagan). On the other hand, investment functions for the EC budget cannot be denied. This poses the question of an institutional reform in order to secure fiscal responsibility, through limiting EC access to capital markets while allowing it to perform its investment functions efficiently.

As can be seen from existing federations, there are indeed possibilities for achieving this policy goal. Both the US model – where no constitutional constraints exist, and budget limitations are negotiable between the president and Congress, with very little success – and the Australian model – with its centristic approach through a Loan Council – seem to be inappropriate for the EC. Yet the German and the Swiss models deserve more attention in this context.

Both European federations limit government loan finance by a cap, the amount of which is defined by investment outlays. Although there may have been attempts at mingling investment outlays with other expenditure categories at the margin, these institutional limits have been binding government decisions effectively for most of the time.[72]

Such a rule could also serve the purpose of the EC budget under EMU. It would *legally* restrict the scope for loan finance to the level of EC investment – which would be comparably small initially. Yet economists must be sceptical as to the validity of legal rules where market forces may become stronger – forcing government to break such rules. The legal constraint should thus be supplemented by *economic constraints* – limiting EC loan finance for an investment project to the regular cashflows earmarked for the serving of the debt. For instance, the regular cashflow servicing derived from the piggy-back tax on national energy consumption (discussed in chapter 4.3.2.2) could be assigned to the financing of an EC investment programme in the realm of transportation policies. Or a regular grant flow accorded by national governments could form the basis for financing an EC investment programme in the area of environmental protection. This would immediately establish an efficiency-enhancing benefit/tax link – that would be more apparent to the taxpayer than such links recommended for the *whole* of Community functions. It would encourage 'sound financing' procedures, and it would limit EC access to capital markets by potential resistance from taxpayers (and governments) – similar to the Swiss model of federalism.

The earmarking of special revenue sources may be objected to by lawyers on the grounds of an abstract universality rule for the budget. Yet this approach to restricting loan finance need not necessarily be in conflict with the rule. All it seems to require is the establishment of an own, but integrated, capital budget *within* the EC budget. Such a capital budget, which would record the amortisation and interest on debt for investment programmes as well as attributed resources, would serve to enhance the clarity of the budget, and it would allow longer-term planning of EC investment programmes.

4.3.7 Some Aspects of Structural Reform for the EC Budget

The need for structural reform of the EC budget has been stressed on several occasions. It seems to be appropriate to summarise some of the main suggestions here.

- A first – and very substantial – point relates to the need to strengthen the role of the European Parliament within budgetary processes. It does not encourage fiscal responsibility on the part of politicians if a large share of the budget is not even subject to parliamentary control. Furthermore, full responsibility of politicians for the EC budget would force them to assess the pros and cons of EC tax and expenditure policies more thoroughly, including the effects this may have on the voters of their respective constituencies. This is likely to limit the size of the EC budget and to enhance the efficiency of budgetary performance.
- A taxing authority should be accorded to the Commission with limited

access to national tax bases and its own responsibilities for EC tax policies – to be controlled by parliament. There seems to be scope for EC taxation in the area of energy taxes, ecotaxes and corporate cashflow taxation. Taxes should be administered conjointly with national tax administrations however.

- There seems to be the need for creating a number of off-balance funds – as discussed more fully in chapter 4.3.3. In particular, a separate fund for CAP (price guarantees) is advisable, since it would permit the abolition of the distinction between compulsory and non-compulsory expenditure, it would strengthen the role of the European Parliament and it would allow the establishment of binding constraints on agricultural expenditures – while protecting other concurrent EC outlay functions. Alternatively, as was stressed by Biehl (1990, p. 98), '[n]o single group of national spending ministers should be allowed in future to decide on EC expenditure, they will always have to sit in a full Council meeting together with all their other spending colleagues and with, above all, the ministers of finance'.

- As to the structure of the budget itself, there seems to be a need for a capital budget if Community policies are to embark on longer-term investment programmes. Also, a more comprehensive EC budget should be formed with regard to functions that now reside outside the normal budget – for example, development funds. This is not at odds with our contention that some operations should be run off-balance according to their own rules where such rules differ from normal budgeting procedures. All other operations should be subject to budgetary control exerted comprehensively by parliament.

- A joint-decision making process for EC taxation should be installed among member states (the Council) and the EC (Parliament and Commission). There is no room to go into the details of such a machinery. The objective of such an institutionalised decision process would seem to be the reconciliation of potentially conflicting interests between member states and the EC – which has grown up to become a public entity with its own independent and supranational policy goals. It would not only relate to matters of EC taxation, tax sharing and grant policies, it would also have a bearing on horizontal fiscal equalisation and specific purpose payments to regions.

- Cohesion within the EC, and related recommendations for appropriate redistribution policies, should become a matter for independent policy advice by an institution similar to the Australian Grants Commission. It would have to discuss and establish criteria for such policies conjointly with the EC and member states' governments.

5 Summary

EMU will have an important impact on the national fiscal systems of member states as it will impinge on European intergovernmental fiscal relations.

Although the structure of government finance in Europe will essentially remain decentralised, the scope for EC policies will widen. Quantitative limits will still be narrow (in the order of 2–3 per cent of GDP), yet the qualitative impact will become very important through the provision of public goods and equalisation measures designed to foster economic and social cohesion in the Community.

Vertical imbalances in the assignment of revenue sources will continue to be corrected by a corresponding enlargement of the tax-sharing formula for VAT in favour of the EC budget. It is unlikely that any of the major existing national taxes will be transferred exclusively to the EC. There will be a tendency toward more uniformity in value-added taxation – national tax autonomy being increasingly sought in the realm of direct taxation. The apportionment of VAT proceeds will require a clearing mechanism, with the flows of funds resulting from this scheme likely to become incorporated in the EC budget. In the longer run, European national VAT systems are not only likely to converge to uniform taxation under the origin principle; it is also probable that it will be transformed into a full-fledged EC tax-sharing scheme with horizontal perequation effects at the national level. The perequation element will be rather weak initially; it may become stronger however as regional economies move toward greater economic cohesion under EMU.

Despite the fact that excise taxation is centralised in many federations, the chances for EC excises are generally small. For the demerit-goods taxes on alcohol and cigarettes, taxation autonomy is strongly expected to remain at national levels of government. Energy taxation is more complex. Mineral-oil taxation is likely to become more and more uniform under EMU. Supported by arguments relating to its instrumental importance for EC energy and transportation policies, the tax can be expected to become accessible to the EC budget in the longer run – either directly or in the form of an EC piggy-back tax on national energy consumption. Energy tax revenue may have to be earmarked for certain EC policies however.

Income tax will remain the cornerstone of national tax policies. It will become the 'core' of member states' tax autonomy given that indirect taxation is likely to be harmonised more strongly within the EC. Income tax fulfils an important role for national policies in the area of redistribution, allocation, stabilisation and specific policy domains such as social policy, housing, education, and family policies. It is thus unlikely that the EC will penetrate into the area of national direct taxation.

The case of corporation tax is very complex. Locational distortions induced by subregional corporate taxation seem to favour a uniform tax, whether levied at regional levels conjointly or administered at the centre level. The Commission has in fact made a number of proposals to harmonise the corporation tax, and it has indicated its interest in appropriating at least part of the funds. Harmonising the corporation tax has so far met resistance from member states' governments however.

The analysis shows that there are indeed a number of arguments in favour of an even stronger integration of corporation taxes with national personal income taxation. This would render it difficult for the EC to penetrate that tax domain in the future. However, tax competition in the area of capital income taxation calls for greater horizontal cooperation in the field of corporate taxes, and even for some clearing mechanism to be established if existing fiscal relativities are to be preserved. The Commission is likely to play an important role as a coordinator in this context.

The case for a European net wealth tax seems to be extremely weak, both on equity and efficiency considerations as well as for administrative reasons. Also, the theory of fiscal federalism would not encourage the EC to engage in user charges on a larger scale. The scope for new tax instruments for the EC budget seems to be wider in the area of ecotaxation, where spillovers could form the basis for a greater use of tax instruments. In particular, a carbon tax – targeted toward reducing the consumption of energy and related carbon emissions – would seem to be commendable to be assigned to the EC budget. The revenue effects of such a tax are likely to entail vertical fiscal imbalances, however, calling for corrective measures through tax sharing or downward-oriented general revenue grants.

There is also a case for an origin-based corporate cashflow tax to be levied at the EC level. Such a tax – apart from its qualities regarding tax neutrality – would skim off inframarginal rates of return in excess of the costs of financing, and/or economic rents. In the international context multilateral adoption of company taxation on a cashflow basis would eliminate nearly all the problems of corporate income tax. Proceeds from such a tax are most likely to be limited, which may render the tax attractive to public-sector minimalists. The tax would exhibit regional reallocation effects in favour of developing regions – to the detriment of more mature regions in the EC. Also, corporate cashflow taxation is not in conflict with existing double-taxation agreements.

A further revenue potential for the EC budget would seem to be related to seigniorage appropriated by the ESCB under EMU. The case for pooling such revenue is extremely strong; yet the eventual horizontal-*cum*-vertical redistribution of ESCB seigniorage will largely depend on political bargaining processes. Although in the beginning there may be political resistance to handing over seigniorage revenue exclusively to the EC, historical evidence from other federations would indicate that such revenue will become centralised in the longer run. The case for EC seigniorage is further strengthened if the Commission compromises by earmarking, initially, all or parts of seigniorage for EMU-related policy objectives – like the serving of debt in national 'wind-up' funds. It is likely, however, that seigniorage revenues will diminish in importance under a system of monetary cooperation in the future.

Finally there would seem to be a need for structural reform of the EC budget under EMU. First, the Community should be given greater access to capital markets – although subject to legal and economic constraints. Second, a number of institutional changes are commendable, notably the strengthening of the role of the European Parliament, the need for an EC taxing authority, the creation of a number of off-balance funds where this is warranted by differing budgetary rules, the inclusion of all other EC functions in a more comprehensive budget subject to parliamentary control, the forming of a capital budget, and the institution of joint-decision machinery for reconciliation and for coordinating policies in the area of fiscal equalisation. Lastly, cohesion within the EC, and related recommendations for appropriate redistribution policies, should become a matter for independent policy advice.

Notes

Chapter 2

1. A basic reference to this model is found in Wheare (1963).
2. This is the so-called 'decentralisation theorem' (Oates 1972, p. 35).
3. For a theoretical discussion of the division of functions among levels of government see, for instance, Oates (1972, ch. 2), and on tax assignment within the 'layer-cake' approach, Spahn (1988). See also, Van Rompuy/Abraham/Heremans (1990).
4. There may be restrictions to mobility by cultural, linguistic and other barriers, yet these can be fully incorporated into the Tiebout model: as long as the benefits (through local public goods *plus* individual earning potentials, cultural and other linkages and so on) from remaining in a given community are considered to be higher than the (opportunity) costs of moving into other jurisdictions, the situation can be described as Pareto-superior to migrating.
5. The EC's initiatives aimed at realising the Single European Market as well as EMU are of course a prerequisite to increasing efficiency and social welfare in Europe. They lead to the abolition of economic, institutional, legal and technical barriers to mobility, enabling taxpayers to react according to the Tiebout view. However, mobility costs are likely to be high in Western Europe even after the abolition of such obstacles.
6. A model that stresses the importance of 'framework legislation' at the centre and policy implementation at the regional level is found in Germany. It has therefore been labelled a 'horizontal model of federalism' in contrast to the (vertical) layer-cake view. Nevertheless there are strong centripetal forces embodied in the German model of federalism, and the central government has successfully increased its functions over the years. See Spahn (1978), and for a more recent assessment, Spahn (1991).
7. This follows from the reduced number of government services entailing a comprehensive coverage of benefits for the whole federation – the most important of which being unusually 'defence' – though not for the Community.
8. Some readers may find fairness to be unrelated to nuisance potentials. For the author, fairness does not exist *per se*, but is part of a consensus designed to stabilise the polity – where potential nuisance is resented as destabilising.
9. It is clear that this possibility hinges on the number of regions within

the federation and on the degree of homogenisation achieved among the regions. In view of a pending expansion of the EC into Eastern Europe, this danger must increase. Yet nuisance strategies may be employed even by regions that are not members of the Community. The effectiveness of such strategies may, however, depend on the region's ability to disturb the institutional decision-making process of the Community. Too rapid an expansion of the EC may thus either require stronger central government intervention – or hinder the European integration process.

10. Nuisance potentials and 'fairness' are related. To the extent that it is possible to convey minority views to individuals of the majority group – through psychological analogies ('put yourself in their position') – nuisance can be culturally 'internalised' through education. It is then unnecessary to exert nuisance potentials directly, because 'fairness' acts as a corrective, protecting minority interests indirectly.

11. This could be the case if political bargaining strengths are distributed unevenly – for example by imbalances in the size of jurisdictions or in economic potentials. German unification provides a good example of the federal government having had to take corrective actions in order to achieve a fair deal as to the distribution of taxes collected among the old and the new states. For further details, see chapter 3.3.7 below.

12. Central government's inability to integrate regional interests can best be demonstrated by pointing to the situation in federations like the former Soviet Union and Yugoslavia, and to a lesser extent, Canada.

13. As can be seen from all federations of Eastern European countries, central government intervention may also be counter-productive if this is considered to undermine state sovereignty. On the importance of federal models for former socialist countries, see the conference report *Financing Federal and State Governments*, edited by the OECD, Centre for Cooperation with European Economies in Transition, Committee on Fiscal Affairs, Paris, 1992.

14. Sometimes this quality is also referred to as 'regional spillovers'. As argued before, regional spillovers could also be dealt with – and usually are – by horizontal cooperation among regional governments. It is thus not automatically a case for centralisation. Where regional spillovers are universal for the whole region, however, they become indistinguishable from supraregional public goods.

15. In the German literature this is usually referred to as 'Popitz's law' (Popitz 1927), yet it became more widely known through the work of Peacock and Wiseman (1967).

16. This argument has been stressed, *inter alios*, by Breton and Scott (1978).

17. Even the German government found it useful, recently, to put the blame for having to announce an increase in VAT rates onto the EC, using the central government as a scapegoat for its policies even before an official

agreement on higher standardised VAT rates had been reached by the Council.

18. The case of Germany illustrates, however, that framework legislation exerted by the centre may result in central government intervention in the longer run – especially *vis-à-vis* weaker regional governments.

19. In Germany, for instance, the states are practising a system of 'brotherly' horizontal equalisation payments by which differences in taxable capacity are reduced without federal government intervention. This model has, however, come under severe strain through the unification of Germany. It is scheduled to be revised in the near future.

20. It should be noted that a distinction has to be made between the right of any one level of government to apportion the proceeds from taxes (*Ertragshoheit*), the right to legislate on taxes (*Gestaltungshoheit*) and the right to administer taxes (*Durchführungshoheit*); Zimmermann/Henke (1990, p. 109). These rights may effectively be split among different tiers of government or exerted jointly in part or in full. In the following, *tax assignment* is meant to include the right both to legislate and to apportion the proceeds from taxes. It is less important, in this context, which level may be charged with administering and collecting taxes.

21. 'Logisch läßt sich die Zuordnung der Einnahmen . . erst nach der Entscheidung über die Aufgaben und die daraus resultierenden Ausgaben bestimmen . . ' (Zimmermann/Henke 1990, p. 108).

22. See also, the general-equilibrium exercise on redistributive taxation at the local level, by Goodspeed (1989), that suggests the possibility of significant regional redistribution policies with restricted efficiency losses.

23. This can best be illustrated with regard to Australia, where New South Wales and Victoria thrive on resources accruing to (and being used by) their residents, whereas the resource-rich states (Queensland, Northern Territory, Western Australia) rely more heavily on origin-based resource taxation.

24. Whereas efficiency neutrality can clearly be characterised as being Pareto-superior (minimisation of the excess burden of taxation), distributive neutrality is a value-laden and hence a vague concept.

25. The German *Reich* (1871) possessed very little in terms of own resources: no more than customs duties and excise taxes. Additional funds had to be transferred to the centre from below (the so-called *Matrikularbeiträge*), general state grants given to finance the expanding functions of the *Reich*.

26. Unless individual preferences are uniform throughout the constituency, the Lindahl-pricing rule (Lindahl 1919) does in fact require different tax rates to be applied to different taxpayers. This contradicts the view – consistently adopted in most countries – that taxation should be legally non-discriminatory against individuals in similar socio-economic conditions (horizontal equity).

27. Questions related to stabilisation policies are not discussed in this book.
28. See, for instance, Spahn/Kaiser (1991) and the literature given there.
29. See Spahn/Kaiser (1991). A number of further arguments in favour of diversifying tax rates are discussed in this paper – in particular as regards indirect taxation. For German VAT, 'optimal' non-standard rates were estimated empirically on the basis of price elasticities for different goods. It is interesting to note that European politics has so much stressed the importance of harmonising indirect taxes, whereas the case for harmonising capital income taxes seems to be much stronger.
30. It will in fact be argued that such a tax should be collected by the Commission. Yet the argument is not based on tax competition; it rests on the instrumental approach.
31. Centralisation of taxes has three distinct dimensions: (i) the centralising of tax legislation, (ii) the centralising of the proceeds from taxes, and (iii) the centralising of tax administration. Administration of taxes is disregarded in this context; it can be assigned to any level of government according to administrative aspects (minimisation of the costs of tax collection and/or of compliance costs).
32. One should note, however, that the instrumental approach to centralising taxes has also played a role in this context.
33. Recent experiences with German unification clearly demonstrate the problem of regional arbitrariness here: Eastern Germany is mainly an importing region; the Western part is predominantly exporting. If national boundaries still existed, the East would collect VAT on the basis of its (imported) consumption; the West would forego tax proceeds relative to its regional export surplus. Under a single market regime with a currency union, tax credits for regional exports to the East disappear. The West then collects taxes on Eastern consumption whereas Eastern regions benefit from VAT only to the extent that there is value added to the imported goods. This massive regional redistribution of tax proceeds calls for a clearing mechanism – as in the case of some proposals relating to the future European system of value-added taxation. The per capita redistribution formula with regard to joint tax collection adopted in Germany acts as a corrective device in this respect. Whether it is sufficient to restore the (hypothetical) initial distribution of tax proceeds remains an open question.
34. Profits can always be shifted from one subsidiary to another through appropriate transfer pricing. This horizontal dimension of tax competition will be addressed later.
35. See, however, Charles Goodhart and Stephen Smith (1992).
36. An impressive example of an abrupt change in the distribution of functions can also be found in president Reagan's new federalism policy, where the federal government's withdrawal from certain areas

of competence was not matched by a concomitant financial compensation of the states.

37. This statement may be rather controversial, given a large body of literature on an alleged 'flypaper effect' of intergovernmental grants. This effect is said to lead to additional public spending for every dollar of unconditional grant money received by the recipient government. Gramlich's (1977) survey of existing empirical work indicates some 40 to 50 per cent additional public outlays for this type of grant. Theoretically unconditional grants must have a pure revenue effect however. Bradford and Oates (1971) have shown formally that – for a wide class of choice rules – unconditional grants have effects on spending identical to those of an increase in private disposable income. A number of authors have therefore claimed that the 'flypaper effect' is some form of mirage. My own empirical work on state-local grants in Australia could not identify the 'flypaper effect' for this constituency (Spahn 1977a). The issue still seems to be unresolved. For a more recent discussion of the effect, see Oates (1991).

38. There is a large body of literature on intergovernmental grants that cannot be reviewed here. See, for instance, Buchanan (1952), Breton (1965), Thurow (1966), Break (1967), Musgrave (1969), Oates (1972), King (1984, chs 3–5),

39. Where the *quid pro quo* principle applies, intergovernmental financial flows correspond to corresponding resource flows in the opposite direction. The net effect for marginal benefits and costs is zero in this case. Often a strict *quid pro quo* principle is not applied in intergovernmental relations however. In this case one would ideally want to separate the *quid pro quo* element from the grant element associated with the resource flow. This distinction is difficult to make in practice. If this distinction is ignored, however, it leads to a large degree of arbitrariness in the definition of grants. Some aspects of this problem will be discussed below.

40. It may be interesting to speculate on whether strings attached to a grant package reflect a 'service' to be rendered to the granting government by the recipient, that is, whether the *quid pro quo* principle is applied in disguise. This is all the more relevant as the grantee government may 'buy' the package or reject it (and often does). However, conditions attached to intergovernmental grant programmes can seldom be realised through the market, which should permit us to retain the distinction made between conditional grants and the pricing of services rendered.

41. See, for instance, Spahn (1977), and the literature given there.

42. These conditions may take various forms: specific minimum contributions by recipient governments, matching requirements, compliance with national standard programmes, and so on.

43. The argument also applies in a dynamic context where the public project under consideration is capable of increasing taxable capacities in the future. With perfect capital markets a government facing an

effective budget constraint is always able to borrow against future increases in taxable capacity. If capital markets are imperfect, however, a possible dynamic deadlock stemming from the inability to pay of one benefiting region may be broken by horizontal government loans or guarantees, not by horizontal grants.

44. In Germany, however, the scheme is the result of central federal legislation, involving state interests, through the second chamber of parliament, the *Bundesrat*, which is the states' House.

45. The process of interstate equalisation in Germany is more fully discussed in chapter 3.3.

46. See the discussion in chapter 3.4 below. Commission of the European Communities (1989, p. 21).

47. For this reason, the introduction of cost elements into the distribution formula may even become an option for Germany after unification – as long as wage rates remain significantly lower in the East. Although there may be a temporary consensus in Germany on the need for regional over-compensation – as long as the public infrastructure is deficient in the new states of the federation – it is doubtful whether this can be realised within the horizontal grants scheme. It certainly implies federal government intervention.

48. As unit labour costs are brought into line, however, distribution schemes taking cost differentials into account will converge towards schemes based on taxable capacity alone.

49. This is a proposal made by Biehl (1985, 1990a,b) for the future financing of the EC budget.

50. Legally a distinction should be made though: tax sharing includes a 'property right' on the tax base, whereas revenue grants are based on political commitments (only).

51. This is definitely true for the distribution of VAT in Germany. Not only is VAT apportioned on a per capita basis (implying strong equalisation effects); two per cent of the tax yield is also used by the federal government to adjust for regional imbalances of taxable capacity through asymmetrical vertical grants.

52. The Australian situation has been described as 'fiscal supremacy' of the Commonwealth. For some writers the Australian states appear to be at the mercy of the central government (see Mathews/Jay 1972, pp. 184 ff). We shall come back to this question more fully in chapter 3.1, where it will become clear that the author does not share this interpretation.

Chapter 3

1. The author wishes to thank Professors R. L. Mathews and Cliff Walsh for comments on an earlier draft of this chapter. The author remains responsible for all remaining errors.

2. The following account is largely based on Mathews/Jay (1972), Hunter (1977), Mathews (1982), Galligan/Walsh (1990), Walsh (1990), Groenewegen (1991).

3. At that time the states' overseas trade connections were generally much more developed than interstate trading within Australia.

4. The High Court has ruled the states out of taxes on goods but not services; it has allowed the states to impose 'franchise fees' on liquor, tobacco and petroleum, which are calculated on the value of sales over the previous period.

5. In the *Wire-netting Case* and the *Steel Rails Case*.

6. 'The real burden of grants (to the Commonwealth) had been at least halved by the increase in prices during the war, and of course was far less than 75 per cent of customs and excise revenue would have been.' (Mathews/Jay 1972, p. 118).

7. Four of the states challenged the validity of the legislation that transferred income taxes to the Commonwealth government. Yet, to the dismay of the states, the High Court declared the essential parts of this legislation valid not merely under defence powers but also under normal peacetime conditions. Mathews/Jay (1972, pp. 173–4).

8. Arguably, the Fraser government's legislation allowing the states to impose surcharges (or give rebates) on federal income taxation accorded greater freedom in revenue raising to the states – which was not taken up however. The Commonwealth scrapped the legislation in 1988 because it feared it might be used.

9. As of 1990–91, half of Commonwealth transfers to the states are specific purpose payments (tied grants).

10. Own calculations on the basis of *Government Finance Statistics Yearbook 1990*, p. 122. Tax assignments were based on *Commonwealth financial relations with other levels of government 1989–90*, Budget Paper No. 4, Canberra, 1989, p. 14.

11. A flat-rate state income tax would, of course, not be in conflict with these policy objectives.

12. At a further Special Premiers' Conference in July 1991 there were signs that the Commonwealth is prepared to accept greater revenue freedom for the states; for a summary of results, see Walsh (1991, pp. 18–20).

13. *Commonwealth financial relations with other levels of government 1989–90*, Budget Paper No. 4, Canberra, 1989, p. 14.

14. The states were thus not prohibited from exploiting this tax base; yet they were encouraged to refrain from doing so (Mathews/Jay 1972, p. 175).

15. This factor was 1.2 per cent in the beginning; it was then raised to 1.8 per cent in 1971 and to 3 per cent in 1975.

16. During the period of revenue sharing (1975–85) the proceeds from income taxes were experiencing high income elasticities through the fiscal drag induced by high inflation rates and a failure to index taxes consistently.

17.   The propensities for taxes to increase in response to this type of grant money were about 35 per cent for grants for recurrent purposes and nearly two-thirds for capital grants (Spahn 1977a, pp. 140–42).

18.   The Australian model also defines relative 'tax effort' as own 'tax effort' relative to standard 'tax effort'. Such a distinction would make little sense in Germany, where legislation governing state taxation is uniform.

19.   A similar conclusion may be drawn on the German horizontal *Finanzausgleich*, to be discussed below.

20.   The federal government has to convince only two states in order to have a motion passed, but, in any case, is able to control the Council's decisions because of its dominating fiscal strength and grant powers.

21.   This was facilitated politically because high real borrowing costs have reduced state desires to borrow.

22.   The author wishes to thank Professor Bernard Dafflon for comments on an earlier draft of this chapter. The author remains responsible for all remaining errors.

23.   Abstraction is made from an intermediate phase, starting in 1798, when the French revolution had invaded the country, creating a unitary state which was heavily resisted, later decentralised by Napoleon, and totally abandoned after his fall.

24.   There are 26 cantons (and half-cantons) today. In addition there is a municipal substructure of about 3000 communes which act under cantonal control. As in Germany – and unlike Australia – this layer of government is very important in Switzerland. Since the cantons may delegate government functions to their communities at extremely varying degrees, it is best to treat the state level in Switzerland as inclusive of communal services (and revenues).

25.   These 'facultative law referenda' were introduced by the important constitutional reform of 1874.

26.   Since these elements are found even in the Swiss – and all other federal – constitutions, it poses the question of whether federations may function at all without such provisions. The gains apparent to be reaped from such arrangements, in terms of political stability, are obviously expected to be greater than those from Pareto-optimality.

27.   A closer look at Swiss experience was also recommended by a prominent Canadian writer, who supposes that this 'may prove to be the most illuminating of all possible comparisons for Canadians' (Bird 1986, p. 245).

28.   Regarding the history of the income tax in the United States this exception is easily understood. The US income tax was developed from a *capitation* – or a (direct) poll tax – to be imposed on citizens in the states according to the *apportionment clause* of the Constitution. It was only after the *Sixteenth Amendment* – which brought the elimination of the clause – that a modern income tax could be introduced in 1913.

29.   Dafflon (1991).

30. The formula apportions 34 per cent of the grant according to cantonal expenditures on roads, 12 per cent according to the length of roads, 43 per cent according to the equalisation yardstick (see below) and the rest in accordance with the canton's relative tax effort regarding the motor vehicle tax and its relative per capita expenditures on roads. (Dafflon 1991).

31. The federal government's contribution to such a 'pool' is zero in Germany, hence the 'pool' must be filled through contributions made by the richer states. As to its impact on horizontal fiscal incidence, the Swiss model is, however, rather similar to that of German *Finanzausgleich*. In particular, if a canton's fiscal capacity falls, the compensating fiscal effect of the revenue-sharing grant is made up by other cantons, not by the Confederation.

32. This tax is paid by male Swiss citizens exempted from military service. It is, essentially, a 'poll tax' that is proportional to income and inversely related to the days of military service accomplished.

33. Recent projections of the Office of Management and Budget (OMB) forecast a deficit of $348 billion in 1992, at 5.8 per cent of GNP, compared with a forecast for fiscal 1991 of $282 billion.

34. Some *de facto* harmonisation has been taking place over the years, since some cantons have tried to tailor their tax laws to the model provided by the federal income tax. There is a strong indication that a centrally levied tax, which competes with similar taxes at the regional level, may become a standard for regional taxation in the long run.

35. *Loi fédérale du 14 décembre 1990 sur l'harmonisation des impôts directs des cantons et des communes.* The cantons and communes are accorded eight years to adapt their respective legislation. After this term, federal rules will apply automatically. At the same time, the federal law on direct taxation has been coordinated.

36. The West German system was characterised as 'unitary' already in the early 1960s; see, for instance, Hesse (1962).

37. Equity considerations are generally derived from the 'social-state principle' (*Sozialstaatsprinzip*) inherent in Article 20 (1) *Grundgesetz*, yet it is spelled out explicitly in Articles 72 (2) and 106 (3) of the Constitution, where the 'maintenance of uniformity of living conditions beyond the territory of any one *Land*' is stressed.

38. Local governments are responsible for two-thirds of all public investment programmes in Germany.

39. The most critical function, in this context, is public welfare (*Sozialhilfe*), which is executed by local governments and paid out of their normal budgets without reimbursements from upper levels of government.

40. According to Article 30 *Grundgesetz*, government responsibility lies in the hands of states unless the Constitution explicitly transfers competences to the federal government. There are, of course, also 'implied powers' at the central level, stemming from the 'nature of the cause' without clear-cut boundaries (BVerfGE 12, 205).

41. See, for instance, the recommendations of a working party ('Martin-Kommission' 1985) or Große-Sender (1990).

42. There is some limited discretion to tax and/or to vary tax rates of national taxes at the communal level though, notably with regard to the local business tax (*Gewerbesteuer*) and the property tax.

43. It should be mentioned, however, that West Berlin has been benefiting from lower income tax rates until now, yet these benefits – which are unique – will be phased out as a result of German unification.

44. Only during Bismarck's Empire and before (in the North German Confederation) do the states seem to have enjoyed more power than today, yet the political weight of Prussia in the *Reich* always jeopardised their constitutional rights.

45. In table 3.3 only the 'shared' part (Federal and State) is recorded as shared business tax (1 per cent). The rest remains in the category of local taxes.

46. Customs duties have been handed over to the EC.

47. The beer tax is the only excise tax remaining at the state level – bearing testimony to Bavaria's successful policy in the *Reichstag* towards the end of last century.

48. Recently, in the context of German unification, the Federal government has introduced vertical general revenue grants (on a per capita basis) for financing local governments in the former GDR. This must, however, be considered to be temporary. It accounts for the fact that these governments – for administrative, legal and economic reasons – have an incomparably lower tax base than their Western counterparts.

49. For a fuller discussion, see, for instance, Reissert (1978).

50. The centralisation of competence, as a consequence of policy coordination for stabilisation purposes, reached its peak at the end of the 60s, when Article 109 *Grundgesetz* was amended (1967), the *Stability and Growth Law* was enacted (1967), a Business Cycle Council (*Konjunkturrat*) and a Finance Planning Council (*Finanzplanungsrat*) were established and the principles governing the budgets of federal and state governments were harmonised (1969).

51. These are (i) university construction, (ii) regional policy, (iii) agricultural structural policy and coast preservation, as well as (iv) the planning of education, and (v) the fostering of research insofar as these are of supraregional importance.

52. The Federal contribution varies however. It is 60 per cent for agricultural measures, and 70 per cent for coast preservation.

53. A last attempt to centralise powers was made in 1973, when the federal parliament set up a commission for a revision of the Constitution (*Enquête-Kommission Verfassungsreform*) the recommendations of which had no further impact on developments.

54. An influential study analysing the effects of responsibility sharing and joint financing was Scharpf/Reissert/Schnabel (1976, 1977). See also, Reissert (1978).

55. *Gesetz über den Finanzausgleich zwischen Bund und Ländern*, as of 18 December 1987 (Equalisation Act), BGBl. I, p. 2764, amended by the *Gesetz zum Ausgleich unterschiedlicher Wirtschaftskraft in den Ländern* of 20 December 1988, BGBl. I, p. 2358.

56. Compare the calculations made in Spahn (1977b), pp. 222 ff.

57. The recent legislation mentioned before was adopted following a ruling of the Court in 1986 (BVerfGE 72, pp. 330ff.). This legislation has provoked new counter-initiatives by Hamburg, Breme and Saarland.

58. These developments have been taking place in spite of the unity-of-the-budget principle controlling German budgetary processes. Similar developments – both the relabelling of outlay (and revenue) categories as well as 'off-budgeting' operations – could also be observed in the United States in response to legislation trying to limit the size of the federal budget deficit.

59. Own estimates. This amount may be distributed as follows: federal government 66 billion; *Länder* 35 billion (of which 20 billion in the East); municipalities 5 billion DM. To this should be added the deficits of special public funds (*European Recovery Fund*, Postal Services, Railways) of 29 billion DM, and the 'shadow' budgets (*Treuhandanstalt*, German Unity Fund and so on) with 58 billion DM.

60. This experience demonstrates vividly – together with the US federal budget deficit – that EMU may have to fear not the relative size of deficits for smaller countries (like Belgium) but the absolute amounts of the larger budgets, to be financed through capital markets and through money creation.

61. East Berlin merged with West Berlin, that had formerly existed as a West German State under special rule (still being controlled by the Western Allies of World War II).

62. This effect is accentuated by special deductions from the tax base accorded to residents of the former GDR.

63. In 1988 total public development aid was US $51 billion (*Weltentwicklungsbericht 1990*, edited by the Weltbank, Washington, D.C., p. 154).

64. Consequently the *Treuhandanstalt* was put under control of the Finance Ministry, not the Economic Ministry – although its activities are far more important for the future structure of the German economy than for revenue raising.

65. This is, of course, heavily resisted by the *Treuhandanstalt*, yet – for political reasons – it could not prevent its having to subscribe capital for the forming of so-called *Beschäftigungsgesellschaften* (which are essentially public-works and job-retraining firms).

66. Council decision of 24 June 1988 concerning budgetary discipline, 88/377/EEC.

67. The history of this crisis is summarised in Commission of the European Communities (1989, ch. 4).

68. The legalistic budgetary principle of 'unity of the budget' is often

evoked against this suggestion. This principle should indeed apply for truly budgetary processes controllable by political decisions. It is questionable, however, whether this principle has a significance where the mechanics of a public function operating in conjunction with market processes are at stake. CAP, as an 'off-balance' operating fund (similar to the ECSC operating budget), would not only contribute to containing agricultural expenditures more effectively; it would also alter the nature of the EC budget, strengthen the role of the European parliament and enhance EC autonomy.

69. For more details, see, for instance, Commission of the European Communities (1989, pp. 21–2).

70. The activities of the European Investment Bank (EIB) – a legally independent bank operating separately from the EC budget – are not considered here.

71. Commission of the European Communities (1989, p. 36). The author's plea for the creation of a capital budget, to be integrated in the normal budgeting process, is *not* in conflict with his advocating putting compulsory expenditures, notably within CAP, 'off-budget'. The latter recommendation is based on a difference in the *nature* of budget operations. Parliamentary control is applicable to both traditional concurrent *and* capital outlays. However, it is not applicable to intrinsically open-ended expenditure that is partly dependent on reactions that cannot be controlled by governments.

72. The fact that the EC has to reimburse member states for their collecting taxes for the EC budget has strengthened this presumption.

Chapter 4

1. Many analysts seem to have been less aware of a further important policy element, the massive fiscal stimulus, in full accordance with Keynes's policy prescriptions, entailing *inter alia* a massive federal debt that remains a persistent problem for the foreseeable future.

2. Whereas Ministers may decide by majority rule for the first group of policy issues, unanimity is required for the second.

3. In the United States the 'equal protection clause' of the Fourteenth Amendment of the Constitution forbids state tax discrimination against US citizens residing in other states. In a similar vein, the EC High Court may rule some provisions of national tax codes as contradicting the spirit of the EC Treaties – for instance, the discriminatory nature of '*begrenzte Steuerpflicht*' of the German income tax applied to EC citizens.

4. The main elements of this reform have been agreed upon in Luxembourg by the Ecofin Council of 24 June 1991.

5. Other writers approach the issue of decentralisation from public decision-making models (public choice), for instance, Downs (1957),

Buchanan and Tullock (1962), and Olson (1963). A more radical approach to decentralisation is found in Brennan and Buchanan (1980), who argue that decentralisation is needed in order to control insatiable governments behaving like revenue-maximising 'Leviathans'.

6.   A case for decentralisation can also be made on grounds of the better revelation of information needed for optimal decisions in distribution policies (Wildasin 1990).

7.   Olson (1983b) p. 23. See also, Olson (1983a), ch. 6.

8.   Germany illustrates this in a particular way: while local governments in West Germany invest two-thirds of total public investment – with a relatively even distribution of economic potentials and incomes resulting – the East has so far neglected local government altogether – with catastrophic effects on the creation and distribution of public infrastructure.

9.   The modesty of the Delors II package has not prevented national governments from reacting vehemently against the proposal of the Commission however.

10. There are $n * (n - 1)$ possible horizontal communication flows between national tax administrations – assumed to be centralised. For the existing member states this would mean $12 * (12 - 1) = 132$. The significant language problem adds to this.

11. The number of communication flows would be $2 * n$ in this case, or 24.

12. It should be noted that the VAT base is usually not fully consistent with private consumption – since parts of public consumption are taxed as well. It is important, however, that parts of the product and of resulting incomes – used for investment and exports – are exempt from VAT. Thus, low producer/high consumer regions (deficit countries) tend to contribute more to the EC budget in relative terms than high producers/low consumers (surplus countries).

13. This contention is supported by the concessions made to the United Kingdom and Germany in the 80s – touched upon in chapter 3.4.3. Notably, the German case was simply based on a 'paying-too-much' kind of argument. The trend for proportional contributions is also reflected in the recent Delors II package, which was briefly discussed above.

14. This does not imply marginal productivity of capital to be below average in the short run. On the contrary, it would usually be higher than average in developing (investing) regions.

15. The Commission is sometimes alleged to politically favour this view through its insisting on 'euro-harmonisation' and centralism for some taxes, notably for the corporation tax. See, for instance, Bird (1989), Cnossen (1990a, pp. 473f.). It is fair to say, however, that the Commission has now firmly adopted the principle of subsidiarity, and it seems to have been altering positions recently. Scrivener (1990, p. 207) – stressing the subsidiarity principle as the prime guideline

for EC policies – concedes, for instance, that 'the Commission might have been overambitious in some of its old proposals on corporate taxation . . '.

16. See, for instance, Article 1, sec. 8 of the US Constitution.

17. The conflict between legalistic and economic views on harmonising VAT (as a potentially central tax) is discussed in Menner/Haufler (1991). Lawyers tend to stress uniformity, economists underscore diversity. A reconciliation of positions has to be sought in the harmonisation of VAT bases and, as is the case, standardised tax-sharing rules for financing the EC budget – with continuing diversity in national tax rates. It is our contention, however, that in the long run VAT diversity *will* vanish within the EC, with continuing diversity in the realm of direct taxation.

18. The argument is more fully developed in Spahn/Kaiser (1991). For recent research results for the UK, see Blundell/Pashardes/Weber (1989), for Italy, Patrizi/Rossi (1989), for France, Baccouche/Laisney (1990), and for West Germany, Kaiser/Spahn (1989), Kaiser/Wiegard/Zimmermann (1989) and Kaiser (1989).

19. Zero-rating for VAT means that no output VAT is charged, and the VAT paid on inputs is all refunded.

20. Zero-rating of exports only applies to goods; see, for instance, 4 No. 1, of the German VAT law, which reserves these concessions to '*Ausfuhrlieferungen*' (according to 6 *Gegenstände*), and '*Lohnveredelungen an Gegenständen*'. Services are generally taxed in the country of origin, hence the *origin principle* applies here.

21. For a review of the destination principle and its counterpart, the origin principle, see Cnossen/Shoup (1987, p. 67ff), Parsche/Seidel/Teichmann (1988, p. 26ff) or Janeba (1988).

22. The system operating in the Benelux states is more fully described in van der Zanden/Terra (1987, pp. 135ff.).

23. This incentive is negligible for the Benelux countries, where tax rates – at least for Belgium and the Netherlands – are reasonably close together (17/19 per cent in Belgium, 18.5 per cent in the Netherlands, *but* 12 per cent in Luxembourg), and border controls continue to play a role for potential cross-checking. Nevertheless there seem to be problems of tax fraud associated with PAS even in the Benelux states; see van der Zanden/Terra (1987, p. 136).

24. In discussing a recent French proposal for the adoption of PAS, Smith (1990, p. 15) underlines the substantial administrative burden, on both government and companies, that is related to an extension of PAS to all EC member states. It would require exports to be accompanied by multiple copies of documents. Entitlement to zero-rate intra-EC exports would require proof of the exported goods being subject to VAT in the country of destination, which could be effected by returning one of the documents – certified by the importer's tax office – to the exporter's tax authorities. Although border controls would be eliminated under

such a system, the transaction costs would be significantly higher on intra-EC transactions compared with those on purely domestic trade; this would effectively discriminate against trade in foreign goods.

25. Cnossen (1991). The proposal was, however, not accepted by the Council of Ministers.

26. For a more detailed discussion of problems associated with the clearing mechanisms proposed see chapter 4.3.3.

27. Since final consumers and VAT-registered traders are subject to different tax rates the scheme was categorised as following a 'mixed tax principle'. See Haufler (1992).

28. Alternatively, a strong diversity in tax rates would distort locational decisions of firms, which would settle in low-tax jurisdictions where cross-border shopping was important.

29. Commission of the European Communities, internal document XXI/311/90–EN.

30. The Cecchini Report (1988, Tables 9.2 and 2.1) estimates economic costs of border controls to be in the order of ECU 8–9 billion.

31. The Commission is required to present a report to the Council on the functioning of the transitory regime as well as on the details of the final regime itself. The Council will have to decide on the definitive scheme before 31 December 1995.

32. This statement seems to contradict actual tendencies as expressed by the Delors II package, which foresees a reduction of the VAT share to the benefit of the GNP-levy. This is induced by the still dominant philosophy of proportional contributions, with VAT suspected of having a regressive regional impact. Once VAT becomes an origin-based turnover tax, in the longer term, this counter-argument will vanish however.

33. According to internal document II-B-1/DC/21.05.1991, Table 4.

34. The proposal seems to contradict the legalistic budget rule of universality. There are exceptions to this rule for the EC budget already, yet it should be stressed that this rule is the dismay of the economist, who would prefer to earmark tax revenue in order to enhance the efficiency of budgetary performance.

35. For a more comprehensive account of personal income tax reforms in OECD countries and the variety of solutions adopted in recent years, see Cnossen/Messere (1990).

36. There are, however, also progressive tax rates, especially for countries applying the classical system.

37. In Germany there is also a local tax on businesses (the *Gewerbesteuer*) which is different in structure from a corporation tax however.

38. Devereux/Pearson (1989) have applied the methodology to transnational investment within the EC, Japan and the United States.

39. Council Directive on the common system of taxation applicable in the case of parent companies and subsidiaries of different member

states. Official Journal of the European Communities, 20 August 1990, L-225.

40. Differences in the tax rates among member states are supposed to reflect differences in the provision of public goods, hence the benefit principle applies, preventing the taxpayer from moving his residence.

41. Countries that do not strictly apply the residence principle are France and the Netherlands.

42. Interests are less balanced between OECD countries as a whole and LDCs – where the latter are typically income-producing, while the former are income-receiving.

43. For a proposal along such lines, see Steuerle (1990).

44. However, there could be no personal tax credit, if the corporation tax should be on cash flow and thus on excess profits only; see chapter 4.3.5.2 below.

45. Commission of the European Community (1967, 1975).

46. Council decision of 23 July 1990 relating to the fiscal treatment of mergers, the imposition of withholding taxes at the repatriation of foreign subsidiaries' profits, and problems of double-taxation. See Vanheukelen (1991, pp. 345f).

47. See, for instance, the various contributions to an IFS symposium on this matter which are published in *Fiscal Studies*, Vol. 13, no. 2 (May 1992).

48. Despite this fact, the government is now prepared to extend wealth taxation to the Eastern states, thus complicating tax administration further and introducing new inequities.

49. This does not mean that other proposals should be discarded from the EC's agenda on tax policies. It simply reflects the author's intellectual limitations (and unwillingness to discuss any detail of further topical proposals that may be on the drawing board).

50. This is true whether government or the agent himself takes care of removing the damage.

51. Qualifications have to be made in the case of marginal cost pricing because this would typically lead to inframarginal 'rents' for the public sector. An ecolevy is, however, typically targeted toward a ceiling. It is levied only *above* the ceiling; its revenue impact would be zero for and below the ceiling.

52. There is a great danger inherent in ecotaxation that governments may overstress the instruments. Too much intervention is likely to create a 'tax jungle' – with uncertain effects on costs and risks, hence inefficiencies.

53. Both an energy tax and the carbon tax could be levied conjointly. Both would reduce energy consumption; yet the carbon tax would additionally lead to energy substitution, fostering low-emission types of energy consumption.

54. Intergovernmental Panel on Climate Change (1990).

55. Quoted in Genser (1992).

56. A distinction must be made between the business and the corporate sectors. The following argument is made for the corporate sector alone, yet a similar reasoning could apply to the business sector *in toto*. Since the tax proposed offers a number of advantages for firms – notably for newly established enterprises with high investment propensities – it is expected that there would be an incentive for firms to incorporate in order to reap these benefits from taxation. Once incorporated, however, they should not be allowed to de-register – unless tax benefits received are redeemed. The author is aware of the fact that this entails complexities for mergers and acquisitions of firms where – for tax purposes – internal accounts showing relative 'participation' of the fisc must be kept.

    Administrative aspects of the tax cannot be fully discussed here. It should be noted, however, that incorporation is likely to become the rule under such a tax – comprising most of the business sector.

57. In the latter case the marginal tax rate on capital income is positive.

58. All forms of assets bought during a period are considered investment.

59. It may help to consider that model as being equivalent to the government partly taking a share of the company, the government's 'investment' being taxes foregone on the company's own investment. By disallowing the deductibility of interest, the government recoups a 'normal' interest rate on this 'tax investment' in the form of taxes on interest payments of the firm. If the company is operating at the margin, in the sense that it cannot concede higher dividends to its shareholders than interest to its debtors, the government will not be able to recoup higher returns on dividends either; the government's return will then not exceed that of any other portfolio investment. If, however, the company has inframarginal profits that are higher than the normal interest rate, and/or a rent – which could even be a windfall profit or a capital gain – the government participates like any other shareholder.

    The government participates in both distributed and undistributed profits, whereas the shareholder is often seen as benefiting from dividends alone. This view ignores the fact, however, that – with perfect capital markets – the value of existing stocks must increase as a function of retained earnings, hence shareholders are in the same position as the taxing government.

60. The proceeds from a cashflow tax would, of course, not be credited against a personal consumption tax.

61. See Spahn (1990) and Spahn/Kassella (1990). This is true because concessions to be made to the idea of comprehensive income taxations have undermined horizontal and vertical equity in many respects, which is unlikely to occur if the tax base firmly rests on a cashflow concept – where manipulations are more difficult.

62. Instead of 'negative revenues' one could also talk of 'investment subsidies'. This term should, however, be avoided in the context of a cashflow corporate tax. Investment subsidies are usually public revenue

foregone – entailing inefficiencies within the concept of comprehensive income taxation. Tax expenditures within the cashflow tax have to be considered as temporary advances to the business sector; they are intrinsically related to future positive cash flows generated through those investments that are taxed. This does not entail inefficiencies; on the contrary: it is neutral as to private investment decisions.

63.　As long as pure profits can be reaped in the whole federation, the net result of the horizontal flows is always positive for the EFTS.

64.　This was, of course, typical of the situation of the *Deutsche Bundesbank* under the Bretton Woods system.

65.　It may in fact be a policy for the ESCB to separate a (monopoly) issue department from a (competitive) banking department. It could well be that central banks – losing some of their monopoly rents through greater competition as well as through developments in transaction technologies (Giovannini, 1991, p. 95) – will be forced to alter their policies *vis-à-vis* the banking industry. For instance, the cash-clearing functions could be separated from policy-oriented central bank operations. The former could then form the centrepiece of a commercial operation to be 'sold' to banks at 'quasi-competitive' rates (assuming that such quasi-competition could be installed, for example by comparison with the banks' own clearing operations). Although such policies may be imaginable, our argument is based on the assumption that the monopoly power of central banking will not be questioned in the near future and that regulatory and commercial functions remain inseparable.

66.　Official reserves – except for gold – may also be held in the form of interest-bearing assets however.

67.　Spain has legislated in 1990 a progressive reduction in the required reserve ratio from 17 to 5 per cent; Commission (1990, p. 121, fn. 58).

68.　Estimates for seigniorage are taken from an internal EC document written by M. Vanheukelen (16 April 1991). An implicit measure was calculated. The steady-state values for 1997 and thereafter were arrived at with the following technical assumptions: *(i)* cash-holdings relative to GNP are constant; *(ii)* interest rates decline linearly to a common 5 per cent in 1997; *(iii)* commercial bank reserves converge to 2 per cent of a broad money aggregate; *(iv)* remuneration of reserves is zero by 1997; *(v)* nominal GDP growth rates converge to 5 per cent by 1997; *(vi)* ratio of representative broad aggregate to GDP remains constant.

　　　Average inflation rates were derived from OECD Economic Outlook, July 1991, and reserve requirements for commercial banks (as per cent of demand deposits) were taken from Grilli (1989) – as quoted in Giovannini (1991, p. 97). The regression results are own calculations.

69.　Apart from this straightforward level effect, demand for EC moneys may also be reduced considerably under EMU because of structural effects. Nowadays demand for exchange is often rerouted through third-party currencies (like the US dollar or the DM) because markets for direct exchange are too small, with little liquidity (Danish krona for Portuguese escudos, for instance). Not only will EMU end the need to hold foreign currencies directly – which are now only imperfect substitutes for national money; it will also end the need for costly deviations through cross-transactions of EC currencies.

70. After all, EMU will form part of a tripolar worldwide monetary system – with the US dollar and the yen forming the other pillars. Coordination of monetary policies within such a system seems to be much easier than at present, since it involves only three dominant (and equally strong) players. If minimum requirements once again become fashionable as a policy instrument, their chances are much better under EMU than under the present system.

71. The Maastricht Treaty, in its article 32, establishes in fact such rules for apportioning monetary income of the ESCB to national governments.

72. If Germany is now successful in circumventing such rules by creating off-balance funds, this should not be taken as a counterexample. It is attributable to the historical challenge of German unification – and it seems to be based on a broad political consensus comprising opposition parties as well.

Bibliography

Aaron, Henry J., Harvey Galper, and Joseph A. Pechman, eds. (1988), *Uneasy compromise: problems of a hybrid income-consumption tax*, Washington D.C. (Brookings).

Andel, Norbert (1990), *Finanzwissenschaft*, 2nd. ed., Tübingen (J.C.B. Mohr).

Baccouche, R., Laisney, F. (1990), 'The simulation of VAT reforms for France using cross-section data', in: *Microeconometrics – Surveys and applications*, edited by J.-P. Florens, M. Ivaldi, J.-J. Laffont and F. Laisney, Oxford (Tito).

Biehl, Dieter (1985), 'A federalist budgetary policy strategy for European Union', *Policy Studies, The Journal of the Policy Studies Institute*, Vol. 6, part 2, October, 66–76.

Biehl, Dieter (1990a), '*Financing the EEC budget*', in *Public finance with several levels of government*, edited by Rémy Prud'homme, Foundation Journal Public Finance, The Hague/Koenigstein, 137–52.

Biehl, Dieter (1990b), 'Deficiencies and reform possibilities of the EC fiscal constitution', in *The Politics of 1992 – Beyond the Single European Market* edited by Colin Crouch and David Marquand, Oxford, 85–99.

Bieri, S. (1979), *Fiscal federalism in Switzerland*, Research Monograph No. 26, Canberra (Australian National University, Centre for Research on Federal Financial Relations).

Bird, Richard (1986), *Federal finance in comparative perspective*, Toronto (Canadian Tax Foundation).

Bird, Richard (1989), 'Tax harmonization in federations and common markets', in *Public finance and performance of enterprises*, edited by Manfred Neumann and Karl Roskamp, Detroit (Wayne State University Press), 139–51.

Blundell, R., Pashardes, P., Weber, G. (1989), *What Do we Learn About Consumer Demand Patterns from Micro-data?*, Institute for Fiscal Studies and London Business School, Micro to Macro Papers No. 3, London.

Bradford, D. F., and Oates, W. E. (1971), 'The analysis of revenue sharing in a new approach to collective fiscal decisions', *Quarterly Journal of Economics*, Vol. 85, 416–39.

Bradford, David F. (1980a) 'The Case for a personal consumption tax', in *What should be taxed: income or expenditure?* edited by Josef Pechman, Washington, D.C. (Brookings), 75–125.

Bradford, David F. (1980b), 'The Economics of tax policy toward saving', in *The government and capital formation*, edited by G. von Furstenberg, Cambridge, Ma., 11–71.

Bradford, David F. (1986), *Untangling the income tax*, Cambridge, Mass. (Harvard University Press).

Break, George F. (1967), *Intergovernmental fiscal relations in the United States*, Washington, D.C. (Brookings).

Brennan, Geoffrey, and James Buchanan (1977), 'Towards a tax constitution for Leviathan', *Journal of Public Economics*, Vol. 8, 255–74.

Brennan, Geoffrey, and James Buchanan (1980), *The power to tax*, Cambridge, Mass. (Cambridge University Press).

Brennan, Geoffrey, and James Buchanan (1983), 'Normative tax theory for a federal polity: Some public choice preliminaries', in *Tax assignment in federal countries*, edited by Charles E. McLure, Jr., Canberra (Australian National University, Centre for Research on Federal Financial Relations), 52–65.

Breton, A. (1965), 'A theory of government grants', *Canadian Journal of Economics and Political Science*, Vol. 31, 175–87.

Breton, A., A. Scott (1978), *The economic constitution of federal systems*, Toronto.

Buchanan, James M. (1952), 'Federal grants and resource allocation', *Journal of Political Economy*, Vol. 60, 208–17.

Buchanan, J. M., G. Tullock (1962), *The Calculus of Consent*, Ann Arbor: University of Michigan Press.

Bundesministerium der Finanzen (1988), *Die wichtigsten Steuern im internationalen Vergleich*, Informationsdienst zur Finanzpolitik des Auslands, Bonn.

Cecchini, Paolo (1988), *1992: The European challenge: The benefits of a single market*, 2nd. ed., Aldershot (Wildwood House).

Cnossen, Sijbren (1981) 'Dutch experience with the value-added tax', *Finanzarchiv*, Vol. 39, 223–54.

Cnossen, Sijbren (1983) 'Harmonization of indirect taxes in the EEC', *British Tax Review*, Vol. 4, 232–53.

Cnossen, Sijbren (1990), 'The case for tax diversity in the European Community', *European Economic Review*, Vol. 34, 471–79.

Cnossen, Sijbren (1991), 'Co-ordination of sales taxes in federal countries and common markets', in *Financing federal and state governments*, edited by the OECD, Centre for Cooperation with European Economies in Transition, Committee on Fiscal Affairs, Paris (forthcoming).

Cnossen, Sijbren and C. S. Shoup (1987), 'Coordination of value-added taxes', in *Tax coordination in the European Community*, edited by S. Cnossen, Deventer (Kluwer), 59ff.

Cnossen, Sijbren and Ken Messere (1990), 'Income tax reforms in OECD Member Countries', in *The income tax – Phoenix from the ashes*, edited by Sijbren Cnossen and Richard Bird, Amsterdam et al. (North-Holland), 17–60.

Commission of the European Communities (1967), *Programme for the harmonization of direct taxes*, Bulletin of the European Economic Community, Supplement 8, Brussels.

Commission of the European Communities (1975), *Proposal for a directive concerning the harmonization of systems of company taxation and of withholding taxes on dividends*, Bulletin of the European Economic Community, Supplement 10, Brussels.

Commission of the European Communities (1989), *Community public finance. The European budget after the 1988 reform*, Brussels – Luxembourg.

Commission of the European Communities (1990), 'One Market, one money – An evaluation of the potential benefits and costs of forming an economic and monetary union', *European Economy*, No. 44 (October).

Commonwealth Grants Commission (1983), *Equality in diversity: Fifty years of the Commonwealth Grants Commission*, Canberra (Australian Government Publishing Service).

Commonwealth Grants Commission (1985), *Report on tax sharing relativities*, Vols. I and II, Canberra (Australian Government Publishing Service).

Cornes, R., T. Sandler (1986), *The theory of externalities, public goods, and club goods*, Cambridge, Cambridge University Press.

Courchène, T., C. Goodhart, A. Majocchi, W. Moesen, R. Prud'homme, F. Schneider, S. Smith, P. B. Spahn, C. Walsh (1992), *Stable money – Sound finances, Community public finance in the perspective of EMU*, Report of an independent group of economists, with M. Vanheukelen as rapporteur (forthcoming).

Dafflon, Bernard (1977), *Federal finance in theory and practice with special reference to Switzerland*, Bern (Paul Haupt).

Dafflon, Bernard (1986), 'Fédéralisme, coordination et harmonisation fiscales: étude du cas suisse', *Recherches Economiques de Louvain*, Vol. 52/1.

Dafflon, Bernard (1989), 'Calcul de la capacité financière des cantons: synthèse et évolution', *Wirtschaft und Recht*, Zürich, 210–20.

Dafflon, Bernard (1991), 'Revenue sharing in Switzerland', in *Financing Federal and State Governments*, edited by the OECD, Centre for Cooperation with European Economies in Transition, Committee on Fiscal Affairs, Paris, (forthcoming).

Deutsche Bundesbank (1992), 'Öffentliche Finanztransfers für Ostdeutschland in den Jahren 1991 und 1992', *Monatsberichte der Deutschen Bundesbank*, Vol. 44, 3, 15–22.

Devereux, M., and M. Pearson, (1989) *Corporate tax harmonization and economic efficiency*, Institute for Fiscal Studies, Report Series No. 35, London.

Diamond, Peter, and James Mirrlees (1971), 'Optimal taxation and public production, I Production efficiency', *American Economic Review*, Vol. 61, 8–27.

Downs, Anthony (1957), *An Economic Theory of Democracy*, New York: Harper & Row.

Fletcher, Christine, and Cliff Walsh (1991), *Intergovernmental relations in Australia: a managerialist revolution?*, Federalism Research Centre, Australian National University, (mimeo).

Frey, René L. (1977), 'The interregional income gap as a problem of Swiss federalism', in *The political economy of federalism*, edited by Wallace Oates, Lexington, Mass., 93–104.

Galligan, Brian, and Cliff Walsh (1990), 'Australian federalism – Developments and prospects', *Publius: The Journal of Federalism*, Vol. 20, No. 4 (forthcoming).

Genser, Bernd (1992), 'Tax competition and harmonization in federal economies', in *European integration in the world economy – Proceedings of the second Konstanz symposium on international economics and institutions*, edited by Hans-Jürgen Vosgerau, Berlin et al. (Springer), (forthcoming).

Giovannini, Alberto (1989), 'National tax systems versus the European capital market', *Economic Policy*, No. 9, October, 364–84.

Giovannini, Alberto (1991), 'Money demand and monetary control in an integrated European economy', in *European Economy*, Special edition No. 1, 'The economics of EMU', Brussels – Luxembourg, 93–106.

Goodhart, C., S. Smith (1992), 'Stabilisation', in 'The Economics of Community Public Finance', *European Economy* (forthcoming).

Goodspeed, T. (1989), 'A re-examination of the use of ability to pay taxes by local governments', *Journal of Public Economics*, Vol. 38, 319–42.

Gordon, Roger H. (1983), 'An optimal taxation approach to fiscal federalism', *Quarterly Journal of Economics*, Vol. 97, 567–86.

Gordon, Roger H. (1990). *Can capital income taxes survive in open economies?*, Working Paper No. 3416, National Bureau of Economic Research, Inc., Cambridge, Mass.

Gramlich, E. M. (1977), 'Intergovernmental grants: A review of the empirical literature', in *The political economy of federalism*, edited by Wallace Oates, Lexington, Mass., 219–40.

Gramlich, E. M. (1987), 'Federalism and federal deficit reduction', *National Tax Journal*, Vol. 40, 299–313.

Grilli, V. (1989), 'Europe 1992: issues and prospects for the financial markets', *Economic Policy*, No. 9 (October), 387–422.

Groenewegen, Peter (1990), 'Taxation and decentralisation. A reconsideration of the costs and benefits of a decentralised tax system', in *Decentralisation, local governments, and markets*, edited by R. J. Bennett, Oxford (Clarendon).

Groenewegen, Peter (1991), 'Financing the States in the Australian federation', in *Financing federal and state governments*, edited by the OECD, Centre for Cooperation with European Economies in Transition, Committee on Fiscal Affairs, Paris, (forthcoming).

Große-Sender, Heinrich A., ed., (1990) *Bericht der Kommission 'Erhaltung und Fortentwicklung der bundesstaatlichen Ordnung innerhalb der Bundesrepublik Deutschland – auch in einem Vereinten Europa'*, Düsseldorf (Landtag Nordrhein-Westfalen).

Haufler, Andreas (1990), 'Die Abschaffung der Steuergrenzen im gemeinsamen Markt: EG-Vorschläge 1989 und alternative Lösungen', *Umsatzsteuer-und Verkehrsteuer-Recht*, No. 5, 131–39.

Haufler, Andreas (1992), 'Indirect tax policy in the European Community: an economic analysis', in *European integration in the world economy*

– *Proceedings of the second Konstanz symposium on international economics and institutions*, edited by Hans-Jürgen Vosgerau, Heidelberg et al. (Springer), (forthcoming).

Helm, D., and S. Smith (1989) 'The assessment: economic integration and the role of the European Community', *Oxford Review of Economic Policy*, Vol. 5, 1–13.

Hesse, Konrad (1962), *Der unitarische Bundesstaat*, Karlsruhe.

Hoeller, Peter, and Markku Wallin (1991), *Energy prices, taxes and carbon dioxide emissions*, OECD, Economics and Statistics Department Working Papers, No. 106, Paris.

Hunter, J. S. H. (1977), *Federalism and fiscal balance*, Canberra (Australian National University: Centre for Research on Federal Fiscal Relations).

IEA (1991), *Energy and the environment: transport system responses in the OECD*, Paris, (forthcoming).

IFS Capital Taxes Group (1991), *Equity for companies: a corporation tax for the 1990s*, IFS Commentary no. 26, London: Institute for Fiscal Studies.

Intergovernmental Panel on Climate Change (1990), *Policymakers' summary of the scientific assessment of climate change*, WMO and UNEP, New York.

Janeba, E. (1988), *Ökonomische Probleme der Umsatzsteuerharmonisierung bei der Vollendung des EG-Binnenmarktes*, Europäisches Parlament, Sammlung Wissenschaft und Dokumentation, Reihe Wirtschaftsfragen Nr. 15, Straßburg.

Kaiser, H., Wiegard, W., Zimmermann, H. (1990), 'Testing the Reliability of Optimal Tax Calculations', *Finanzarchiv*, Vol. 48, Heft 1, 77–96.

Kaiser, H. (1989), *On labour supply, commodity demands, and taxation of households*, Sfb 3–Working Paper No. 300, Frankfurt/Main.

Kaiser, H., Spahn, P. B. (1989), 'On the efficiency and distributive justice of consumption taxes', *Zeitschrift für Nationalökonomie/Journal of Economics*, Vol. 49, No. 2, 199–218.

Kaldor, Nicholas (1955), *An expenditure tax*, London.

Kay, John, and Mervyn King (1986), *The British tax system*, 4th ed., Oxford (Oxford University Press).

Kenen, Peter (1987), 'Global policy optimization and the exchange-rate regime', *Journal of Policy Modelling*, Vol. 9 (1), 19–63.

King, D. (1984), *Fiscal tiers: the economics of multi-level government*, London (Allen & Unwin).

King, Mervyn and David Fullerton (1984), *The taxation of income from capital: a comparative study of the United States, the United Kingdom, Sweden and West-Germany*, Chicago (The University of Chicago Press).

Krupp, Hans-Jürgen (1991), *Political change and intergovernmental fiscal relations: the case of German unification*, in *Public finance with several levels of government*, edited by Rémy Prud'homme, Foundation Journal Public Finance, The Hague/Koenigstein, 368–78.

Lindahl, E. (1919), *Die Gerechtigkeit der Besteuerung*, Lund.

MacDougall, D. et al. (1977), *Report of the study group on the role of public finance in European integration*, Office for official publications of the EC, Luxembourg.

Martin-Kommission (1985), Landtag Rheinland-Pfalz, *Drs. 10/1150*, January 1985.

Mathews, Russell L. (1977), 'Mechanisms for fiscal equalisation in an integrating European Community', ch. 13, Vol. II of the *McDougall Report*, 401–32 (reproduced in *The economics of federalism*, edited by B. S. Grewal, G. Brennan, and R. L. Mathews, Canberra (ANU Press), 1980).

Mathews, Russell L. (1978), 'Issues in Australian federalism', *Economic Papers* (March).

Mathews, Russell L. (1982), *The Commonwealth-State contract*, Reprint no. 46, Canberra (Australian National University: Centre for Research on Federal Fiscal Relations).

Mathews, Russell L., and W. R. C. Jay (1972), *Federal finance. Intergovernmental financial relations in Australia since federation*, Melbourne.

McLure, C.E., J. Mutti, V. Thuronyi, and G. R. Zodrow (1988), *The taxation of income from business and capital in Colombia*, Bogotá.

Meade, James (1978), ed., *The structure and reform of direct taxation*, London (The Institute for Fiscal Studies).

Menner, S. and A. Haufler (1991), *Wettbewerbsverzerrungen und Harmonisierung der Umsatzsteuer in Europäischen Binnenmarkt*, Diskussionsbeiträge, Sonderforschungsbereich 178 Serie II/127, Konstanz.

Musgrave, R. A. (1969), 'Theories of fiscal federalism', *Public Finance*, Vol. 24, 521–32.

Musgrave, R. A. (1983), 'Who should tax, where, and what?', in *Tax assignment in federal countries*, edited by Charles McLure, Canberra (Australian National UP), 2–19.

Nutter, G. Warren (1978), *Growth of government in the West*, Washington (American Enterprise Institute for Public Policy Research).

Oates, Wallace (1991), 'The theory of fiscal federalism: revenue and expenditure issues – A survey of recent theoretical and empirical research', in *Public finance with several levels of government*, edited by Rémy Prud'homme, Foundation Journal Public Finance, The Hague/Koenigstein, 1–18.

Oates, Wallace E. (1972), *Fiscal federalism*, New York et alia (Harcourt-Brace-Jovanovich).

OECD (1986) *Personal income tax systems under changing economic conditions*, Report by the Committee on Fiscal Affaris, Paris.

OECD (1989), *Tax revenue statistics of OECD member countries 1965– 87*, Paris.

OECD (1991), *Taxing profits in a global economy: domestic and international issues*, Paris.

Olson, Mancur (1983a), *The rise and decline of nations*, New Haven.

Olson, Mancur (1983b), 'The political economy of comparative growth rates', in *The political economy of growth*, edited by Dennis C. Mueller, New Haven (Yale University Press), 7–52.

Patrizi, V., Rossi, N. (1989), *The European internal market and the welfare of Italian consumers*, University of Venice, Working Paper No. 89/06, Venice.

Parsche, R., B. Seidel, and D. Teichmann (1988), *Die Beseitigung der Steuergrenzen in der Europäischen Gemeinschaft*, DIW Sonderheft Nr. 145, Berlin (Duncker & Humblot).

Peacock, Alan T., and Jack Wiseman (1967), *The growth of public expenditures in the United Kingdom*, 2nd ed., London.

Pearson, M., and S. Smith (1990), *Taxation and environmental policy*, IFS Commentary No. 19, London (The Institute for Fiscal Studies).

Pechman, Josef A. (1988), *World tax reform: a progress report*, Washington D.C. (Brookings).

Pisani-Ferry, J., A. Italianer (1992), 'Regional Stabilisation Properties of Fiscal Arrangements', *Economic and Social Cohesion in the EC*, edited by the Centre for Economic Policy Research (CEPS), Brussels, (forthcoming).

Ploeg, Frederick van der (1989), *Monetary interdependence under alternative exchange-rate regimes: A European perspective*, Discussion Paper No. 358, Centre for Economic Policy Research, London.

Ploeg, Frederick van der (1991), 'Macroeconomic policy coordination during the various phases of economic and monetary integration in Europe', in *European Economy*, Special edition No. 1, 'The economics of EMU', Brussels – Luxembourg, 136–64.

Pommerehne, Werner W. (1977), 'Quantitative aspects of federalism: A study of six countries', in *The political economy of fiscal federalism*, edited by Wallace E. Oates, Lexington, 105–13.

Popitz, J. (1927), 'Der Finanzausgleich', *Handbuch der Finanzwissenschaft*, 2. Bd., 1. Aufl., Tübingen, 348 ff.

Poterba, J.M. (1990), *Designing a carbon tax*, Massachusetts Institute of Technology, mimeo.

Pryor, Frederic L. (1968), *Public expenditures in communist and capitalist nations*, London.

Razin, Assaf, and Efraim Sadka (1989), *International tax competition and gains from tax harmonisation*, NBER Working Paper no. 3152, October.

Reissert, Bernd (1978), 'Responsibility sharing and joint tasks in West German federalism', in *Principles of federal policy co-ordination in West Germany: basic issues and annotated legislation*, edited by P. Bernd Spahn, Research Monograph, Centre for Research on Federal Financial Relations. The Australian National University, Canberra, 24–41.

Ruding Committee (1992), *Report of the committee of independent experts on company taxation*, Brussels: Commission of the European Communities.

Samuelson, Paul A. (1954), 'The theory of public expenditure', *Review of Economics and Statistics*, Vol. 36, 386–89.

Samuelson, Paul A. (1955), 'Diagrammatic exposition of a theory of public expenditures', *Review of Economics and Statistics*, Vol. 37, 350–56.

Scharpf, Fritz W., Bernd Reissert and Fritz Schnabel (1977), Eds., *Politikverflechtung II. Kritik und Berichte aus der Praxis*, Kronberg.

Scharpf, Fritz W., Bernd Reissert and Fritz Schnabel (1976), *Politikverflechtung: Theorie und Empirie des kooperativen Föderalismus in der Bundesrepublik*, Kronberg.

Scrivener, Christiane (1990), 'Corporate taxation in Europe and the Single Market', *Intertax*, 207–8.

Sinn, Hans-Werner (1987), *Capital income taxation and resource allocation*, Amsterdam et. al. (North-Holland).

Sinn, Hans-Werner (1990), 'Tax harmonisation and tax competition in Europe', *European Economic Review*, Vol. 34, No. 2/3, 489–504.

Smith, Stephen (1990) *The European Community's priorities in tax policy*, Institute for Fiscal Studies, Working Paper Series No. W90/2, London.

Smith, Stephen (1991) 'Excise duties and the Internal Market', *Journal of Common Market Studies*, Vol. 27, 147–60.

Solomon, David (1982), *Constitution and politics: conflict restrained*, Paper presented to the Australian Institute of Political Science, Canberra.

Spahn, P. Bernd (1977a), 'Federal grant policy and state-local taxation', in *State and local taxation*, edited by Russell L. Mathews, Australian National University Press, Canberra, 125–42.

Spahn, P. Bernd (1977b), 'The pattern of state and local taxation in the Federal Republic of Germany', in *State and local Taxation*, edited by Russell L. Mathews, Australian National University Press, Canberra, 190–241.

Spahn, P. Bernd (1978), 'The German model of horizontal federal decentralisation' in *Principles of federal policy co-ordination in West Germany: basic issues and annotated legislation*, edited by P. Bernd Spahn, Research Monograph, Centre for Research on Federal Financial Relations. The Australian National University, Canberra, 3–23.

Spahn, P. Bernd (1988), 'La réforme fiscale aux Etats-Unis: Un modèle pour le monde industrialisé?, *Revue Française de Finances Publiques*, Vol. 24, p. 11–36.

Spahn, P. Bernd (1988), 'On the assignment of taxes in federal polities', in *Taxation and federalism: essays in honour of Russell Mathews*, edited by Geoffrey Brennan, Bhajan S. Grewal, Peter Groenewegen, Pergamon/Press/ANU Press, Sydney et al., 148–65.

Spahn, P. Bernd (1989), *Agenda für eine Reform der Haushaltsbesteuerung um die Jahrtausendwende*, Sfb-3–Arbeitspapier Nr. 279, Frankfurt – Mannheim.

Spahn, P. Bernd (1990), 'L'impôt direct sur la consommation: une utopie pour toujours?', *Revue Française de Finances Publiques*, No. 29, 1990, 85–101.

Spahn, P. Bernd (1991), 'The choice of own taxes, shared taxes and grants to finance state governments – The experience of Germany –', in *Financing federal and state governments*, edited by the OECD, Centre for Cooperation with European Economies in Transition, Committee on Fiscal Affairs, Paris, (forthcoming).

Spahn, P. Bernd, H. Kaiser (1991), 'Tax harmonization or tax competition as means to integrate Western Europe', *Konjunkturpolitik*, 37. Jg., H. 1/2, 1–44.

Spahn, P. Bernd, T. Kassella (1990), *Ius summum saepe summa malitia: Über die Ungerechtigkeit der Einkommensteuer*, Sfb-3–Arbeitspapier Nr. 319, Frankfurt – Mannheim.

Spaventa, L., L. Koopmans, P. Salmon, S. Smith, and P. B. Spahn (1986), *The future of Community finance*, Centre for European Policy Studies, CEPS Paper Nr. 30, Brussels.

Stern, Klaus (1980), *Das Staatsrecht der Bundesrepublik Deutschland*, Bd. II, Munich.

Steuerle, Eugene (1990), 'Capital income and the future of the income tax', in *The income tax – Phoenix from the ashes*, edited by Sijbren Cnossen and Richard Bird, Amsterdam et al. (North-Holland), 211–33.

Thurow, L. C. (1966), The theory of grants-in-aid', *National Tax Journal*, Vol. 22, 486–95.

Tiebout, Charles (1956), 'A pure theory of local expenditure', *Journal of Political Economy*, Vol. 64, 416–26.

Tresch, R. W. (1981), *Public finance: a normative theory*, Texas: Business Publications.

United States Advisory Commission on Intergovernmental Relations (1981), *Studies in comparative federalism: Australia*, Washington, D.C.

United States Department of the Treasury (1992), *Integration of the individual and corporate tax systems: taxing business income once*, Washington D.C.: Bureau of National Affairs.

Van Rompuy, Paul, Filip Abraham, and Dirk Heremans (1990), 'Economic federalism and the EMU', in *European Economy*, Special edition No. 1, 'The economics of EMU', Brussels – Luxembourg, 109–35.

Vanheukelen, Marc (1991), 'Corporate tax harmonization in the European Community', in *Public finance with several levels of government*, edited by Rémy Prud'homme, Foundation Journal Public Finance, The Hague/Koenigstein, 343–57.

Walsh, C. (1992), 'Fiscal federalism: an overview of issues and a discussion of their relevance to the European Community', in 'The economics of Community public finance', *European Economy* (forthcoming).

Walsh, Cliff (1991), *Reform of Commonwealth-State relations 'No representation without taxation'*, Federalism Research Centre, Australian National University, Discussion Paper No. 2, (August).

Walsh, Cliff, ed. (1990), 'State taxation and vertical fiscal imbalance – the radical reform options', in *Issues in State Taxation*, Canberra (Australian National University, Centre for Research on Federal Financial Relations), 1–22.

Wheare, K. C. (1963), *Federal government*, 4th ed., London (Oxford University Press).

Wildasin, D. E. (1990), 'Budgetary Pressures in the EEC: A Fiscal Federalism Perspective', *American Economic Review* (Papers and Proceedings),

Vol. 80.

Wilson, John (1986), 'A theory of interregional tax competition', *Journal of Urban Economics*, Vol. 19, 296–315.

Wissenschaftlicher Beirat beim Bundesministerum der Finanzen (1989), *Die Einheitsbewertung in der Bundesrepublik Deutschland – Mängel und Alternativen*, Schriftenreihe Heft 41, Bonn (Bundesminister der Finanzen).

Zanden, J. B. van der, and B. J. M. Terra (1987), 'The removal of tax barriers: The White Paper from the Commission to the European Council', *Intertax*, No. 6, 130–42.

Zimmermann, Horst, and Klaus-Dirk Henke (1990), *Finanzwissenschaft*, 6th edition, Munich.

Index